Digital Media Law

Digital Media Law

Rights, Rules, and Regulations in the Age of AI

Michael E. Jones

University of Massachusetts Lowell

BLOOMSBURY ACADEMIC
NEW YORK • LONDON • OXFORD • NEW DELHI • SYDNEY

BLOOMSBURY ACADEMIC
Bloomsbury Publishing Inc, 1359 Broadway, New York, NY 10018, USA
Bloomsbury Publishing Plc, 50 Bedford Square, London, WC1B 3DP, UK
Bloomsbury Publishing Ireland, 29 Earlsfort Terrace, Dublin 2, D02 AY28, Ireland

BLOOMSBURY, BLOOMSBURY ACADEMIC and the Diana logo
are trademarks of Bloomsbury Publishing Plc

First published in the United States of America 2026

Copyright © Bloomsbury Publishing Inc, 2026

Cover design: Dustin Watson
Cover image © iStock/Getty Images Plus/KrulUA

All rights reserved. No part of this publication may be: i) reproduced or transmitted in any form, electronic or mechanical, including photocopying, recording or by means of any information storage or retrieval system without prior permission in writing from the publishers; or ii) used or reproduced in any way for the training, development or operation of artificial intelligence (AI) technologies, including generative AI technologies. The rights holders expressly reserve this publication from the text and data mining exception as per Article 4(3) of the Digital Single Market Directive (EU) 2019/790.

Bloomsbury Publishing Inc does not have any control over, or responsibility for, any third-party websites referred to or in this book. All internet addresses given in this book were correct at the time of going to press. The author and publisher regret any inconvenience caused if addresses have changed or sites have ceased to exist, but can accept no responsibility for any such changes.

Library of Congress Cataloging-in-Publication Data
Names: Jones, Michael E., author.
Title: Digital media law : rights, rules, and regulations in the age of AI / Michael E. Jones, University of Massachusetts Lowell.
Description: New York : Bloomsbury Publishing, Inc, 2025. | Includes bibliographical references and index. |
Summary: "This textbook explores the evolving legal landscape where digital media and AI intersect, offering crucial insights into copyright, data privacy, ethics, and regulatory frameworks shaping the media industry's future"– Provided by publisher.
Identifiers: LCCN 2025016132 (print) | LCCN 2025016133 (ebook) |
ISBN 9781538196908 (hardback) | ISBN 9781538196915 (paperback) |
ISBN 9781538196922 (epub) | ISBN 9798765154366 (pdf)
Subjects: LCSH: Digital media–Law and legislation–United States. | Intellectual property–United States. | Artificial intelligence–Law and legislation–United States. | Online social networks–Law and legislation–United States. | Copyright and electronic data processing–United States. | Privacy, Right of–United States.
Classification: LCC KF2985.D54 J66 2025 (print) | LCC KF2985.D54 (ebook) |
DDC 343.7309/944–dc23/eng/20250404
LC record available at https://lccn.loc.gov/2025016132
LC ebook record available at https://lccn.loc.gov/2025016133

ISBN:	HB:	978-1-5381-9690-8
	PB:	978-1-5381-9691-5
	ePDF:	979-8-7651-5436-6
	eBook:	978-1-5381-9692-2

Typeset by Integra Software Services Pvt. Ltd.
Printed and bound in the United States of America

For product safety related questions contact productsafety@bloomsbury.com.

To find out more about our authors and books visit www.bloomsbury.com
and sign up for our newsletters.

Contents

List of Figures vii
Preface ix
Acknowledgments xi

1 **Charting the Digital Media Law Landscape**   1

2 **Voices and Echoes: Balancing Freedom and Control in the Social Media Sphere**   15

3 **Behind the Digital Curtains: Safeguarding Privacy in an Online World**   51

4 **Content Control: Copyrights and the Future of Digital Distribution**   87

5 **Brand Protection in Pixels: Managing Trademarks and Online Identities**   131

6 **Defamation, Deceit, and Disparagement in the Digital Age**   167

7 **Data Protection, National Security, and Hacking: Defending the Digital Frontier**   201

8 **Digital Media Contracts, Blockchain Technology, Cryptocurrencies, NFTs, and the Metaverse**   235

9   Big Data Battles: Antitrust Law in an Age of Tech Giants and Market Dominance   263

10 The Future of Digital Media Law: Navigating Ethics, AI, and Beyond   289

Index   316
About the Author   335

Figures

1.1	This swagged-out image of Pope Francis shared across social media is an AI fake	7
1.2	News consumption by social media site	9
2.1	What's driving the digital media	19
2.2	E-commerce sales worldwide	22
2.3	Most breached countries	36
4.1	AI-generated image not qualifying for copyright protection in the United States	97
4.2	This was one of the first popular posts using the "Distracted Boyfriend" meme on Reddit, gaining over 31,000 upvotes within twenty-four hours	113
4.3	Warhol's silkscreen magazine cover image of Prince and Goldsmith's photo of Prince	119
5.1	"Fuct" trademark registered by Brunetti	139
5.2	Examples of MetaBirkins: The NFTs sold online by Mason Rothschild for $450 apiece	143
5.3	Xbox series X logo vs. Twitter X logo vs. Musk's XAI logo	148

5.4	Document from a US Trademark Notice of Opposition filed by DC Comics and Marvel over the use of the terms *Superman* and *Batman*	150
5.5	Jack Daniel's vs. parody Jack Daniels	156
8.1	Beeple non-fungible token for sale by Christie's Auction House	241
8.2	On the left is the BAYC "Bored Apes" image, and on the right is the "RR/BAYC" image in dispute	245
8.3	CryptoPunks	246
10.1	A synthetic media interactive display of a deceased Salvadore Dalí at the Dalí Museum, St. Petersburg, Florida	296
10.2	False reporting article using an image of Clint Eastwood	303

Preface to *Digital Media Law*

After teaching and studying digital media law and emerging technologies for many years, I felt compelled to write a book addressing the legal challenges awaiting students and professionals in this rapidly changing field. *Digital Media Law* is intended as a guide to understanding the evolving legal landscape of digital media, especially as it intersects with emerging technologies, ethics, and artificial intelligence.

As digital media evolves, legal and ethical concerns shift swiftly. The rise of artificial intelligence, blockchain, and social media platforms has given birth to unprecedented challenges around intellectual property, data privacy, content regulation, and ownership. AI-generated content raises significant questions about originality and copyright, while blockchain and cryptocurrency pose concerns over transparency and security. Meanwhile, deepfakes, misinformation, and hacking highlight how malicious actors can manipulate digital content.

Jurisdictional boundaries further complicate regulation as content flows across borders, challenging traditional legal frameworks. These hurdles emphasize the need for comprehensive laws and regulatory oversight to keep up with the pace of digital transformation. Smart contracts, intellectual property rights, data security, and algorithm-driven technologies all require careful consideration.

At the same time, ethical dilemmas around inclusivity, fairness, and misinformation must be resolved to foster safer, more equitable digital spaces. The dynamism of digital media often outstrips the adaptive capacity of existing legal frameworks, creating regulatory gaps and uncertainties. For example, the rapid development of AI technologies challenges traditional notions of authorship and creativity, yet copyright laws remain grounded in concepts developed before these technologies existed. Blockchain provides revolutionary ways to track and manage digital transactions, yet legal systems worldwide grapple with jurisdictional and enforcement issues.

Emerging technologies like facial recognition and predictive analytics bring forth intense scrutiny regarding surveillance and privacy rights. Here, the tension between innovation and individual rights requires legal intervention and a broader ethical discourse.

This disconnect between technological innovation and legal responsiveness underscores a crucial point: laws must not only adapt to the current landscape but also be crafted with the flexibility to address future developments. Digital Media students, academics, policymakers, and professionals must recognize these gaps and actively shape laws that effectively govern the digital age.

In this book, I aim to bridge this understanding by dissecting how current laws apply to new technologies and proposing pathways toward more effective and nimble legal structures. By exploring these challenges through recent cases, ongoing policy debates, and the philosophical underpinnings of law, *Digital Media Law* seeks to equip readers with the knowledge and tools necessary to navigate this complex and ever-evolving field.

Michael E. Jones

Acknowledgments

The creation of this book has been a collaborative endeavor, enriched by the generous contributions of numerous individuals who have shared their expertise, insights, and unwavering support throughout this journey.

I owe a debt of gratitude to the experts and scholars whose scholarly input and constructive feedback have significantly enhanced the content of this book. Special recognition goes to Pavel Romaniko, whose leadership as the director of the Digital Media program at the University of Massachusetts Lowell has afforded me the privilege of guiding and instructing hundreds of students over the span of my tenure in university teaching.

Heartfelt appreciation is extended to the professionals, practitioners, and industry leaders who generously shared their real-world experiences and insights, infusing this book with context and practical wisdom. Your firsthand knowledge has been instrumental in bridging the gap between theory and practice in the realms of digital media law, ethics, and artificial intelligence.

I am especially grateful to my academic colleagues and peers at the University of Massachusetts at Lowell and the University of Massachusetts School of Law, whose camaraderie, guidance, and encouragement have been constant sources of motivation throughout the writing process. Your unwavering enthusiasm fueled my determination to overcome the myriad challenges encountered along the way.

A special acknowledgment goes to the editorial and production team at Rowman & Littlefield, whose dedication, expertise, and meticulous attention to detail have played a pivotal role in bringing this project to fruition. Their commitment to excellence ensured the integrity and quality of the final product.

Lastly, my warmest gratitude goes to my family, particularly my spouse, Christine M. Jones, and my friends, whose love, encouragement, and understanding have been the driving force behind this endeavor, while offering thoughtful suggestions and recommendations. Their patience and belief in me have been pillars of support throughout this journey.

To all those mentioned, as well as the countless others, especially my students who have contributed in ways both seen and unseen, I extend my sincerest thanks for your invaluable Gen Z insight and encouragement to share our lecture conversations in book form. This book stands as a testament to the collective efforts of a diverse and dedicated community committed to advancing knowledge and understanding in the dynamic fields of digital media law, ethics, and artificial intelligence.

Michael E. Jones

1
Charting the Digital Media Law Landscape

> *In the era of constant connectivity, studying digital media law is a crucial step towards reclaiming our autonomy. It's about recognizing that our digital choices are governed by legal frameworks that shape the very fabric of our online interactions.*
>
> —Sherry Turkle, professor of the social studies of science and technology, MIT

Navigating the Digital Media Legal Landscape

In the midst of the digital age, the contours of media have undergone a profound metamorphosis, giving rise to an unprecedented legal domain, as articulated by Professor Turkle. This comprehensive guidebook—*Digital Media Law*—is designed to lead you through the intricate terrain of legal and ethical quandaries that have surfaced alongside the ascent of digital media since the 1990s.

Digital media encompass content encoded in machine-readable formats and transmitted through digital binary signals (0s and 1s) over cables or satellites. This expansive array of content includes text, video, audio, and graphics, accessed through a myriad of devices such as computers, tablets, and smartphones via web-based systems and applications. The digital media landscape spans videos, articles, advertisements, music, podcasts, audiobooks, virtual reality, artificial intelligence, and digital art.

As we find ourselves on the brink of a new era, the significance and complexity of digital media, including the immersive metaverse, have burgeoned, reshaping the very fabric of society and the legal frameworks tasked with its governance. The digital revolution not only revolutionizes how we communicate, conduct business, and interact with the world but introduces a multitude of legal challenges that evolve at a rapid pace.

In the contemporary digital landscape, individuals armed with a computer, modem, and basic software possess the capability to broadcast their opinions globally through blogs and podcasts. This marks a seismic shift from the traditional feedback mechanisms of letters to the editor or phone calls seen in traditional media. This transformative phenomenon enables news consumers to provide instantaneous responses through User Generated Content (UGC) and social networks like X, Facebook, Reddit, and Snapchat, thereby amplifying citizen engagement in democratic processes. However, the unbridled expression by bloggers, citizen journalists, and amateur reporters occasionally blurs the line between free speech rights and potential overreach, with digital anonymity serving as a protective shield. In stark contrast to traditional media, where only professional journalists were subject to media laws and ethics, the contemporary digital era seemingly lacks any clear and universally accepted legal and ethical publishing standards other than holding accountable those who stray into defamatory statements, copyright and trademark infringements, or obscene speech.

Digital Media Law intends to unveil the intricate interplay between the dynamic landscape of digital media and the multifaceted legal challenges it presents. As we navigate this terrain, we'll delve into the nuances of digital expression, its impact on democratic processes, and the evolving ethical considerations that accompany this unprecedented era. Welcome to the forefront of the digital revolution, where legal understanding is not just a matter of professional necessity but a crucial facet of being an informed participant in the digital age.

The Early Evolution and Emerging Complexities of Digital Media Law

In the formative years of the internet, the legal landscape surrounding digital media grappled with issues like plagiarism, copyright infringement,

Chapter 1: Charting the Digital Media Law Landscape

and cyberbullying—predicaments that, though substantial, were initially contained in their scope. However, with the maturation of the digital landscape, a new wave of formidable challenges has surfaced:

1. **Hate Speech:** The rampant proliferation of online hate speech has ignited fervent debates, challenging the boundaries of free speech and underscoring the responsibilities borne by digital platforms.
2. **Disinformation Campaigns:** Deliberate campaigns disseminating false information, particularly orchestrated by foreign state actors, have raised alarms regarding their profound impact on democracy and global stability.
3. **Information Wars:** The strategic deployment of digital media to manipulate public opinion or influence government policy has become a paramount concern for national security.
4. **Market Domination:** The ascendancy of tech giants has prompted intensified scrutiny, focusing on potential monopolistic practices and their far-reaching influence on competition and consumer choice.

Building upon these existing concerns, contemporary challenges now include profound issues related to privacy and algorithmic bias:

1. **Privacy:** The digital age has witnessed an exponential surge in the collection and analysis of personal data. Heightened concerns center on the usage, accessibility, and protection of these data. While legal responses, such as the General Data Protection Regulation (GDPR) in the European Union and the California Consumer Privacy Act (CCPA) in the United States, have sought to address these concerns, the ongoing adequacy of these regulations remains a subject of intense debate.
2. **Algorithmic Bias:** With the increasing integration of AI and machine learning into digital media, the potential for bias within algorithms making decisions based on data patterns has emerged as a significant and nuanced issue. This bias can manifest in discriminatory outcomes in realms such as job advertising, credit scoring, and law enforcement.

As we maneuver through the ever-evolving landscape of digital media law, these multifaceted challenges underscore the dynamic nature of the digital age and emphasize the pressing need for legal frameworks that adapt to the complexities presented by technological advancements and societal shifts.

The Legal Conundrum in the Digital Era

The legal challenges posed by digital media stem from its stark departure from traditional forms of media, such as print and broadcast. Unlike traditional media, characterized by top-down systems and limited public access, digital media operates on a crowd-sourced model, offering an abundance of easily accessible, freely copied content often published without traditional filters, editing, or ethical oversight. Social media platforms, in particular, have become the linchpin for the production and dissemination of information across various news genres, regardless of reliability or accuracy.

A pivotal shift in legal perception occurred with the landmark case of *Reno v. ACLU* (1997), marking the recognition that the regulatory factors justifying control in traditional media do not apply in cyberspace. This laid the groundwork for a less regulated internet, solidified by **Section 230 of the Telecommunications Act**, granting immunity to internet service providers for user-generated content, subject to a narrow exception from blanket immunity for copyright infringement under the **Digital Millennium Copyright Act (DGMA)**. Individuals, however, remain accountable under existing laws, including those against libel, privacy breaches, obscene speech, and incitement to violence.

The case of *Packingham v. North Carolina* in 2017 spotlighted unique legal challenges in the digital realm. The Supreme Court invalidated a statute barring registered sex offenders from accessing social media, emphasizing the role of these platforms as modern public squares and highlighting the importance of safeguarding First Amendment rights in the digital age.

In a recent development, the Supreme Court's decision in *303 Creative LLC v. Elenis* has significant implications for online free speech and antidiscrimination laws. The ruling, in favor of a Christian website designer who claimed that her free speech rights were at risk of being compromised by state laws requiring her to create websites for same-sex weddings, underscores the delicate balance between protecting artistic freedom and preventing discrimination. However, critics argue that this decision may inadvertently pave the way for discrimination under the guise of free speech, impacting various artistic services beyond web design.

Beyond these legal milestones, the role of tech giants like Mark Zuckerberg (Meta, formerly Facebook) and Elon Musk (X) as gatekeepers for social media speech has become a contentious issue. As digital media evolves, the legal landscape is under constant scrutiny, with ongoing debates about the adequacy of existing laws, particularly in the realms of privacy, intellectual property rights, and potential misuse of personal data by technology behemoths such as X, TikTok, Snapchat, Meta, YouTube, Instagram, and even Amazon with its AI-assisted personal shopper.

Policymakers, legal experts, and society at large engage in discussions about balancing the benefits of digital media with the imperative to protect individual rights and maintain a fair and competitive marketplace. These debates extend to concerns about the impact of social media on the mental health of young people, highlighting a pressing need for effective regulation and accountability by both the government and social media companies. Research increasingly links social media use to a rise in mental health issues among adolescents, emphasizing the urgency of establishing a legal framework prioritizing the well-being of children and teenagers in the digital age.

The Evolving Role of Artificial Intelligence in Digital Media

The integration of artificial intelligence (AI) has ushered in a transformative era within the digital media landscape, presenting unparalleled capabilities in content creation, distribution, user behavior analysis, and personalized experiences. However, these advancements also usher in profound legal implications, particularly within the realms of copyright and privacy.

1. **Copyright and AI Ownership:** The emergence of AI-generated content poses intricate questions about copyright ownership. Determining whether it lies with the AI programmer, the user who initiated the creation, or the AI itself remains a complex and evolving legal challenge. The legal community grapples with defining the boundaries of ownership in this dynamic landscape.

2. **Privacy Concerns in AI-Driven Personalization:** AI's capacity to track and analyze user behavior for tailored content raises significant privacy concerns. The collection, storage, and utilization of data by AI systems necessitate robust data protection measures and informed consent from users. Balancing the benefits of personalized experiences with the protection of user privacy becomes a pivotal legal consideration.
3. **Bias and Content Moderation:** The implementation of AI in content moderation brings forth concerns about bias and potential censorship. The automated decision-making processes of AI can inadvertently suppress legitimate speech, challenging the principles of freedom of speech and fairness. Navigating the legal dimensions of AI-driven content moderation requires a delicate balance between mitigating bias and upholding fundamental rights.

As the influence of AI continues to permeate the digital media sphere, the legal landscape must adapt to address these multifaceted challenges. Crafting frameworks that strike a balance between fostering innovation and safeguarding individual rights will be pivotal in addressing the complex intersection of AI, copyright, and privacy in the ever-evolving digital media ecosystem.

AI and the Deceptive Realm of Deepfakes

Deepfakes, synthetic media generated by sophisticated AI algorithms, have emerged as a powerful yet concerning facet of the digital landscape. Typically manifesting as convincing videos or images, deepfakes employ deep learning algorithms trained on extensive datasets of real face or voice data. This technology, while holding promise for positive applications, raises alarming issues related to consent, psychological harm, political stability, and business disruption.

1. **Creation and Deceptive Realism:** Deepfakes leverage AI's ability to convincingly depict someone else's likeness or voice, often without their knowledge or consent. These deceptive media pieces are crafted

through the meticulous training of deep learning algorithms, leading to startlingly realistic portrayals. The process involves manipulating visual and auditory elements, giving rise to content that can betray the viewer's senses of sight and sound.
2. **Malicious Applications and Societal Impact:** The weaponization of deepfakes poses serious threats, ranging from reputational harm to national security risks. Malicious actors can utilize deepfakes to spread disinformation, manipulate public opinion, and even perpetrate revenge porn. The ability to create false narratives, often undetectable by the human eye and ear, introduces an

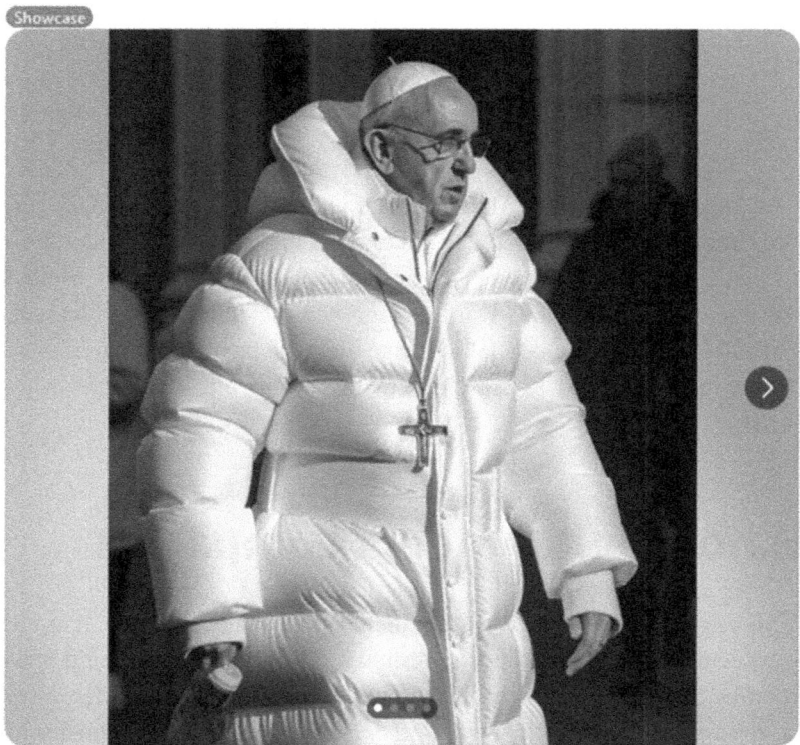

Figure 1.1 This swagged-out image of Pope Francis shared across social media is an AI fake.

unsettling divergence in shared reality, impacting individuals and societies.
3. **Legal and Legislative Responses:** In response to the growing concerns around deepfakes, there is a call for legislative measures to address their creation, especially for malicious purposes like nonconsensual pornography. The proposed **No Artificial Intelligence Fake Replicas and Unauthorized Duplications Act** aims to criminalize the generation of deepfake images, providing a regulatory framework to combat their detrimental consequences.
4. **Commercial Applications and Ethical Considerations:** On a contrasting note, the commercial realm has witnessed a positive application of AI with start-ups like Rembrand (playing off the name of the Dutch artist Rembrandt). This digital company is rejuvenating the age-old practice of product placement by seamlessly integrating realistic images of products like shampoo bottles into social media videos starring celebrity influencers. While this introduces new opportunities for content creators and advertisers, it also raises ethical considerations regarding the transparency of digitally enhanced content.

As the capabilities of AI continue to advance, the challenges and opportunities presented by deepfakes demand careful consideration, especially in a world where AI experts like Professor Ethan Mollick maintain AI detectors don't work. Balancing innovation with ethical and legal safeguards will be crucial to harnessing the positive potential of AI while mitigating the risks associated with deceptive technologies in the digital era.

Major Digital Media Companies

Apple Inc. has transformed from a niche computer manufacturer into a prominent technology giant. Established in 1976 by Steve Jobs and Steve Wozniak, Apple faced early challenges in the computer industry. However, the release of the iMac in 1998 and the iPod in 2001, combined with Jobs's marketing brilliance, propelled Apple to the forefront of consumer electronics. The subsequent introduction of products like the iPhone, iPad, Apple Watch, and Vision Pro headset solidified Apple's dominance.

% of U.S. adults who **regularly** get news on each social media site
Facebook 30%
YouTube 26
Instagram 16
TikTok 14
X (Twitter) 12
Reddit 8
Nextdoor 5
LinkedIn 5
Snapchat 4
WhatsApp 3
Twitch 1
Source: Survey of U.S. adults conducted Sept. 25–Oct. 1, 2023.
PEW RESEARCH CENTER

Figure 1.2 News consumption by social media site.

Services such as iTunes and Apple TV play integral roles in the digital media consumption habits of millions.

In the realm of social media, platforms like Facebook, X (formerly Twitter), Instagram, YouTube, Snapchat, and TikTok wield substantial influence with vast user bases. Ownership is concentrated among major corporations, with **Meta Platforms Inc.** (formerly Facebook) overseeing Instagram and WhatsApp, while **Google** owns YouTube. The ongoing expansion of social media usage is driven by younger generations growing up with these platforms and the continual influx of new users.

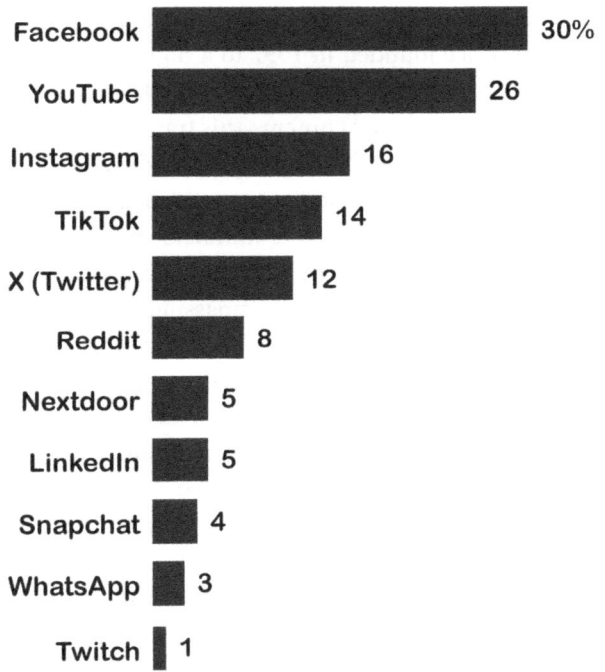

Amazon has emerged as a digital commerce and media behemoth, recognized as one of the world's most valuable companies. Its reach spans from the Prime streaming service to cloud computing and digital advertising.

Netflix has undergone a significant evolution, transitioning from an online DVD rental service founded in 1997 to a digital media giant. The introduction of streaming video on demand in 2007 marked a pivotal shift from physical DVDs to digital content. This transformation involved producing original content, and like other digital media content provider giants such as **Hulu** and **Disney+**, Netflix faces the ongoing challenge of innovating to sustain growth in subscriber numbers and revenue.

The **Walt Disney Company's** media influence extends beyond streaming content and cable networks, encompassing theme parks, global distribution of live-action and animated pictures, interactive media development, and licensing and retailing of iconic names and characters.

Comcast holds a global presence in digital media, with its UK-based Sky network offering high-speed internet, voice, and wireless phone services. It also operates NBC Universal, involved in film and television production, alongside its original Comcast Cable services providing wireless, video, internet, and voice services in the United States.

Once a media powerhouse, **Fox** divested its entertainment business to Disney, along with a substantial stake in Hulu and FX. Currently, Fox is recognized for operating the Fox News Channel and Fox Broadcasting Company.

Summary: The Significance of Studying Digital Media Law

In our interconnected world, where media has seamlessly woven itself into the fabric of our daily lives, the study of digital media law holds profound significance. This book transcends the boundaries of traditional analog media and burgeoning digital start-ups. It meticulously examines the far-reaching impact of law, ethics, and culture on a diverse spectrum of individuals in the digital age—from amateur podcasters to tech behemoths, from social media influencers to Pulitzer Prize–winning journalists, and from filmmakers and musicians navigating the realm of

AI-generated content to video gamers seamlessly integrating celebrities and trademarked goods into their virtual landscapes.

As we embark on this intellectual journey through the pages of this book, we will unravel the complex relationship between digital media and the law. The discussions within will delve into ongoing debates surrounding the adequacy of current legal frameworks and the compelling need for novel regulations that can effectively grapple with the constantly evolving challenges presented by the digital landscape. In a world where anyone can assume the role of an anonymous digital publisher, possessing a comprehensive understanding of digital media law becomes not just advantageous but essential for every well-informed individual. This includes not only mass communication students, business entrepreneurs, or judges but also anyone who engages with the digital world.

This book will investigate some of the most pressing legal and ethical issues of our time. From safeguarding politically charged free speech rights in the digital public square to striking a delicate balance between protecting reputation and the public's right to know, it will scrutinize questions like the right to erase one's digital past; the boundaries of privacy in the age of digital news and online advertising; the complexities of whistleblowing, leaks, and national security; and the intricate web of publicity rights surrounding celebrities and historical figures in the realm of AI-generated content. Additionally, it will explore the accountability of tech companies for potential mental health harm inflicted upon social media users.

Welcome to the exploration of *Digital Media Law*, where change is the only constant, and the future unfolds with each technological leap, social media reaction, and judicial decision. This journey promises to be a thought-provoking exploration of the legal landscape in the ever-evolving digital frontier.

Discussion Questions

1. How has the landscape of media transformed in the digital age, and what role does digital media law play in regulating this new realm?
2. In what ways has the rise of digital media since the 1990s given birth to intricate legal and ethical issues? Provide examples to illustrate the complexity.

3. Define *digital media* and its various forms, emphasizing the transmission of content through digital binary signals. How does this differ from traditional media formats?
4. Explore the significance and complexity of digital media in reshaping society and the legal frameworks that govern it.
5. How has the digital revolution impacted communication, business, and societal engagement?
6. Discuss the evolution of legal challenges associated with digital media, highlighting the dynamic nature of these issues in the rapidly changing digital landscape.
7. Analyze the democratization of media in the digital era, emphasizing how anyone with basic tools can broadcast globally.
8. Delve into the potential challenges arising from the unrestricted expression in digital media, particularly focusing on the blurred line between free speech rights and overreach. Provide examples of situations where digital anonymity may shield individuals from accountability.
9. Compare the accountability structures in traditional media with the current scenario where anyone posting online can be held responsible for legal violations. How has this shift impacted the understanding and application of media laws and ethics?
10. Investigate the implications of digital anonymity on legal violations such as defamatory statements or obscene images. How can the legal system adapt to address these challenges while respecting the principles of free speech in the digital era?

Works Referenced

Calfas, Jennifer. "Social Media Could Pose 'Profound Risk of Harm' to Young People's Health, Surgeon General Warns." *The Wall Street Journal*, May 23, 2023, accessed at https://www.wsj.com/articles/social-media-could-pose-profound-risk-of-harm-to-young-peoples-mental-health-surgeon-general-warns-db9eaaf8

Communications Law and Ethics: Media Law and Ethics, accessed at https://revolutionsincommunication.com/law/digital

Digital Media Law Project (blog) accessed at https://www.dmlp.org

Jones, Michael. *Art Law*, 2nd ed. Rowman & Littlefield, Lanham, MD, 2023.

Maheshwari, Sapna. "A.I. Fuels a New Era of Product Placement." *The New York Times*, February 2, 2024, accessed at https://www.nytimes.com/2024/02/01/business/media/artificial-intelligence-product-placement.html?searchResultPosition=1

Mollick, Ethan. *Co-Intelligence*. Penguin Books, New York, 2024.

Seth, Shobhit. "The World's Top Media Companies." *Investopedia*, October 22, 2022, accessed at https://www.investopedia.com/stock-analysis/021815/worlds-top-ten-media-companies-dis-cmcsa-fox.aspx

2

Voices and Echoes: Balancing Freedom and Control in the Social Media Sphere

> *Congress shall make no law respecting an establishment of religion, or prohibiting the free exercise thereof; or abridging the freedom of speech, or of the press; or the right of the people peaceably to assemble, and to petition the government for a redress of grievances.*
>
> —First Amendment, US Constitution

The bedrock of American democracy, the **First Amendment** to the **US Constitution**, is a cornerstone within the Bill of Rights, explicitly preventing Congress from enacting laws that encroach upon the freedom of speech, press, religion, assembly, and the right to petition the government for a redress of grievances. This expansive safeguard of speech not only encompasses spoken or written words but extends to diverse forms of expression, including the complex landscape of digital media. As technology and societal norms evolve, the US Supreme Court has been tasked with reviewing the application of **First Amendment** protections in the face of emerging digital and social media platforms. Additionally, freedom of expression is a fundamental human right recognized in numerous international human rights treaties.

This chapter endeavors to provide an expansive exploration of the legal contours surrounding freedom of expression, synthesizing constitutional underpinnings, contemporary issues, and pertinent case law. Its objective is to furnish readers with a thoughtful and balanced comprehension of the complexities and confusion inherent in freedom of expression within the digital age, addressing restrictions imposed by both governments and digital media platforms' terms and conditions of use. The discussion underscores the necessity for a judicious legal framework that not only upholds individual rights but also adeptly tackles the evolving challenges presented by the digital era.

In the dynamic terrain of digital media, the amalgamation of technology and communication has brought forth an era characterized by unparalleled access to information and global connectivity. Within this dynamic realm, the fundamental right to freedom of expression assumes a pivotal role, presenting both unprecedented opportunities and intricate challenges. This examination reveals that the digital age has not only magnified the potency of individual expression but has also prompted profound inquiries into the boundaries and constraints of such freedoms. From the unbridled dissemination of user-generated content on social media platforms to the intricate interplay between privacy and expression, the legal dimensions of digital media demand meticulous analysis, a task not always requisite in traditional media with well-established legal boundaries and ethical norms.

Importance of Freedom of Expression in the Digital Age

In recent years, the emergence of social media platforms, such as Twitter, now X, and Facebook, now Meta, has provided individuals with unprecedented opportunities to express their opinions and engage in public discourse. For instance, the Arab Spring, MeToo, and Black Lives Matter movements demonstrated the transformative power of digital media in amplifying dissenting voices and catalyzing political change.

Moreover, citizen journalism has flourished in the digital landscape, with ordinary individuals becoming reporters and disseminators of information. During events like the Occupy Wall Street protests and even the Israeli-Palestinian conflict, citizens used platforms like YouTube and blogs to share firsthand accounts, challenging traditional media narratives and contributing to a more refined yet politically charged understanding of the issues at hand.

Within the sphere of innovation and creative expression, platforms such as Kickstarter and Patreon have ushered in a transformative era, empowering artists, writers, and creators to establish direct connections with their audiences, sidestepping conventional gatekeepers. A striking illustration of this paradigm shift can be observed in the music industry. Approximately a decade ago, nearly 90 percent of the music content available on streaming platforms was dominated by major record label companies. In contrast, today, the landscape has undergone a significant transformation. Emerging artists now leverage platforms like TikTok and YouTube to create music independently, challenging the traditional support and power structures of major music labels like Universal Music Group, Sony, and Warner Music. This shift is reflected in their current contribution, which constitutes around 10 percent of the total music content available. This democratization of creativity has engendered a flourishing environment for diverse voices and niche content, providing an invaluable platform for those who might otherwise struggle for visibility within the confines of traditional media structures.

Nevertheless, amid these favorable advancements, the trajectory of digital media has introduced its set of challenges. One notable concern is the emergence of the echo-chamber effect, where individuals are exposed primarily to information that reinforces their existing beliefs, potentially contributing to the polarization of public discourse. The algorithms embedded in social media platforms, strategically designed to optimize user engagement, may inadvertently prioritize sensational content at the expense of nuanced discussions, thereby shaping the nature of the information ecosystem. In the realm of music, the scenario is equally daunting, with an influx of over a hundred and twenty thousand music tracks posted daily on streaming platforms. This surge, driven by aspiring artists seeking algorithmic recognition, inundates these platforms with an overwhelming abundance of songs, posing a distinct challenge in navigating and curating content effectively.

In addition, instances of hate speech, fueled by the anonymity provided by digital platforms, have sparked debates on the limits of free expression. The prevalence of misinformation, again amplified by social media algorithms, has raised concerns about the potential impact on public opinion and democratic processes. Additionally, revelations about mass surveillance and data breaches have heightened privacy concerns, prompting a reevaluation of the delicate balance between protecting personal privacy and preserving the principles of free speech.

Evolution of Digital Media and Its Impact on Freedom of Expression

In the analog era, people traditionally received their news, information, and entertainment through established media such as newspapers, television, and radio. These time-honored outlets acted as gatekeepers, controlling the flow of information and shaping public narratives. Broadcasting networks determined the news agenda, and print publications decided which stories made it to the front page. The information ecosystem was characterized by a one-to-many communication model, where a select few controlled the dissemination of content to mass audiences.

The shift to digital media began to gain momentum with the advent of the internet in the late twentieth century. The proliferation of personal computers and the development of the World Wide Web democratized access to information, allowing individuals to create and share content on a global scale. The transition accelerated in the early twenty-first century with the rise of social media platforms, marking a groundbreaking moment in how people engage with news, information, and each other.

Leading the charge in this digital revolution are tech giants such as Google, Facebook, and X. Google, with its search engine dominance, became the go-to platform for accessing information, fundamentally changing how people discover news and content. Facebook revolutionized social interaction, fostering a digital space where individuals could share personal updates, articles, and opinions with their social networks. X, with its succinct format, emerged as a real-time news-sharing platform, influencing public discourse in 280 characters or less.

In the early to mid-2000s, the growth of mobile internet and the widespread adoption of mobile applications have played a pioneering role in shaping the digital media landscape, fostering an era of unprecedented connectivity and information accessibility. The advent of smartphones and the proliferation of high-speed mobile networks have empowered individuals with "always-on" access to information and communication, fundamentally altering how people interact with content.

This constant connectivity has fueled a surge in content creation and sharing across various digital platforms. The convenience of accessing the internet anytime, anywhere has led to a democratization of information dissemination, allowing individuals from diverse backgrounds to participate actively in shaping the digital narrative. Social media platforms, blogging sites, and multimedia-sharing apps have become powerful tools for expressing ideas, opinions, and experiences, not without consequences.

Freedom of expression has particularly flourished in this environment. The immediacy of mobile communication enables individuals to share their thoughts, perspectives, and creativity instantaneously with a global audience. This has resulted in a rich tapestry of diverse voices contributing

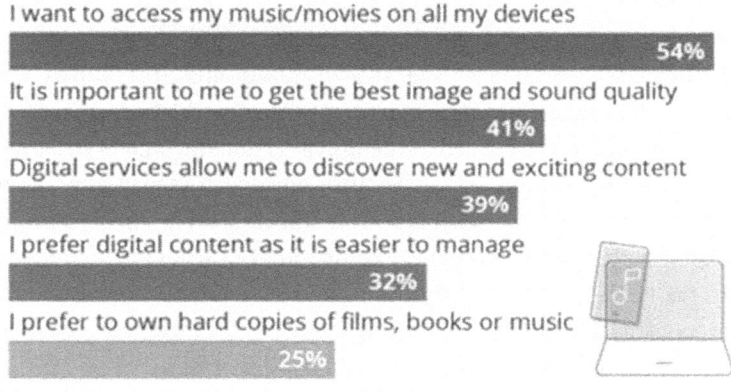

Figure 2.1 What's driving the digital media.

to the digital discourse, breaking away from traditional custodians and allowing for a more inclusive representation of viewpoints.

Moreover, the visual and interactive nature of mobile apps has expanded the scope of creative expression. From multimedia storytelling to user-generated content on platforms like YouTube, Instagram, and LinkedIn, individuals now have versatile means to convey their messages and narratives. The "never-off" nature of mobile connectivity has effectively dismantled temporal and geographical barriers, creating a dynamic space where digital expression knows no bounds. However, alongside the positive aspects, challenges such as misinformation, digital divides, and privacy concerns have also emerged.

More recently, emerging technologies, including artificial intelligence (AI), blockchain, and the metaverse, are catalyzing a disruptive shift in the digital landscape at unprecedented speed and societal impact. Here are working definitions for each of these new technologies.

Artificial Intelligence (AI): AI refers to the development of computer systems that can perform tasks that typically require human intelligence. This encompasses activities such as problem-solving, learning, language understanding, and decision-making. Machine learning, a subset of AI, involves the use of algorithms that enable systems to learn and improve from experience without being explicitly programmed. AI applications range from virtual assistants and chatbots to complex systems used in health care, finance, and autonomous vehicles.

Blockchain: Blockchain is a decentralized and distributed ledger technology that records transactions across a network of computers. Each transaction, or block, is linked to the previous one through cryptographic hashes, forming a chain. This structure ensures transparency, security, and immutability of the recorded data. Blockchain is most commonly associated with cryptocurrencies like Bitcoin, but its applications extend to diverse fields such as supply chain management, voting systems, and smart contracts. The decentralized nature of blockchain challenges traditional models of centralized control and ownership.

Metaverse: The metaverse is a collective virtual shared space that is created by the convergence of physical and virtual reality. It is a space where users, represented by avatars, can interact with a computer-generated environment and with each other in real-time. The metaverse goes beyond traditional virtual reality by encompassing augmented reality, 3D graphics, and immersive technologies. It is envisioned as a fully realized digital universe where people can engage in various activities, such as work, socializing, gaming, and commerce, blurring the lines between the physical and digital realms.

As these technologies advance, they bring to the forefront critical issues related to ownership, control, privacy, and ethics. In the context of AI, questions arise about the ethical use of algorithms, bias in decision-making, and the potential impact on employment. For example, advanced AI tools like ChatGPT and ElevenLabs enable the training of chatbots to mimic the realistic voices of deceased children from gun violence. Used in a campaign for gun safety and stricter control measures by the parents of the deceased, these deepfake voices raise ethical concerns, prompting a critical examination of the moral implications tied to this emerging technology. Blockchain challenges conventional notions of centralized authority, introducing decentralized governance models and redefining concepts of ownership and trust. In the metaverse, concerns revolve around data privacy, security, social connections, and the implications of a virtual space where individuals increasingly conduct real-life activities bypassing face-to-face interactions.

As we examine the evolving landscape of these technologies, a careful consideration of their ethical implications and societal impact becomes imperative. Balancing innovation with safeguards to protect individual rights, privacy, and freedom of expression will be pivotal in ensuring a responsible and inclusive digital future.

In addition to their impact on personal expression and social dynamics, digital media have become indispensable in shaping modern business and communication landscapes. Platforms such as LinkedIn, owned by tech giant Microsoft with a market capitalization over $3 trillion, have undergone a metamorphosis in the realm of professional networking, redefining how individuals connect with peers, colleagues, and potential employers. LinkedIn has not only transformed the job search process but has also become a dynamic space for knowledge sharing, industry discussions, and professional development. The platform's influence extends beyond traditional networking, playing a pivotal role in career growth and personal branding.

Spotify has developed a new feature that enables subscribers to become DJs by offering tools to speed up, mash up, and creatively edit songs from their favorite artists. In this digital age, recording artists and music publishers often struggle to receive proper compensation when altered versions of their songs are used across platforms like Instagram Reels, where such modifications are difficult to track. However, Spotify's new tool aims to address this issue by ensuring that rights holders—including labels, publishers, and artists—are paid whenever fans stream modified versions of their music. This initiative creates a space for creative musical experimentation while maintaining a fair compensation system for the original creators.

Simultaneously, e-commerce giants like Amazon have revolutionized the retail industry through the seamless integration of digital media. These platforms offer consumers an unparalleled shopping experience, leveraging advanced algorithms, personalized recommendations, and user reviews to enhance customer engagement. Amazon, in particular, has reshaped the retail landscape, fostering a shift toward online shopping that has had profound implications for brick-and-mortar businesses. The convenience and accessibility afforded by digital media platforms have transformed consumer behavior, creating a new era of e-commerce that transcends geographical boundaries.

Nevertheless, the expansion of online retailers encompasses rapidly emerging start-ups such as Temu and Shein, both of which US lawmakers

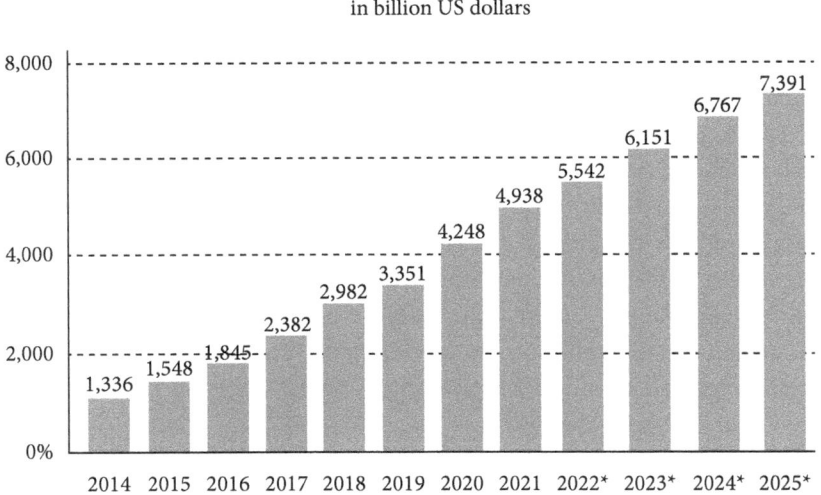

Figure 2.2 E-commerce sales worldwide.

have previously criticized for allegedly exploiting specific trade rules due to their affiliations with China. Lawmakers have been raising data privacy and national security concerns regarding these Chinese companies, as well as the social network TikTok, owned by ByteDance, also a Chinese company. The recently enacted law that would compel ByteDance to divest TikTok to a non-Chinese owner or risk being banned in the United States altogether has been challenged by free speech First Amendment advocates in federal court.

The advent of digital media has not only transformed consumer-facing industries but has also revolutionized the way businesses operate internally. The accessibility and connectivity offered by digital platforms have played a crucial role in facilitating remote work and online collaboration. Platforms like Zoom, Microsoft Teams, and Slack have become integral to the modern workplace, enabling seamless communication and collaboration irrespective of geographical distances. The rise of remote work, accelerated by digital media, has redefined traditional avenues and venues of work, emphasizing flexibility and work-life balance.

Furthermore, digital media have become catalysts for global business transactions. International trade and commerce now rely heavily on digital platforms for communication, negotiation, and transaction facilitation. E-commerce platforms serve as global marketplaces, connecting buyers and sellers across continents. Cryptocurrencies and blockchain technologies, while fundamentally altering financial transactions, have also played a role in fostering secure and transparent global business interactions.

In essence, the innovative power of digital media has not only impacted personal expression and social dynamics but has also become an integral force in the realms of business and communication. The continuous evolution of these platforms presents both challenges and opportunities, shaping the future landscape of work, commerce, and global connectivity. As businesses adapt to these digital shifts, the synergy between technology and commerce is likely to redefine industries, fostering innovation and efficiency in ways previously unimaginable.

The transition from analog to digital media has reshaped how people receive news, share information, connect, and conduct business. The evolution of digital media providers has not only democratized access to information but has also raised critical questions about the concentration of power, information integrity, and the delicate balance between freedom of expression and responsible content dissemination in the interconnected digital age.

Defining Digital Discourse: Supreme Court Landmark Decisions in Speech, Online Expression, and Creativity

The **First Amendment** to the **US Constitution** provides that the government must not "abridge the freedom of speech, or of the press." Free speech has long been considered one of the pillars of a democracy. Explaining its importance, Justice Oliver Wendell Holmes Jr. declared that "the best test of truth is the power of the thought to get itself accepted in the competition of the market." A faith in this marketplace of ideas continues to buttress **First Amendment** law; however, in light of the online efforts by bad faith actors to create fake news, advance white supremacist ideas, sow propaganda, and engage in disinformation and misinformation campaigns to weaken national security, this bedrock principle critical to the defense of democracy is under threat.

Examples of disinformation or false data abound, such as when Twitter mistakenly verified an imposter posing as drugmaker Eli Lilly with a blue check mark of authenticity. The imposter tweeted, "We are excited to announce insulin is free now," and this misleading information was retweeted thousands of times. Additionally, various false statements regarding the safety, efficacy, and origins of Covid-19 vaccines were disseminated on various social media platforms, including Facebook and X.

Recently, the Food and Drug Administration (FDA) issued a health and safety warning about "Nyquil chicken," a recipe posted on TikTok that involved marinating raw chicken in Nyquil. In another instance, a survey conducted by the Royal Society for Public Health in Britain asked individuals aged 14 to 24 how social media platforms impacted their health and well-being. The survey revealed that Snapchat, Facebook, Twitter, and Instagram all contributed to increased feelings of depression, anxiety, poor body image, and loneliness.

These instances raise the critical question of whether the foundational constitutional assumption about free speech still holds true in the context of social media or, as the president of Microsoft writes in his book *Tools and Weapons*, if unbridled freedom in social media might be the technology that drives us apart.

The delicate balance between individual expression and societal interests is particularly relevant when it comes to creativity or artistic expression. While the **First Amendment** guarantees the freedom of speech and press without government interference, these rights are not absolute. In democratic societies, there is a need to prevent harm to reputation, violations of copyright and moral rights, exposure to indecent speech, and threats to peace.

Initially, the framers of the Constitution focused on protecting spoken words. However, it took almost 150 years for the US Supreme Court to recognize that non-spoken communication, such as paintings, posters, or comics, as well as symbolic speech embodied in flag burning or wearing an armband, are also protected by the Constitution. Courts have generally been reluctant to regulate the content of nonverbal messages but have been more willing to accept regulations that serve a legitimate societal goal and are unrelated to the message's meaning.

The distinction between content-based and content-neutral laws has played a key role in free speech cases. Content-based laws regulate speech based on its substance, while content-neutral laws generally control the time, place, and manner of speech. The government bears a heavy burden in defending content-based restrictions since they are subject to strict scrutiny. In contrast, content-neutral regulations are reviewed under a form of intermediate scrutiny, which means that they are more likely to survive a challenge, especially when public safety is a concern.

Below are the key US Supreme Court cases that examine restrictions on the government's censorship of different types of speech, with a particular focus on online expression.

Schenck v. United States (249 U.S. 47 (1919)) is a landmark case in US constitutional law that played a crucial role in shaping the boundaries of free speech, particularly during times of war. The case centered on Charles Schenck, a socialist and member of the Socialist Party of America, who distributed leaflets urging resistance to the military draft during the First World War. The US government charged Schenck under the **Espionage Act of 1917**, arguing that his actions presented a clear and present danger to the nation's military efforts.

The Supreme Court, in a unanimous decision authored by Justice Oliver Wendell Holmes, established the "clear and present danger" test as a standard for evaluating restrictions on free speech. The key principle of this test is that the government can limit speech only when it poses a direct and imminent threat to the country or its citizens. In Schenck's case, the Court held that his anti-draft advocacy presented a clear and present danger, justifying the government's restriction on his speech.

Justice Holmes famously wrote in the opinion that "the most stringent protection of free speech would not protect a man falsely shouting fire in a theater and causing a panic." This analogy illustrates that certain forms of expression can be restricted if they create a danger that is both clear and present.

While Schenck's conviction was upheld, the case's significance lies in the establishment of the "clear and present danger" test as a guiding principle for evaluating **First Amendment** rights. Over time, subsequent cases have refined and clarified the application of this test, but Schenck remains a foundational precedent in the constitutional analysis of free speech, especially in the context of national security and wartime circumstances.

In *Zeran v. America Online, Inc.* (129 F.3d 327 (4th Cir. 1997), cert. denied, 524 U.S. 937 (1998)) a federal appeals court established that online platforms are not treated as the publishers of user-generated content, providing them with immunity from liability for content posted by third parties. This immunity has been crucial in fostering the growth of online platforms as spaces for diverse expression without imposing an undue burden on their operators to monitor every user submission.

The same year as the *Zeran* decision by a lower court, the Supreme Court decided *Reno v. American Civil Liberties Union* (521 U.S. 844 (1997)). In this case, the focus was on the regulation of indecent and patently offensive content on the internet, particularly under the **Communications Decency Act (CDA)**. The Supreme Court played a pivotal role by striking down crucial provisions of the **CDA**, underlining the internet's unique and expansive nature as a medium for free expression. The Court emphasized that internet companies are not broadcasters, therefore, they are not subject to regulatory control by government agencies like the **Federal Communications Commission**. The decision emphasized the protection of **First Amendment** rights for adults to access and disseminate information online, setting a crucial precedent in favor of online free speech.

In the 2015 case of *Elonis v. United States* (575 U.S. 723 (2015)), Anthony Elonis found himself at the center of a legal battle after being convicted for posting threatening messages on Facebook. The pivotal issue in the case revolved around whether Elonis's intent to instill fear could be established without considering his subjective state of mind. The Supreme Court, in a unanimous decision, ruled that mere recklessness was insufficient for a conviction of making criminal threats. The verdict underscored the significance of considering an individual's subjective intent and mental state, particularly in the realm of online expression. This recognition highlighted the complexities of applying traditional legal standards to the ever-evolving dynamics of communication in the digital age.

In another landmark decision the focus was on a state law in North Carolina that prohibited registered sex offenders from using certain social media platforms. Lester Packingham, a registered sex offender, contested the law, arguing that it infringed upon his **First Amendment** rights. The Supreme Court, in a unanimous ruling re *Packingham v. North Carolina* (582 U.S. 98 (2017)), declared the North Carolina law overly broad, stating that it impinged on individuals' fundamental right to participate in protected speech on social media platforms. The decision highlighted the contemporary importance of online platforms as essential avenues for communication and the exchange of ideas, characterizing them as the modern equivalent of the public square.

In the 2019 split-decision case of *Manhattan Community Access Corp. v. Halleck* (139 S.Ct.1921 (2019)), the dispute centered on Manhattan Community Access Corp. (MCAC), a private, nonprofit organization responsible for overseeing public access channels on a cable system in New York City. Producers DeeDee Halleck and Jesus Papoleto Melendez contended that MCAC violated their **First Amendment** rights by limiting access to public access channels. In a decision authored by Justice Brett Kavanaugh, the Supreme Court clarified that when a private entity such as MCAC manages public access channels on a cable system, it does not perform a traditional, exclusive public function. The act of opening its property for speech by others does not transform MCAC into a state actor, exempting it from **First Amendment** constraints on its editorial discretion.

The decision emphasized that MCAC's operation of public access channels did not constitute a traditional, exclusive public function and clarified the state actor doctrine. It reinforced that private entities managing public access channels are not automatically transformed into state actors subject to **First Amendment** restrictions.

Masterpiece Cakeshop v. Colorado Civil Rights Commission (138 S. Ct. 1719 (2018)): The Masterpiece Cakeshop case introduced a complex legal scenario involving the clash between antidiscrimination laws and the **First Amendment's** protection of free exercise of religion and free speech. Jack Phillips, the owner of Masterpiece Cakeshop, argued that designing a wedding cake for a same-sex couple would violate his Christian beliefs and constitute compelled speech by the government, infringing upon his free speech rights. The Supreme Court ruled in favor of Jack Phillips, but the decision was narrow, leaving the broader conflict between antidiscrimination laws and religious freedom unresolved.

The Supreme Court's decision in *303 Creative LLC v. Elenis* (600 U.S. 570 (2023)) addressed the complex issue of when and how the **First Amendment's** protection of free speech applies to artists and creative professionals in the context of public accommodation laws within the digital space. The case centered on Lorie Smith, a Christian website designer and owner of 303 Creative LLC, who argued that being compelled by Colorado's Anti-Discrimination Act (CADA) to create wedding websites for same-sex couples would violate her religious beliefs and her **First Amendment** rights to free speech and expression. The Supreme Court, in a 6–3 decision, ruled in favor of Smith, holding that the **First Amendment** prohibits Colorado from forcing a website designer to create expressive designs that convey messages with which the designer disagrees. The Court's opinion, authored by Justice Gorsuch, emphasized that the **First Amendment** protects individual rights to speak one's mind, regardless of the government's views, and that this protection extends to "all manner of speech," including "pictures, films, paintings, drawings, and engravings," as well as speech conveyed over the internet.

The *303 Creative LLC v. Elenis* case illustrates the Supreme Court's struggle with defining who is considered an artist or creative person deserving of **First Amendment** protection. The decision underscores the balance the Court seeks to maintain between protecting free speech and expression in the digital space and upholding the principles of public accommodation and nondiscrimination.

Also in 2023, against the backdrop of the defendant Mr. Counterman sending Facebook messages implying potential harm, the Supreme Court, led by Justice Elena Kagan, in a content-based decision ruled that the **First Amendment** demands proof of the speaker's "subjective understanding" for true threat convictions. In the matter of *Counterman v. Colorado* (600 U.S. 66 (2023)), the state needs to prove "recklessness," indicating a conscious disregard for a substantial risk of the messages being perceived as threats. This decision raises the evidentiary bar for prosecutors seeking true threat convictions, emphasizing protection for more speech, even if offensive, as long as the speaker lacked the intent to threaten violence.

Expanding on this, the Supreme Court declared that Colorado's law concerning "true threats" ran afoul of the **First Amendment**. In order to secure a conviction for such threats, the government is now required to establish only a subjective component, involving the defendant consciously disregarding a substantial risk of their speech being perceived as threatening, introducing a "recklessness" standard. The ruling underscores the significance of upholding free speech, especially in the digital sphere, and places the responsibility for managing harmful or offensive nonviolent speech on social media platforms. This management is achieved through specific standards outlined in their terms and conditions of use, rather than relying on an objective test.

However, it would be unjust to focus solely on the Court's legal analysis, disregarding the significant harm inflicted by online stalker Billy Raymond Counterman on the victim, Coles Whalen. Over two years, Counterman sent numerous aggressive Facebook messages to musician Whalen, persisting even after being blocked by creating new accounts on various platforms to continue sending threatening messages. This relentless stalking induced fear in Whalen for her life and that of her children, leading her to modify her behavior by avoiding solo walks, declining social engagements, and canceling performances. Whalen reported Counterman's actions, resulting in charges, including stalking for credible threats and causing emotional distress, as well as harassment. While Colorado dismissed most cases, the stalking charge remained the focus of the Court's litigation. Now, victims of online stalking, like Whalen, must maneuver through social media restrictions on harmful speech for some level of protection, presenting a significant, if not impossible, challenge.

In two additional significant 2023 Supreme Court cases, *Gonzalez v. Google* (598 U.S. 617 (2023)) and *Twitter v. Taamneh* (598 U.S. 471 (2023)), the court dismissed the idea of holding social media giants, YouTube and Twitter, responsible for alleged involvement in terrorist violence stemming from user-generated content on their platforms. The case against YouTube, which is owned by Google, raised concerns as the families of those harmed by terrorists aimed to limit the application of **Section 230** of the **Communications Decency Act**, a crucial law protecting internet users' speech. The court, emphasizing the enduring significance of **Section 230**, which shields online services and users from legal consequences related to content created by others, affirmed the law's integrity. Importantly, the court chose not to explore the extent of **Section 230**, confirming that online platforms, as a general rule, cannot be held accountable under the **Anti-Terrorism Act**. These decisions safeguard the legal framework that shields internet users and online services from unwarranted censorship, ensuring a resilient and unrestricted online experience, while leaving families harmed by terrorists' online posting without an adequate remedy.

These influential cases collectively impact the contours of online free speech rights, establishing precedents that will influence how the law addresses the intersection of government censorship, digital media, and freedom of expression. The decisions will shape the balance between protecting speech and addressing legitimate societal concerns in the evolving landscape of online communication. The Supreme Court's rulings will serve as benchmarks for future legal considerations, reflecting the ongoing efforts to adapt constitutional principles to the intricacies of the digital age making the task of regulators increasingly complex and difficult.

Individual States' Attempts to Regulate Social Media

In 2018, Mark Zuckerburg, in testimony before Congress famously said: "My position is not that there should be no regulation. I think that the real question as the internet becomes more important in people's lives, is what is the right regulation, not whether there should be or not."

Disappointed by the perceived inability of Congress to address the technical, free speech, censorship, and privacy issues on social media, lawmakers in thirty-four states have introduced hundreds of legislative proposals. The most recent impetus for the call for regulation of social media access and content stemmed from a whistleblower consultant for

Meta disclosing to a 2023 Congressional Committee that Mark Zuckerberg and other executives were aware that one in eight social media users under the age of 16 reported experiencing unwanted sexual advances on the platform within the previous week. The whistleblower argued that for the well-being of its users, Meta needed to pivot its approach. Instead of relying solely on a flawed system of rules-based policing, the company should focus on addressing these negative experiences. The bills being proposed, as highlighted by National Conference of State Legislatures' data, are designed to establish regulations governing how social media companies, including prominent platforms such as Facebook (Meta), Instagram, TikTok, and X, act to prevent individual and national security harm.

One of the primary concerns also is exemplified by the tragic mass shooting of fifty-one Muslims in Christchurch, New Zealand. The assailants initially shared details of the attack on X, posted announcements on message boards, and live-streamed the event on Facebook. The distressing footage was subsequently re-uploaded on platforms like YouTube, X, and Reddit, prompting social media platforms to race to remove the clips as they resurfaced. In the same year as this appalling act of terrorism, a collaborative effort between Oxford University and an American data-analytics firm analyzed testimony from Instagram, Facebook, YouTube, and X, provided to a Senate investigative committee. The findings revealed that Russia's Internet Research Agency (IRA) orchestrated a comprehensive and ongoing attack on the United States. Using computerized propaganda, the IRA aimed to misinform and polarize American voters—an online assault on democracy that the Russians and other foreign adversaries continue to this day.

Despite the high number of proposed bills, only a handful have successfully become law. Notably, these include statutes in Texas and Florida designed to penalize social media platforms accused by Republicans of censoring conservative voices. Nevertheless, federal courts have intervened and blocked the implementation of these measures in Texas and Florida, citing concerns related to violating the First Amendment.

The clash between state lawmakers and tech giants over the regulation of online speech underscores the complex legal landscape surrounding free expression on digital platforms. The tension between the desire to address perceived biases or censorship and the constitutional protection of free speech sets the stage for ongoing legal battles that will likely shape the future of social media regulation in the United States, yet any proposed state legislation seem doubtful to overcome Supreme Court scrutiny.

Social Media Platforms' Policies on Regulating Online Speech

The content moderation policies of major social media companies in the United States continue to evolve in light of increased legislative pressure. In general, these platforms attempt to prohibit hate speech, racist speech, and content harmful to children to create a safer online environment. Here are some basic standards embedded in policy statements and terms-and-conditions agreements for regulating content by the largest social media companies:

1. **Facebook:**
    - Facebook has community standards that explicitly prohibit hate speech, including content that directly attacks people based on characteristics such as race, ethnicity, and religion.
    - Racist speech and content harmful to children are also against Facebook's community standards, albeit without significant enforcement.
    - Facebook uses a combination of technology and human review to enforce these policies with imperfect success.
2. **Twitter or X:**
    - X prohibits hate speech and any content that promotes violence or harassment against individuals or groups based on attributes such as race and ethnicity. However, in contrast to stated policy, Elon Musk, who identifies as a staunch advocate of absolute free speech, has escalated his efforts to silence critics, aligning with an online movement associated with white nationalists and anti-Semitic propagandists. In a recent tweet, Musk targeted the Anti-Defamation League (ADL), an organization committed to countering anti-Semitism. Musk has issued legal threats against the ADL, attributing the departure of advertisers from his declining social media platform to the organization.

- The platform also has policies against child sexual exploitation and abuse.
3. **Instagram:**
   - As a subsidiary of Facebook, Instagram follows similar community standards, including the prohibition of hate speech and content harmful to children.
   - Instagram also has guidelines against bullying, harassment, and content that promotes self-harm.
4. **YouTube:**
   - YouTube's policies include restrictions on hate speech, which encompasses content that promotes violence or discrimination against individuals or groups based on attributes like race.
   - The platform has guidelines to protect minors from harmful content, and it tries to enforce policies against content that endangers the well-being of children.
5. **Snapchat:**
   - Snapchat prohibits hate speech, including content that promotes discrimination or violence based on characteristics like race.
   - The platform also has community guidelines to protect against the sharing of explicit content involving minors.

Notwithstanding the user policy statements of these social media platforms, investigative reporting by *The Wall Street Journal* uncovered insights from Facebook's internal message board. The reviewed content emphasized the significant impact of Instagram on the self-perception and descriptions of young women. Over the last few years, Facebook has been actively engaged in studies assessing the influence of its photo-sharing app on its extensive user base, particularly focusing on the well-being of teenage girls.

Facebook's own research discovered that its Instagram app had a significant detrimental impact on teenage girls. Some of the identified concerns include:

1. **Negative Impact on Body Image:** The report suggested that the use of Instagram contributes to negative perceptions and descriptions of body image among young women.
2. **Mental Health Issues:** Instagram was found to be linked to mental health problems, with concerns about the platform's impact on the well-being of teenage girls.

3. **Comparisons and Self-Esteem:** The internal message board content revealed that comparisons on Instagram could lead to changes in how young women view and describe themselves, indicating potential issues with self-esteem.

The *Journal*'s reporting highlights significant shortcomings in the platform's content moderation and safety measures, as harmful content affecting vulnerable users was reportedly prevalent. The ability of social media platforms to strike a balance between providing a space for self-expression and protecting users, especially young and impressionable ones, remains a complex ongoing challenge. Facebook's use of algorithms is designed to optimize user engagement, often by presenting content that aligns with users' preferences, interests, and behaviors. They create a continuous stream of content reinforcing unrealistic beauty standards, potentially impacting self-esteem. Instagram's advertising algorithms may also contribute to the issue by delivering targeted ads based on user behavior. If the algorithms identify a user's vulnerability to certain body image concerns, they might expose them to ads that capitalize on these insecurities, exacerbating the problem. The findings underscore the importance of more robust content moderation policies, and continuous efforts by platforms to address the negative consequences associated with their services, and accountability for failing to perform these duties, particularly when it comes to the well-being of young users.

Challenges to Regulating Social Media Content

The landscape of the internet, especially social media, has undergone a profound transformation since the 1990s, with a shift in content creation dynamics and power. While individual users still contribute to social media content, the pivotal role played by algorithms, serving as the blueprints for intelligence systems employed by companies in shaping and amplifying content, cannot be understated. This raises pertinent questions about the accountability of these platforms, including whether to impose a legal duty of care to make them accountable for harm to its users, particularly when it comes to the dissemination of viral and promoted content.

In comparison to traditional media companies, which have traditionally been held liable for damages arising from any defamatory content they propagate, the responsibility of social media platforms for the amplification of such content is increasingly being scrutinized. The rise of algorithms as key arbiters of content distribution prompts a crucial inquiry into the point at which these platforms should be held liable for the impact of their algorithms.

Legislative action, particularly through the proposed **Platform Accountability and Transparency Act (PATA**), emerges as a potential partial solution to address pressing concerns in the realm of social media. **PATA** advocates for heightened transparency, proposing that social media platforms should mandatorily furnish data to independent researchers. This includes disclosing, along with original raw data, the content most amplified by their algorithms regularly.

Empowering independent scrutiny becomes essential to combat issues such as the spread of misleading information, ensuring compliance with laws preventing children under 13 from having social media accounts, and preventing algorithm-driven content that negatively impacts the mental health of younger users. Additionally, the proposed **Online Safety Act,** which is akin to the United Kingdom's recently enacted legislation of the same name, aims to protect children from sexual exploitation on social media platforms.

Relying solely on the self-regulation efforts of tech giants and social media companies, as proposed by transparency measures, may prove insufficient in effectively addressing a diverse range of issues. Critics of social media self-regulation voice concerns about potential impacts on unbridled free speech. On one side, conservative politicians argue that social media platforms frequently censor conservative thought and opinion. On the other side, liberal politicians contend that these platforms often fail to adequately remove or moderate harmful content, as well as postings of misinformation and disinformation.

The prospect of repealing **Section 230** is perceived as a potential threat to the ongoing growth of the digital economy. Nonetheless, adopting more refined approaches has become crucial to insuring the continuation of a democratic republic. For instance, tailoring regulatory requirements based on platform size or holding companies legally accountable for algorithmically promoted hate speech or harmful content, along with addressing issues like the exposure of adolescents to indecent or illegal images and texts, can initiate steps toward addressing these concerns. Striking an equilibrium between effective content moderation and the preservation of free speech rights necessitates thoughtful regulatory frameworks. This may require federal legislators to work directly with social media platforms and high-tech companies to find an appropriate and constitutionally permissible balance.

What is clear is that while the evolution of technology, particularly in the realm of social media, has undergone substantial changes, the law remains two steps behind any meaningful content regulation because of the "hands-off" approach by current jurisprudence interpretations who are also asked to interpret pre-algorithm statutes in a post-algorithm online world. To emphasize the point, Justice Kagan famously remarked during oral arguments in *Gonzalez v. Google* (598 U.S.___(2023)) drawing laughter from the audience, that we are not "the nine greatest experts on the internet."

Compounded by the global nature of the internet, with its cross-border issues such as foreign interference and cyber threats, effective regulation becomes challenging for individual countries when bad actors reside outside sovereign boundaries making jurisdiction nearly impossible. The negative influence of social media on society has grown significantly, impacting areas such as elections—with no better example than the attempt to disrupt the certification of presidential elections—public discourse, and

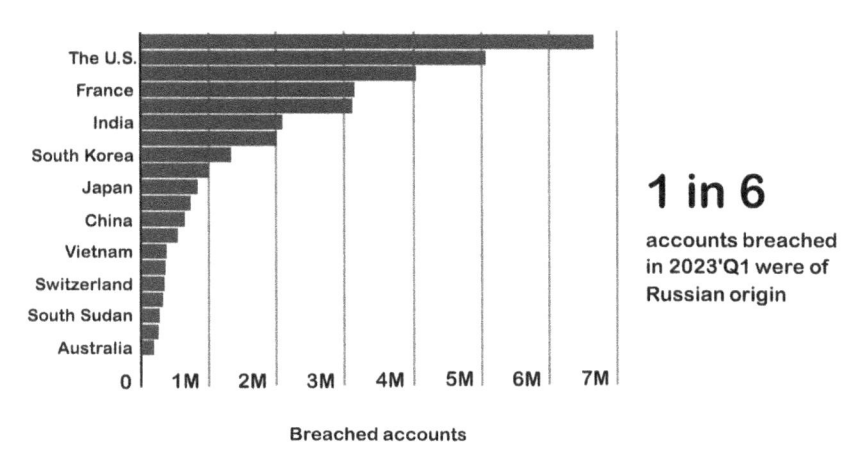

Figure 2.3 Most breached countries.

mental health, prompting a critical reevaluation of regulations to ensure alignment with contemporary needs across the world.

Furthermore, the concentration of power in large tech companies—Apple, Microsoft, Amazon, Meta, Google, NVIDIA, along with Tesla constitute significantly more than 25 percent of the market capitalization of all the S&P 500 firms—surpassing that of traditional media and all twenty-three energy stocks on the S&P gas and oil index, has raised concerns about accountability and monopolistic practices, necessitating consideration of antitrust regulatory measures to level the playing field.

Incidents like data breaches by Russian hackers targeting social media data bases, privacy scandals, and the spread of public health misinformation have fueled public outcry, reinforcing the assertion that the current regulatory status quo is inadequate. This growing recognition underscores the imperative for regulatory frameworks, whether instituted by government or by social media companies, to adapt to the dynamic nature of the digital landscape and effectively address emerging challenges, without compromising the democratic traditions of free speech enshrined in the **First Amendment**.

International Perspectives on Online Free Speech

Addressing the regulation of social media in today's global community is a formidable task, marked by a myriad of challenges. As these digital platforms seamlessly connect individuals across continents, the complexities of enforcing consistent standards become apparent. The borderless nature of the internet, combined with diverse cultural, legal, religious, and political landscapes, creates a dynamic environment where determining what constitutes acceptable speech, combating harmful content, and protecting fundamental rights pose significant hurdles.

Striking a balance between fostering free expression and preventing the spread of misinformation, hate speech, or other forms of online harm demands a focused and collaborative approach on a global scale. The challenges extend beyond legal considerations, encompassing technological advancements, varying definitions of harm, and the inherent tension between universal principles and contextual sensitivities.

Addressing these multifaceted challenges is crucial for developing effective and ethical frameworks that govern social media use in our interconnected world.

For example, within the European Union (EU), hate speech is deemed a criminal offense subject to **Article 10** of the **European Human Rights Convention**, which states that everyone has the right to freedom of expression. This right includes freedom to hold opinions and to receive and impart information and ideas without interference by public authority and regardless of frontiers. The United Kingdom also has specific laws targeting expressions of hatred and threats based on protected group membership, subject to the broader guarantees of the right to express and receive opinions, ideas, and information. In contrast, the United States, guided by **First Amendment** rights as discussed above, affords considerably broader protection to a wide spectrum of speech, even if it is perceived as harmful.

While the lack of a standardized terminology for identifying terms like *hate speech* contributes to the complexity of addressing the issue, discrepancies persist not only in defining what constitutes hate speech but also in gauging the severity of the harms it inflicts and the legal standards required to prove violations.

The challenges are further compounded by the online environment's unique characteristics, where harmful speech can proliferate rapidly, reaching a vast audience. The speed and global reach of online dissemination amplifies the impact of harmful speech, making it crucial to develop effective regulatory frameworks. As described earlier, even in a global context striking a balance between safeguarding freedom of expression and curbing the detrimental effects of harmful speech remains a delicate and contentious task.

Below are examples of how governments outside the United States are addressing the issue of managing online speech.

In late 2023, the United Kingdom's **Online Safety Act** was enacted. It stands as a pivotal milestone in digital regulation, ushering in a comprehensive framework to enhance online safety, particularly for children and addresses a spectrum of online harms. This landmark legislation places new responsibilities on online service providers, encompassing social media platforms and search engines, compelling them to proactively manage and mitigate risks associated with illegal and harmful content.

The Act prioritizes the protection of both children and adults online. It mandates online platforms to implement measures preventing children from accessing harmful content, such as pornography, bullying, and materials promoting self-harm, suicide, and eating disorders. Simultaneously, it aims to empower adults with greater control over the content they encounter in the digital realm.

The legislation addresses the swift removal of illegal content and introduces new offenses related to contemporary online phenomena like revenge pornography and the nonconsensual sharing of intimate images. It establishes a duty of care, unlike in the United States, requiring online services to conduct risk assessments and implement systems to enhance user safety, tackling both illegal content and protecting children from harmful material.

Regulation and enforcement of the **Online Safety Act** fall under the purview of Ofcom, the UK's communications regulator. Ofcom will publish codes of practice covering illegal content, child safety, and additional duties for specific services in phased releases. Noncompliance with the Act could result in fines reaching up to $22 million or 10 percent of global annual turnover, with potential criminal action against senior managers. In comparison, administrative bodies in the United States have limited regulatory authority. Although in 2024, the **Federal Communications Commission** made it unlawful to use AI-generated audio deepfakes in scam robocalls, stating that people have been tricked by voices that sounded like known relatives or colleagues. However, its enforcement within the global digital media community is questionable.

Given its extraterritorial reach, affecting any online service accessible to UK users regardless of location, the Act presents substantial compliance challenges for international businesses. To date there have been no reported cases of failure to comply.

Despite its noble objectives, the **Online Safety Act** has encountered criticism from diverse quarters. Privacy advocates, tech companies, and free speech organizations have expressed concerns regarding potential implications:

1. **Impact on Encryption:** Critics argue that the Act might undermine end-to-end encryption, posing risks to privacy and security. Messaging apps like WhatsApp and Signal have hesitated to comply with potential requirements that could compromise encryption.

2. **Free Speech and Overreach:** Fears persist that the Act's broad provisions could infringe on free speech, leading to over-censorship as platforms strive to avoid penalties.
3. **Implementation and Enforcement Challenges:** The phased implementation approach and the need for detailed guidance from Ofcom raise questions about the effectiveness of enforcing the Act's provisions and whether platforms can comply without significant operational changes.

The UK's **Online Safety Act** is a bold regulatory endeavor with a crucial focus on protecting children and combating online harms. While its objectives are widely endorsed, the Act's broad scope, potential impacts on privacy and free speech, and the global compliance challenges have triggered substantial debate. As Ofcom progresses with the phased implementation, the Act's effectiveness and its implications for online safety and digital rights will become clearer.

Across the North Sea from the United Kingdom, is the European Union (EU). It is founded on values such as respect for human dignity, freedom, democracy, equality, the rule of law, and respect for human rights. All forms of hatred and intolerance are incompatible with these fundamental rights and values. From the EU's perspective, hatred not only affects the individual victims, but it also represents a threat to vibrant democracies and a pluralistic society.

In the context of online social media speech and hate-motivated crimes, the legal standards of proof under EU law involve demonstrating elements that establish the commission of the offense. The specifics may vary, but generally, the legal standards include:

1. **Content and Expression:** Prosecutors must establish that the online content or expression in question constitutes hate speech, involving public incitement to violence or hatred against specific groups based on protected grounds like race, color, religion, national or ethnic origin, and descent.
2. **Identification of Perpetrator:** The prosecution needs to attribute the online speech to a specific individual or entity, demonstrating their involvement in the creation or dissemination of the content.
3. **Intent or Mens Rea:** Just as in traditional hate crimes, the prosecution may need to prove that the perpetrator acted with intent, knowledge, or recklessness regarding the hate-motivated nature of their online speech. In contrast, the current legal standard of proof

in the United States as articulated in the *Counterman v. Colorado* Supreme Court decision requires a showing of "recklessness," not proving knowledge or intent to harm another person.
4. **Criminal Act or Actus Reus:** There must be evidence that the online speech constitutes a criminal act, such as incitement to violence or hatred, as defined by EU law.
5. **Protected Groups:** Hate speech online typically involves discrimination against specific protected groups. The prosecution needs to establish that the online speech was motivated by prejudice against one or more of these groups. More recently, the European Union has enacted regulations seeking to combat online anti-Semitism and anti-Muslim hate speech.
6. **Causal Link to Harm:** If harm is caused by the online speech, the prosecution may need to establish a causal link between the hate-motivated content and the harm suffered by individuals or groups.
7. **Admissible Digital Evidence:** Given the online nature of the speech, the admissibility of digital evidence, such as screenshots, metadata, or records of online interactions, is crucial. The evidence must meet legal standards for reliability and relevance.
8. **Compliance with EU Law:** Ensuring that the case aligns with EU law, including the criminalization of hate-motivated crimes and speech as mandated by the 2008 Framework Decision, is an essential aspect of the legal standards.

EU Voluntary Code of Conduct

The relationship between the European Commission and major IT companies in a voluntary Code of Conduct to counter illegal hate speech online signifies a collaborative effort to address the challenges posed by hate speech on digital platforms. This initiative, which began in 2016, demonstrates a shared commitment to combating the spread of illegal hate speech within the European Union. Here's an elaboration and expansion on this relationship:

Elaboration:
1. **Voluntary Code of Conduct:** The Code of Conduct is a set of guidelines and commitments voluntarily adopted by major IT companies operating within the European Union. The companies

agree to take proactive measures to identify and remove illegal hate speech from their platforms.
2. **Commitments by IT Companies:** Participating IT companies commit to reviewing the majority of valid notifications for removal of illegal hate speech within twenty-four hours and removing or disabling access to such content. They also pledge to provide transparency reports on their efforts.
3. **Scope of Cooperation:** The cooperation between the European Commission and IT companies extends beyond mere removal of content. It involves fostering an environment where hate speech is not tolerated, raising awareness about community guidelines, and empowering users to report offensive content.
4. **Monitoring and Reporting:** The companies involved are subject to monitoring by the European Commission to ensure compliance with the Code of Conduct. Regular reporting mechanisms and transparency initiatives help assess the effectiveness of the measures taken by IT companies.
5. **Balancing Act:** While combating hate speech is a shared goal, there is a delicate balance between curbing harmful content and protecting freedom of expression. The voluntary nature of the Code allows companies to adapt their content moderation policies while adhering to the overarching principles of the European Union.

Expansion:
1. **Evolution of the Code:** Since its inception in 2016, the Code of Conduct has evolved to address emerging challenges in the online environment. This includes adapting to new forms of hate speech and incorporating advanced technologies for content moderation.
2. **Global Impact:** The cooperation between the European Commission and major IT companies has implications beyond the EU borders. Companies often implement global changes to their policies and practices influenced by the Code, impacting users worldwide.
3. **Public-Private Partnership:** The collaboration exemplifies a public-private partnership where governmental bodies work alongside private entities to address complex issues. It recognizes the influence and responsibility that major IT companies hold in shaping online discourse.

4. **Lessons for Regulation:** The voluntary nature of the Code provides insights into how regulatory approaches can be shaped to effectively address hate speech online. It serves as a learning experience for policymakers seeking to strike a balance between regulation and industry cooperation.

Related Cases:
1. **Facebook, X, and YouTube:** Major social media platforms such as Facebook, X, and YouTube are among the key companies that have actively participated in the voluntary Code of Conduct. Their involvement has been crucial in shaping industry standards.
2. **Challenges and Criticisms:** The relationship has faced challenges and criticisms, including concerns about the effectiveness of self-regulation and the need for more robust enforcement mechanisms. Instances of false positives and removal of inoffensive content have also been subjects of scrutiny.

The EU hate speech law, particularly the **2008 Framework Decision** on combating certain forms of expressions of racism and xenophobia, aims to criminalize public incitement to violence or hatred based on various grounds. The specific groups protected under EU hate speech law include:

1. **Race:** The Framework Decision addresses expressions of racism, targeting individuals or groups based on their race.
2. **Color:** Discrimination or hatred based on color is considered a form of hate speech under EU law.
3. **Religion:** Expressions of hatred or incitement to violence based on religion are covered, protecting individuals from discrimination on religious grounds.
4. **Descent:** Hate speech based on descent, which can include factors such as ethnic or national origin, is prohibited.
5. **National or Ethnic Origin:** Individuals or groups facing discrimination or hatred due to their national or ethnic origin are protected.

The law reflects the EU's commitment to upholding fundamental rights and values, including the principles of respect for human dignity, freedom, democracy, equality, and the rule of law. The protection afforded by this legislation contributes to fostering a diverse and inclusive society within the European Union; however, the two most noteworthy European Court of Human Rights decisions reflect conflicting rulings leaving the application of these directives unclear.

Illustratively, when the European Court of Human Rights (ECHR) examined a case (*Carl Jóhann LILLIENDAHL v. Iceland* Application no. 29297/18) originating from Iceland's legal system, it concluded that the conviction and subsequent penalties imposed on the defendant, Lilliendahl, for posting homophobic remarks beneath an online news article did not violate his freedom of expression under **Article 10** of the **European Human Rights Convention**. In the Icelandic legal proceedings, Lilliendahl faced charges for publicly disseminating "serious, severely hurtful, and prejudicial" comments related to sexual orientation and gender identity. This occurred within the broader context of increased educational initiatives and counseling about LGBTI issues in schools. While the comments in question did not explicitly advocate violence, their employment of derogatory language and explicit expressions of disgust were deemed tantamount to promoting intolerance toward homosexual individuals, thereby constituting hate speech.

In contrast, the European Court of Human Rights ruled differently in the case of *Savva Terentyev v. Russia* (Application no. 10692/09). In this instance, the Court determined that the imposition of a suspended sentence on an individual for posting a provocative comment online, criticizing police abuse, constituted a violation of the right to freedom of expression under **Article 10** of the **European Convention on Human Rights**. The post in question was a response to a press release detailing a politically motivated police search of a newspaper's premises during an election period. Terentyev's comment, posted on a blog referencing the press release, referred to the police as "cops," "pigs," and "hoodlums," also alluding to the burning of police officers "like at Auschwitz." Initially sentenced to one year suspended, the ECHR ultimately reversed the decision, challenging the charges of publicly inciting hatred, enmity, and humiliating the dignity of a social group based on their membership.

Unlike in the United States, where legislators have failed to enact meaningful laws or regulations to protect children on social media from harmful or inappropriate content, the European Union has taken steps to do so through the **Digital Services Act (DSA)**. The **DSA**, which is a comprehensive piece of legislation aimed at regulating digital services, includes provisions to enhance the protection of minors online. Here are key aspects related to the protection of children under the **Digital Services Act**:

1. **Age-Appropriate Settings:**
   The **DSA** introduces requirements for online platforms to implement age-appropriate settings. This aims to ensure that children are provided with services and content suitable for their age.
2. **Protection Against Harmful Content:**
   Online platforms are obligated to take measures to protect users, including minors, from illegal content and activities. This includes content promoting self-harm, suicide, eating disorders, and other harmful behaviors.
3. **User Reporting Mechanisms:**
   Platforms must establish user-friendly mechanisms for reporting harmful content. This includes procedures for users, including parents or legal guardians, to report content that may be inappropriate or harmful to minors.
4. **Transparency and Accountability:**
   The DSA emphasizes transparency and accountability, requiring platforms to provide clear information about their policies, content moderation practices, and measures taken to protect minors.
5. **Risk Assessments and Mitigation Measures:**
   Online services are required to conduct risk assessments, particularly regarding potential harm to minors, and implement mitigation measures to enhance user safety.
6. **Enforcement by Regulatory Authorities:**
   The legislation empowers national regulatory authorities to enforce the **DSA**, ensuring that online platforms comply with the provisions related to the protection of minors. Authorities may impose sanctions for noncompliance.
7. **Codes of Conduct:**
   The **DSA** allows for the establishment of codes of conduct by representative organizations, including those focused on child protection. These codes provide additional guidance on protecting minors online.

The **Digital Services Act** reflects the EU's commitment to creating a safer online environment, especially for vulnerable groups like children. By imposing obligations on digital service providers, the legislation aims to strike a balance between preserving the freedom of expression and ensuring the well-being of users, including minors, in the digital realm.

Under the **Digital Services Act**, the European Commission is charged with investigating potential violations of the **DSA** by certain online platforms and search engines, such as Google, YouTube, and X. The **DSA** imposes strict regulations on digital services, including marketplaces and online platforms. The law establishes a framework for cooperation between the Commission and national authorities to ensure enforcement and monitoring of its obligations. The **DSA** also includes fines of up to 6 percent of global annual turnover for violations.

The enforcement procedure of the **DSA**, after the designated digital services entities comply with annual reporting requirements, involves an investigation, potential interim measures, noncompliance decisions, and the imposition of fines. X's Elon Musk is on a collision course with EU regulators by refusing to comply.

Summary

Our exploration of free speech in the digital age has brought to light the intricate and multifaceted landscape that defines this crucial aspect of our modern society. The chapter delved into the complexities surrounding the regulation of online content, highlighting the delicate balance between preserving free expression and addressing the perils of harmful and misleading information prevalent on digital platforms.

A significant theme revolved around the protection social media enjoys from government regulation, a unique position that places immense responsibility on these platforms. The tension between the call for unrestricted free speech and the necessity to prevent digital spaces from becoming havens for misinformation and hate speech remains a central point of ongoing discourse.

Moreover, the chapter examined the concept of self-regulation by social media platforms, particularly in the context of the United States, where **First Amendment** rights impose limits on government intervention.

The material scrutinized how platforms grapple with the challenges of effectively moderating echo-chamber content, considering the global nature of digital communication and the diverse cultural, legal, and ethical contexts in which they operate.

On the international stage, our exploration extended to the intricate web of challenges and regulations governing digital speech. The absence of universal definitions, particularly concerning terms like *hate speech*, injected complexity into global conversations. Insights were provided into the endeavors of international bodies, such as the European Union, to establish frameworks that combat online harm while respecting fundamental rights. The varying approaches and regulatory landscapes across different regions underscored the complexities inherent in harmonizing global standards.

In summary, this chapter has examined the diverse dimensions of free speech in the digital era, addressing challenges, regulatory dilemmas, and the evolving role of social media platforms in shaping the contours of online discourse. The ongoing dialogue on these issues reflects the continuous evolution of our understanding and approach to preserving the principles of free expression in our rapidly changing digital landscape.

Discussion Questions

1. How has the landscape of free speech evolved with the advent of digital platforms, and what challenges does this pose for traditional legal frameworks?
2. Discuss the concept of self-regulation in the context of social media platforms. How effective is this approach in balancing free speech with responsible content moderation?
3. Explore the international perspectives on free speech and regulation discussed in the chapter. How do cultural, historical, and political differences influence these perspectives?
4. What are the specific challenges posed by regulating online content, particularly in terms of hate speech and harmful speech? How can legal systems adapt to effectively address these challenges?
5. Analyze the role of social media platforms in protecting users' free speech from government regulation. To what extent should platforms be responsible for policing content on their platforms?

6. Discuss the implications of the Online Safety Act in the United Kingdom and the Digital Services Act in the European Union. How do these regulations strike a balance between free speech and the need to protect users from harmful content?
7. Explore the controversies and criticisms surrounding online speech regulations. How can lawmakers address concerns related to privacy, free speech, and potential overreach?
8. Consider the challenges of regulating harmful speech globally, given the lack of universal definitions and varying cultural norms. How can international cooperation and agreements contribute to a more standardized approach?
9. Examine the role of major social media companies in regulating hate speech and speech harmful to children in the United States. What standards and policies do these companies currently have in place?
10. How can the international community work together to address hate speech and hate crimes online? Discuss initiatives, such as the EU's Code of Conduct, and their effectiveness in combating online hatred.

Works Referenced

Bollinger, Lee C., and Stone, Geoffrey R. "Social Media, Freedom of Speech, and the Future of our Democracy." *Columbia News*, accessed at https://news.columbia.edu/content/social-media-freedom-speech-and-future-our-democracy

Chin, Kyle. "Biggest Data Breaches in U.S. History (Updated 2024)." *UpGuard*, January 11, 2024, accessed at https://www.upguard.com/blog/biggest-data-breaches-us

Cope, Sophia, Greene, David, Mackey, Aaron, and Gilligan, Brendan. "The U.S. Supreme Court's Busy Year of Free Speech and Tech Cases: 2023 Year in Review." Electronic Frontier Foundation, December 27, 2023, accessed at https://www.eff.org/deeplinks/2023/12/2023-year-review-us-supreme-courts-busy-year-free-speech-and-tech-cases

"Council Framework Decision 2008/913/JHA of November 28, 2008, on Combating Certain Forms and Expressions of Racism and Xenophobia by Means of Criminal Law." *EUR-Lex*, accessed at https://eur-lex.europa.eu/legal-content/EN/TXT/?uri=celex%3A32008F0913

Cusumano, Michael A., Gawer, Annabelle, and Yoffie, David B. "Social Media Companies Should Self-Regulate Now." *Harvard Business Review*, January 15, 2021, accessed at https://hbr.org/2021/01/social-media-companies-should-self-regulate-now

Ehmke, Rachel. "How Using Social Media Affects Teenagers." Child Mind Institute, accessed at https://childmind.org/article/how-using-social-media-affects-teenagers

"Hate Crime Recording and Data Collection Practice across the EU." European Union Agency for Fundamental Rights, June 19, 2018, accessed at http://fra.europa.eu/en/publication/2018/hate-crime-recording-and-data-collection-practice-across-eu

Jones, Michael, *Art Law*, 2nd ed. Rowman & Littlefield, Lanham, MD, 2023.

Kern, Rebecca. "Push to Rein in Social Media Sweeps the States." *Politico*, July 1, 2022, at accessed https://www.politico.com/news/2022/07/01/social-media-sweeps-the-states-00043229

Matthews, Luke J., Williams, Heather J., and Evans, Alexandra T. "Protecting Free Speech Compels Some Form of Social Media Regulation." *TheRANDblog*, October 20, 2023, accessed at https://www.rand.org/pubs/commentary/2023/10/protecting-free-speech-compels-some-form-of-social.html

Miller, Gaby. "Elon Musk Will Test the EU's Digital Services Act." *Tech Policy Press*, September 11, 2023, accessed at https://www.techpolicy.press/elon-musk-will-test-the-eus-digital-services-act

Norton, Kim. "Chips vs. Oil: Nvidia Now Outweighs the S&P 500's Entire Energy Sector." *Investor's Business Daily*, February 6, 2024, accessed at https://www.investors.com/news/sp500-chips-vs-oil-nvidia-now-outweighs-the-sp-500s-entire-energy-sector

Pop-Wyatt, Mihaela. "The Challenges of Regulating Online Speech." *Policy @ Manchester* (blog), July 27, 2023, accessed at https://blog.policy.manchester.ac.uk/posts/2023/07/the-challenges-of-regulating-online-speech

Richter, Felix. "What's Driving the Digital Media Revolution." Statista, March 24, 2023, accessed at https://www.statista.com/chart/29572/attitudes-towards-digital-media

Smith, Brad, and Browne, Carol Ann. *Tools and Weapons*. Penguin Books, New York, 2021.

Steele, Anne. "Spotify Has Plans to Let Users Play DJ." *The Wall Street Journal*, April 12, 2024.

Stern, Joanna. "'I Died That Day'—AI Brings Back Voices of Children Killed in Shootings." *The Wall Street Journal*, February 14, 2024, accessed at https://www.wsj.com/tech/ai-brings-back-voices-of-children-killed-in-shootings-7d72cb8d?mod=hp

Taye, Mohammad Mustafa. "Understanding of Machine Learning with Deep Learning: Architectures, Workflow, Applications and Future Directions." *Computers*, April 25, 2023, accessed at https://www.mdpi.com/2073-431X/12/5/91

Taylor, Russell, and Tudor, Sarah. "Freedom of Expression Online: Communications and Digital Committee Report." House of Lords Library, October 19, 2022, accessed at https://lordslibrary.parliament.uk/freedom-of-expression-online-communications-and-digital-committee-report/#heading-1

Wells, Georgia, Horwitz, Jeff, and Seetharaman, Deepa. "Facebook Knows Instagram Is Toxic for Teen Girls, Company Documents Show." *The Wall Street Journal*, September 14, 2001, accessed at https://www.wsj.com/articles/facebook-knows-instagram-is-toxic-for-teen-girls-company-documents-show-11631620739

3

Behind the Digital Curtains: Safeguarding Privacy in an Online World

In the digital world, a right to privacy is no less essential than the right to breathe.

—Jan Philipp Albrecht, German politician and digital privacy protection advocate

Privacy as a Right

Louis Brandeis and Samuel Warren's groundbreaking article, "The Right to Privacy," published in the *Harvard Law Review* in 1890, stands as a foundational document that significantly influenced the development of the right to privacy in the United States. This seminal work not only marked a turning point in legal discourse but also laid the intellectual groundwork for the expansion of individual liberties, contributing to the evolution of privacy rights and later influencing the concept of the right of publicity.

In their article, Brandeis and Warren responded to the challenges posed by technological advancements and the rise of mass media in the late nineteenth century, particularly the intrusive nature of the press. They argued for the recognition of a new legal right, the "right to be let alone," to protect individuals from unwarranted intrusions into their private lives.

The article was grounded in a societal shift and an acknowledgment of the changing nature of privacy due to the growing influence of newspapers, tabloids, intrusive journalism, and new technology. Two years before their article an advanced technology was introduced: a Kodak camera. This camera was not only compact enough to be easily carried but also affordable, operable with a simple button press, and preloaded for one hundred shots. The newfound portability of this camera marked a significant shift, making intrusions that were once impractical now effortlessly achievable. Brandeis and Warren articulated the idea that technological advancements should not come at the expense of personal privacy and autonomy. They eloquently expressed the need for legal protection against the sensationalized and invasive reporting that was becoming prevalent at the time.

The concept of the "right to be let alone" introduced by Brandeis and Warren set the stage for a broader understanding of privacy rights. It provided a theoretical foundation for recognizing privacy as a fundamental aspect of individual autonomy, separate from physical intrusions or property rights. This intellectual framework became crucial in shaping subsequent legal interpretations and debates on privacy.

Dean William L. Prosser, in his influential law review article titled "Privacy," published in the *California Law Review* in 1960, expanded on the concept of privacy initially introduced by Warren and Brandeis.

In his article, Prosser categorized privacy into four distinct torts or legal wrongs:

1. **Intrusion upon Seclusion:** Prosser extended the concept of intrusion upon seclusion, emphasizing that individuals have a right to be free from unwarranted and offensive invasions of their private affairs or physical solitude.
2. **Public Disclosure of Private Facts:** Prosser elaborated on the idea that individuals have a right to keep certain private matters confidential. Public disclosure of private facts involves the dissemination of information that is highly offensive and not of legitimate concern to the public.
3. **False Light:** Prosser introduced the concept of false light, which involves presenting individuals in a misleading or false manner that would be highly offensive to a reasonable person.
4. **Appropriation of Name or Likeness:** Prosser extended the right to privacy by discussing the unauthorized use of an individual's name

or likeness for commercial purposes without their consent to what we now view as the right of publicity.

Prosser's work served to modernize and expand the scope of privacy law, providing a more comprehensive framework for understanding and addressing privacy-related issues in the legal context. His categorization of privacy torts has had a lasting impact on privacy jurisprudence in the United States that exists today.

Early Constitutional History of Privacy

Following the publication of the Brandeis and Warren law review article in 1890, the concept of the right to privacy gradually gained legal recognition. While the Supreme Court did not explicitly address the right to privacy until the mid-twentieth century), there were several early cases that laid the groundwork for the eventual recognition of privacy rights. These cases, though not always directly referencing the right to privacy, dealt with related issues such as freedom from unwarranted intrusion and protection of personal autonomy.

Mugler v. Kansas (127 U.S. 623 (1887)):

While predating the Brandeis and Warren article, this case is noteworthy for establishing the principle that the state cannot interfere with the private lives of individuals without a justifiable reason. The decision recognized the importance of personal autonomy.

Union Pacific Railway Co. v. Botsford (114 U.S. 250 (1891)):

This case emphasized an individual's right to control their body and medical information. It laid the groundwork for the later development of medical privacy rights.

Roberson v. Rochester Folding Box Co., 171 N.Y. 538, 64 N.E. 442 (1902):

Roberson v. Rochester Folding Box Co is a significant early case, although it did not reach the United States Supreme Court. Instead, it was decided by the New York Court of Appeals, and it played a crucial role in establishing the early principles of the right to privacy, specifically in the context of unauthorized use of one's likeness for commercial purposes.

The case involved a young girl whose photograph was taken without her consent and used in a commercial context, a common occurrence in the digital world. A private company, engaged in the business of manufacturing and selling educational materials, had taken her photograph and used it without her permission in an advertisement for its educational products. Her parents filed a lawsuit, claiming that the unauthorized use of her image was a violation of her privacy.

The New York Court, in its decision, recognized a new legal principle related to privacy. While the court did not explicitly frame it as a "right to privacy" case, the ruling acknowledged the importance of protecting individuals from unauthorized commercial exploitation of their likeness, which is akin to what we now call the right of publicity. The decision emphasized the individual's right to control the use of their image, particularly in the context of advertising and commercial exploitation. The court suggested that obtaining consent before using someone's likeness for commercial purposes was a fundamental aspect of respecting an individual's rights.

This decision set a precedent and contributed to the growing recognition of privacy rights in various legal contexts. It foreshadowed later cases that would explicitly recognize a broader right to privacy, such as the influential law review article by Louis Brandeis and Samuel Warren in 1890 and the subsequent Supreme Court decision in *Griswold v. Connecticut* (381 U.S. 479 (1965)).

Olmstead v. United States (277 U.S. 438 (1928)):

Olmstead v. United States (1928) was a landmark case that dealt with the constitutionality of wiretapping and electronic surveillance, raising important questions about the scope of privacy protections in the **Fourth Amendment**.

The case ultimately resulted in a ruling against the right to privacy in the context of wiretapping, but Justice Louis Brandeis's dissenting opinion is particularly notable for articulating a broader view of the right to privacy, foreshadowing future developments in constitutional jurisprudence.

In the 1920s, Roy Olmstead, a suspected bootlegger during the Prohibition era, was the subject of wiretapping conducted by federal law enforcement officials. The evidence obtained through these wiretaps was used against Olmstead in court, leading to his conviction. The central issue in the case was whether the evidence obtained through warrantless wiretapping violated the Fourth Amendment's protection against unreasonable searches and seizures.

In a 5-4 decision, the Supreme Court, in an opinion written by Chief Justice William Howard Taft, held that the use of wiretaps without a physical intrusion into a constitutionally protected area (like a person's home) did not constitute a violation of the Fourth Amendment. The majority opinion narrowly interpreted the Fourth Amendment, focusing on the physical aspect of trespassing and concluded that the use of wiretaps, even without a warrant, did not constitute a search within the meaning of the constitutional protection.

Justice Louis Brandeis, in a powerful and influential dissent, disagreed with the majority's narrow interpretation of this constitutional prohibition. Rather than focusing solely on physical trespass, Brandeis argued for a more expansive understanding of privacy rights. He contended that the framers of the Constitution intended the Fourth Amendment to protect not only physical spaces but also individuals' right to be secure in their "persons, houses, papers, and effects."

What is most noteworthy about Brandeis's dissent is that it introduced the concept of the "right to be let alone," echoing the sentiments expressed in his earlier law review article with Samuel Warren. He emphasized the importance of protecting the individual's right to privacy from government intrusion and, foreshadowing a high-tech future, highlighted the potential threats posed by technological advancements, such as wiretapping.

Griswold v. Connecticut (381 U.S. 479 (1965)):

Griswold v. Connecticut is a milestone Supreme Court case that is often regarded as the first to explicitly recognize a constitutional right to privacy. The case challenged a Connecticut law that criminalized the use of contraceptives, even by married couples, except for medical reasons. The Supreme Court, in a 7–2 decision, struck down the law, asserting the existence of a right to marital privacy and laying the groundwork for the subsequent expansion of privacy rights.

In a majority opinion written by Justice William O. Douglas, the Supreme Court held that the Connecticut law was unconstitutional. The Court did not explicitly rely on the word "privacy" in the Constitution, but Justice Douglas, in his opinion, articulated a broader concept of privacy inherent in several constitutional amendments.

The majority opinion identified a "zone of privacy" created by the **First, Third, Fourth,** and **Ninth Amendments**. While none of these amendments explicitly mention privacy, nor does the term appear anywhere in the US Constitution, the Court reasoned that when taken together, they implied a fundamental right to privacy. The First Amendment's protection of freedom of association, the Third Amendment's prohibition against quartering soldiers in homes, the Fourth Amendment's protection against unreasonable searches and seizures, and the Ninth Amendment's recognition of unenumerated rights collectively formed the basis for the right to privacy.

This case had a profound impact on the development of privacy rights in the United States. While the decision specifically addressed the right to marital privacy in the context of contraceptive use, the recognition of a broader "zone of privacy" laid the groundwork for future cases expanding the right to privacy in various areas.

Katz v. United States (389 U.S. 347 (1967)):

Katz v. United States is a pivotal Supreme Court case that dramatically expanded privacy protections under the Fourth Amendment. The case involved the use of electronic surveillance, specifically wiretapping, by law enforcement to gather evidence against a suspected gambler, Katz. The Court's decision reshaped the understanding of the Fourth Amendment's protections against unreasonable searches and seizures, particularly in the context of emerging technologies.

Katz was suspected of transmitting wagering information across state lines, a violation of federal law. To gather evidence against him, the FBI placed a wiretap on a public payphone booth that he frequently used. The authorities believed that because Katz was using a public phone booth, his conversations were not subject to Fourth Amendment protections against unreasonable searches and seizures.

The majority opinion, written by Justice Potter Stewart, rejected the notion that the physical location alone determined the Fourth Amendment's applicability. Instead, the Court focused on whether an individual had a "reasonable expectation of privacy."

The Court held that individuals have a reasonable expectation of privacy in their conversations, even in public places. Justice Stewart famously stated that the Fourth Amendment protects "people, not places." He argued that the government's use of electronic surveillance to eavesdrop on Katz's private conversations, even in a public phone booth, constituted a search and seizure within the meaning of the Fourth Amendment.

The decision established the "reasonable expectation of privacy" test, which became a key criterion for determining whether government actions violated the Fourth Amendment. The Court emphasized that privacy interests should be evaluated based on societal expectations, and not solely on the physical location of the individual.

Forms of Recognized Privacy

Today privacy is a multifaceted concept that encompasses various dimensions of individual autonomy and control over personal information. Recognized forms of privacy can be broadly categorized into several types:

1. **Physical Privacy:**
   - **Bodily Privacy:** Protection of one's physical body from unwanted intrusions, such as unwarranted searches or bodily examinations.
   - **Spatial Privacy:** The right to control access to one's personal space, including the home, and the freedom from unwarranted surveillance.
2. **Informational Privacy:**
   - **Data Privacy:** The protection of personal information, including collection, storage, and use of data, often in the context of technology and the internet.
   - **Financial Privacy:** Safeguarding information related to an individual's financial transactions and status.

- **Medical Privacy:** Protection of personal health information and medical records.
3. **Communicational Privacy:**
   - **Wiretap Privacy:** Protection from unauthorized interception of communications, such as wiretapping.
   - **Email and Correspondence Privacy:** Ensuring the confidentiality of private communications, including emails and letters.
4. **Decisional Privacy:**
   - **Autonomy:** The right to make personal decisions without external interference, particularly in matters of personal beliefs, lifestyle choices, and reproductive choices.
5. **Associational Privacy:**
   - **Social Privacy:** The ability to control access to and disclosure of personal information within social circles and networks.
   - **Family Privacy:** Protection of familial relationships and the right to keep family matters private.
6. **Visual Privacy:**
   - **Surveillance Privacy:** Protection from unwarranted monitoring and surveillance, whether by the government, employers, or other entities.
   - **Facial Recognition Privacy:** Concerns related to the collection and use of facial images for identification purposes.
7. **Privacy of Personal Relationships:**
   - **Intimacy Privacy:** Protection of intimate and personal relationships from unwarranted intrusion.
   - **Marital Privacy:** The right to privacy within the context of marriage and family life.
8. **Corporate Privacy:**
   - **Workplace Privacy:** Protection of personal information and privacy rights in the workplace.
   - **Consumer Privacy:** The right to control how personal information is collected and used by businesses.
9. **Publicity Rights:**
   - **Right of Publicity:** The right to control the commercial use of one's name, image, or likeness.
10. **Temporal Privacy:**
    - **Temporal Autonomy:** The right to control the use and disclosure of personal information over time, including the right to be forgotten.

Among the listed rights, Data Privacy, encompassing a host of these recognized forms or dimensions of privacy, is a critical concern in the digital media age, with various instances highlighting the need for vigilant protection of personal information.

Online platforms, such as social media, websites, and apps, routinely collect vast amounts of user data encompassing personal preferences, behaviors, and interactions, as described below in the "cookies" section. Companies employ advanced analytics tools for processing large datasets, often containing personal information, to inform targeted advertising and decision-making. Since the advent of the internet for commercial purposes, the escalating threat of cybersecurity incidents and data breaches poses risks to individuals' personal information, leading to unauthorized access and potential misuse (see Table 3.1).

"Cookies"

Cookies play a crucial role in online advertising by aiding advertisers in gathering information about users' online behavior and preferences. These small pieces of data, stored on users' devices when they visit a website, allow advertisers to track users' activities across different sites. This tracking helps create detailed profiles of users' interests, behaviors, and demographics. With this information, advertisers can craft targeted advertising campaigns, displaying ads that are more likely to be relevant to users based on their browsing history and preferences. Additionally, cookies enable retargeting, where ads are shown to users who previously visited a website but did not complete a desired action, such as making a purchase.

Furthermore, cookies contribute to a personalized online experience by facilitating the retention of small details across web pages or visits, acting as a temporary memory for the internet. Advertisers can tailor content and ads based on users' preferences, making the ads more relevant and engaging. However, concerns about user privacy prompted legislative actions, leading to the implementation of the European Union's (EU) **ePrivacy Directive** in 2011, commonly known as the "**Cookie Law.**" This directive addressed privacy issues associated with cookies and required websites to inform visitors and obtain their consent.

Table 3.1 How Businesses Use Cookies

Industry	Strictly Necessary	Functional	Performance	Advertising
Technology, Media, & Communications	34%	12%	18%	36%
Consumers	33%	10%	23%	34%
Energy, Resources, & Industrials	29%	16%	23%	32%
Financial Services	39%	10%	19%	32%
Life Sciences & Healthcare	34%	21%	16%	29%
Government & Public Services	27%	21%	25%	27%

Source: Deloitte Cookie Benchmark Study, 2020.

In 2018, the European Union introduced the **General Data Protection Regulation (GDPR)** strongly advocated by the fore-quoted Jan Philipp Albrecht, which, combined with the Cookie Law, establishes fundamental principles for personal information collection and imposes significant penalties for violations. The GDPR treats any data linked to an identifiable individual as personal data, requiring consent before collection and granting individuals rights over their personal data. This global wave of privacy legislation aligning with the EU's standards highlights the escalating importance and sensitivity of personal data in the digital age.

The impact of EU cookie laws extends globally, influencing data privacy legislation, even in the United States. The EU's stringent data privacy regime, including the ePrivacy Directive and GDPR, has influenced US developments like the **California Consumer Privacy Act (CCPA)** and the subsequent **California Privacy Rights Act (CPRA)**. These state-level laws echo the EU's approach to data privacy, introducing more robust data protection measures. The GDPR, setting a high standard for data protection, has played a pivotal role in shaping global data protection laws, with many countries adopting rules influenced by the European Union. The adoption of "cookie banners" on websites in the United States, informing users about cookie usage and seeking their consent, reflects the EU's impact on data privacy practices worldwide. Despite historical differences, there is a growing convergence, particularly at the state level in the United States, toward the EU model, driven by the global influence of the EU's comprehensive data protection laws.

Big Data and Analytics

A notable example of big data and analytics concerns involved the Federal Trade Commission (FTC) and the Department of Justice (DOJ) charging Amazon with violating the **Children's Online Privacy Protection Act (COPPA)** (15 U.S.C. §§ 6501–6506). The Act is a federal law in the United States designed to address the online collection of personal information from children under the age of 13.

COPPA imposes specific requirements on operators of websites or online services directed to children under 13 or those with actual knowledge of collecting personal information from such children. The primary objective of COPPA is to empower parents by giving them control over the online information collected from their children. Key provisions include the necessity for operators to have a clear and comprehensive privacy policy, providing direct notice to parents, obtaining verifiable parental consent before collecting information, allowing parental access to review or delete their child's personal data, offering the choice to consent without disclosing information to third parties, and maintaining the confidentiality, security, and integrity of the collected information. COPPA also extends its jurisdiction to foreign websites targeting US children or knowingly collecting information from them. Violations of COPPA can result in civil penalties.

The FTC revealed that Amazon failed to adequately protect children's privacy on its Alexa platform by not consistently deleting children's voice recordings upon parental requests. Amazon was subsequently ordered to pay a $25 million civil penalty. This case underscores the ongoing challenges in maintaining data privacy and serves as a reminder of the continuous efforts required to safeguard personal information in the digital landscape.

The controversy surrounding Amazon's data collection practices extends beyond failing to protect children's data privacy. Criticism has been directed at Amazon for instances of improperly storing millions of credit card numbers and allowing a Chinese data firm access to consumer information. An investigation has also revealed a troubling level of carelessness within Amazon, with reports of widespread sharing of consumer data within the company, leading to allegations of employees spying on celebrity purchases and accepting bribes to undermine a seller's business.

The sheer volume of data collected by Amazon is another point of contention, encompassing names, addresses, search histories, order details, and interactions with the Alexa voice assistant. Users who have requested their data from Amazon have been surprised by the extensive information provided to them, raising questions about the scope and depth of the company's data collection practices.

The potential for abuse is a significant concern arising from Amazon's extensive data collection. There are worries that Amazon's data could be used to predict personal details about individuals, such as pregnancy, allowing for targeted advertising. Additionally, the risk of the data being stolen or subpoenaed by government entities further underscores the potential misuse of this vast reservoir of information.

Privacy and security failings have been highlighted through internal documents and investigations, exposing Amazon's decentralized accountability and ownership model as a factor that complicates effective management of the company's data. These shortcomings pose risks to the privacy and security of the vast amounts of sensitive information held by Amazon.

Legal and regulatory challenges have also emerged in response to Amazon's data practices, including a substantial fine of 746 million euros for alleged violations of the European Union's data privacy laws. This regulatory scrutiny reflects the growing recognition of the need for robust oversight and accountability in the face of concerns surrounding data privacy and security within large corporations like Amazon.

In the ever-evolving landscape of online services and e-commerce, privacy concerns have become increasingly prominent, with major players in the tech industry utilizing big data analytics for targeted advertising. Companies like Google, Facebook (Meta), Amazon, Adobe Analytics, and Salesforce leverage user data to enhance their advertising strategies. While these practices aim to deliver personalized content, they have raised significant privacy-related controversies and developments, leading to legal scrutiny and public concern.

Google employs targeted advertising by leveraging user data to enhance the relevance of ads. Advertisers on the Google platform can target their ads based on user searches, with Google selling this valuable data to ensure that advertisements align more closely with individual interests. The process involves auctions on search keywords, aiming to match relevant ads to user queries, creating a more personalized and effective advertising experience.

However, Google has not been without privacy controversies. The company faced legal action from forty states regarding its location-tracking policies, resulting in a substantial $392 million settlement. The dispute revolved around the lack of transparency in Google's location-tracking policies and the continuous collection of location data even when users believed they had disabled such tracking. This incident underscored the importance of clear communication and user consent in data privacy practices.

Meta, formerly known as Facebook, has found itself embroiled in controversies surrounding targeted advertising, notably following the Cambridge Analytica scandal. The company, a behemoth in the realm of social media, has been under scrutiny for its utilization of personal data in targeted political advertising. The misconduct, which erupted in 2018, exposed how the personal data of as many as 87 million users was illicitly harvested and exploited for political campaign purposes.

At the heart of the matter was Cambridge Analytica, a British political consulting firm hired by various campaigns, including those of Donald Trump's 2016 presidential bid and the pro-Brexit movement. Exploiting Facebook's data policies, Cambridge Analytica accessed and amassed vast quantities of user information, breaching privacy boundaries. The revelation shook the digital landscape, sparking widespread debate about the ethical boundaries of data usage in advertising and prompting calls for tighter regulations to safeguard user privacy.

The incident unfolded when it was unveiled that Cambridge Analytica had acquired the personal data of millions of Facebook users without their explicit consent. These data were originally sourced through a personality quiz app named "This Is Your Digital Life," created by Aleksandr Kogan, a researcher associated with Cambridge Analytica. Despite its initial academic intent, Kogan and Cambridge Analytica repurposed the app to harvest not only the quiz takers' data but also the data of their unsuspecting Facebook friends.

Subsequently, Cambridge Analytica used this trove of information to craft intricate psychographic profiles of individuals, with the aim of understanding and influencing their political inclinations. Allegedly, these data were leveraged to target users with tailor-made political advertisements, shaping the messaging of political campaigns.

The unethical practices of Cambridge Analytica raised profound concerns regarding privacy, data protection, and the ethical utilization of personal information in political contexts. Consequently, it prompted investigations into Facebook's data management practices and intensified scrutiny of social media platforms' handling and safeguarding of user data. This scrutiny, in turn, fueled discussions about the imperative need for more stringent regulations to ensure responsible and transparent handling of user data by technology firms.

In 2023, Salesforce found itself embroiled in privacy controversies that underscored the critical need for stronger security measures. One notable incident involved a misconfiguration in Salesforce Community sites, resulting in the unintended exposure of sensitive data from various organizations, including government agencies, banks, and health care providers. The misconfiguration allowed unauthenticated users to gain access to private information that should have been protected by login credentials. The compromised data included extensive details such as full names, Social Security numbers, addresses, phone numbers, email addresses, and even bank account numbers. Despite being alerted by security researchers, several organizations, particularly in the government sector, demonstrated a sluggish response in addressing and rectifying these vulnerabilities.

Adding to the privacy concerns, Salesforce faced a class-action lawsuit related to a data breach that involved the sale of consumer data on the dark web. The lawsuit asserted that Salesforce failed to adequately protect private data, employed insufficient security practices, and neglected to warn consumers about these shortcomings. Once more, this particular breach brought to light the importance of implementing and maintaining better security measures in the digital age. It emphasized the severe

Chapter 3: Behind the Digital Curtains: Safeguarding Privacy in an Online World 65

consequences that can arise when organizations fall short in safeguarding sensitive information, especially as it can lead to unauthorized access and exploitation of private data on illicit platforms such as the dark web. The incidents surrounding Salesforce underscore the ongoing challenges and responsibilities that companies face in ensuring the security and privacy of the data they handle.

As reported by a recent *FasterCapital* article on digital privacy the revelation that aggregated bulk data can be-which allows for an individual to be directly identified from their name, address, postcode, telephone number, photograph or image, or some other unique personal characteristic, raises profound concerns, challenging the prevailing belief that anonymity remains intact when personal identifiers are excluded. Researchers consistently demonstrate the ability to pinpoint individuals' identities within such datasets by cross-referencing information from various sources, which becomes increasingly possible when linking data stored in the cloud with the search capabilities of artificial intelligence. Notably, matching location data during a person's commute or tracking purchasing habits can expose identities, evading legal privacy protections applicable solely to explicitly labeled "personally identifiable information," which includes names or Social Security numbers.

Alarming instances vividly highlight the inherent risks and potential abuses associated with the mishandling of personal data. The controversy surrounding the widely used gay dating app Grindr serves as a stark illustration of this issue. The revelation that Grindr engaged in the sale of user data led to the deanonymization of individuals, exposing them to unwarranted invasions of privacy. A notable incident involved the outing of a priest, where meticulous tracking of his visits to gay bars and a bathhouse led to the deanonymization process. This case underscores the far-reaching consequences of data exploitation, particularly in the context of sensitive personal information and the potential harm it can inflict on individuals.

Similarly, the involvement of phone companies in the sale of real-time location data adds another layer of concern. Reports indicate that these data ended up in the hands of bounty hunters and stalkers, raising serious questions about the responsibility and ethical considerations surrounding the trade of individuals' real-time location information. The repercussions of such practices extend beyond mere privacy violations, touching on the potential for misuse and harm in the hands of malicious actors. These incidents emphasize the need for heightened scrutiny, enhanced regulations, and ethical standards to safeguard individuals from the perils of data exploitation and the resulting threats to their personal security and well-being.

Even ostensibly reputable companies have been involved in questionable practices, as illustrated by Uber's tracking of journalists and the publication of data analyses revealing potential one-night stands in major cities. The risks associated with such practices extend beyond privacy invasion, potentially exposing sensitive situations, such as women arranging access to abortion pills or seeking support.

Traditional strategies to mitigate these dangers, including leaving phones at home or adjusting app settings, prove inadequate. Turning off location tracking in apps does not prevent data collection by the phone or cellular network. Burner phones, though conceptually appealing, are impractical in execution, requiring extensive technical knowledge for maintenance. Leaving phones behind provides little assurance, as commercially available biometric databases with vast image collections can facilitate facial recognition at scale, even without digital devices.

The Supreme Court's decision in *Dobbs v. Jackson Women's Health Organization* (597 U.S. 215 (2022)) overturning the long-standing right of a woman to have an abortion under the constitutional right to privacy established by *Roe v. Wade* (410 U.S. 113 (1973)) poses significant risks to privacy, particularly concerning the role of big data companies in collecting and using health care data. The decision, marking a departure from the constitutional protection of a woman's right to choose abortion within specific limits, has broader implications for individual privacy, data security, and the potential exploitation of sensitive health information.

1. **Erosion of Privacy Rights:**
   The reversal of *Roe v. Wade* diminishes the privacy rights established for women in their reproductive health care decisions. This erosion of privacy extends beyond the specific context of abortion, raising concerns about the broader interpretation of privacy rights in various domains, including health care.
2. **Increased Surveillance and Data Collection:**
   The decision may lead to increased surveillance and data collection related to individuals' reproductive health choices.

As the legal landscape changes, there is a risk that personal information regarding reproductive health decisions may become subject to heightened scrutiny, potentially leading to increased data collection by health care providers, insurers, and other entities, which could be hacked or leaked to social media.

3. **Role of Big Data Companies:**
Big data companies, known for their extensive data-analytics capabilities, could exploit the changing legal landscape to intensify the collection and analysis of sensitive health care data. This includes tracking patterns, preferences, and decisions related to reproductive health, posing privacy risks for individuals.

4. **Potential for Targeted Advertising and Profiling:**
With the availability of detailed health care data, big data companies may engage in targeted advertising and profiling. Individuals' reproductive health decisions could become a focal point for personalized advertisements, potentially influencing opinions and behaviors while raising ethical concerns about the use of such sensitive information.

5. **Security and Consent Challenges:**
The increased collection and utilization of health care data by big data companies raises security and consent challenges. Individuals may find their health information vulnerable to breaches, and concerns about the lack of informed consent in sharing such intimate details with third-party entities could arise.

6. **Impact on Health Insurance and Employment:**
Big data companies, through their analytical capabilities, may influence health insurance decisions and employment opportunities based on individuals' reproductive health choices. This could result in discrimination and the potential misuse of personal health information, further compromising privacy.

Even federal health privacy laws, such as the **Health Insurance Portability and Accountability Act (HIPAA)**, may not provide an adequate level of privacy protection for health information in diverse circumstances. Concerns arise in the realm of third-party data sharing, exemplified by instances like GoodRX selling users' medication search and purchase data, which reveal potential vulnerabilities. Despite HIPAA's oversight of covered entities, entities like GoodRX may not fall directly under its jurisdiction if they do not meet the criteria outlined for covered entities or business associates.

It is noteworthy that certain health apps or websites collecting health-related information may exist beyond the purview of HIPAA's regulatory framework. This recognition underscores the need for review of existing health privacy policies by Congress, considering the evolving landscape of health care data management and the diverse big data entities involved in handling sensitive health information.

An eye-opening report by one of America's leading media publications, *The Wall Street Journal*, uncovered the fact that US intelligence agencies have been purchasing vast amounts of personal data from Americans from third-party data brokers, which includes information from smartphone apps, vehicles, and internet-connected household appliances. These data, often collected through common technologies, are readily available for purchase not only by US agencies but also by foreign governments, raising significant privacy and surveillance concerns. The data acquired include geolocation data, phone records, and internet browsing histories. Such information can reveal sensitive personal details such as political affiliations, religious activities, and intimate details of individuals' lives.

The widespread availability of these data and their acquisition without a warrant have sparked debates about potential violations of privacy rights and warrantless searches. Critics argue that the unchecked collection and use of such data could lead to abuses by both domestic and foreign entities, potentially undermining civil liberties. The concerns are amplified by the ease with which the data can be de-anonymized and linked to individuals, despite being initially collected as "anonymized" data. In response to these concerns, US spy agencies agreed to limit how they buy and use troves of data about Americans that many critics argue is still not sufficient data privacy protection.

Big Data and AI

The impact of AI technology on data collection and usage is tremendously significant. AI systems, designed to learn and enhance their capabilities

Chapter 3: Behind the Digital Curtains: Safeguarding Privacy in an Online World

through extensive data analysis, continuously raise privacy and data protection concerns. Generative AI tools, like ChatGPT and Stable Diffusion, underscore how personal data, including copyright-protected articles, images, and videos, are often used without owners' explicit consent.

Among the myriad issues, invasive surveillance stands out as a threat to individual autonomy, contributing to power imbalances that will be discussed more fully in another chapter. Simultaneously, unauthorized data collection exposes sensitive personal information, rendering individuals susceptible to cyberattacks. For instance, AI systems have the capability to infer sensitive information from inexplicit data, such as predicting personal attributes like sexual orientation, political views, or health status from unrelated data, leading to privacy violations.

Compounding these concerns is the lack of transparency in AI systems. Complex algorithms make it challenging for individuals to comprehend how their data contribute to decisions affecting them, fostering a sense of unease and distrust. Addressing these issues requires organizations utilizing AI to implement better data security measures, ensuring data are used solely for their intended purpose and aligning AI systems with ethical principles.

Transparency emerges as a crucial element in building trust, allowing individuals to comprehend and control the use of their data by AI systems. Providing mechanisms for opting out of data collection and requesting data deletion empowers individuals, fostering a future where AI technologies contribute positively to society while safeguarding privacy and data protection. These proactive measures are vital for shaping a future where technological advancements benefit humanity at large, promoting ethical AI practices and protecting individuals' privacy in the digital age.

In contrast to the lack of national privacy standards in the United States, the European Union has enacted legislation providing extensive data protection for its citizens. The European Union (EU) data privacy laws, particularly articulated through the General Data Protection Regulation (GDPR) as described earlier, establish vigorous safeguards for the personal data of EU citizens. These regulations extend their reach to encompass organizations operating within the EU, as well as those situated outside the EU but providing goods or services to, or monitoring the behavior of,

EU residents. The GDPR confers key protections and rights, including the requirement for explicit consent or adherence to specific lawful bases for the collection and processing of personal data. These lawful bases include contractual necessity, legal obligations, vital interests, public tasks, or legitimate interests.

Transparency is also integral to the GDPR, necessitating that individuals be informed in a clear and comprehensible manner about the entity collecting their data, the purpose of collection, and how the data will be used. Moreover, individuals hold the right to receive their personal data in a structured, commonly used format, and are empowered to transfer this data to another person or entity responsible for processing personal data like a credit card or phone company. The right to access one's personal data and obtain information about its processing is enshrined, alongside the right to rectify inaccuracies.

Under very specific conditions, the GDPR grants individuals the right to request the deletion of their personal data, also known as the "Right to Erasure" or "Right to be Forgotten." The regulation imposes restrictions on the transfer of personal data outside the European Union, permitting such transfers only to non-EU countries, ensuring an adequate level of data protection, or through the implementation of specific safeguards.

Organizations processing data on a large scale or handling special categories of data are obligated to appoint a Data Protection Officer (DPO) to oversee compliance with the GDPR. In the event of a data breach, organizations are required to promptly notify the relevant data protection authority and, in certain cases, the affected individuals. The GDPR also includes provisions for significant fines as a deterrent for noncompliance, emphasizing the importance of adherence to these comprehensive data protection measures.

Across the globe, Facial Recognition Technology (FRT) has rapidly integrated into various facets of daily life, serving functions from unlocking smartphones to surveillance by law enforcement. However, this widespread adoption has given rise to substantial privacy concerns, stemming from several critical issues. One significant challenge lies in the fact that faces, unlike other forms of data, cannot be encrypted. This inherent vulnerability of facial recognition data makes it susceptible to breaches, intensifying the risks of identity theft, stalking, and harassment. The consequences of such breaches are particularly severe, as faces,

Chapter 3: Behind the Digital Curtains: Safeguarding Privacy in an Online World 71

unlike passwords or credit card information, cannot be easily altered or replaced.

Another prominent privacy concern revolves, once more, around the lack of transparency and consent in the deployment of FRT. The technology's capacity to identify individuals without their knowledge or agreement raises ethical red flags, especially considering the uniqueness of biometric data for each person. The potential for facial scans to be captured remotely and covertly amplifies the magnitude of privacy issues.

Imagine, for example, a technologically advanced shopping mall, with surveillance cameras linked to a cloud-based system equipped with facial recognition software, and how this process could play a pivotal role in tracking and analyzing shoppers. Strategically positioned throughout the mall, these cameras continuously capture facial images, which are then transmitted to the cloud for real-time processing. The facial recognition software meticulously examines these images, discerning unique facial features and associating them with individual profiles stored in a comprehensive database.

Store owners, granted access to this cloud-based system, gain the ability to monitor customers' movements and scrutinize their behaviors. The system, in turn, identifies specific individuals, generating detailed customer profiles based on their shopping history, preferences, and demographic information. Leveraging these data, store owners can provide a personalized shopping experience by utilizing AI algorithms to forecast a customer's potential interests and preferences. As recognized customers enter participating stores, the system has the capability to dispatch tailored offers, discounts, or recommendations either to store associates or directly to the customers' mobile devices.

This intricate process is reinforced by predictive analytics, allowing the AI system to continuously refine its predictions over time. Despite the potential for enhancing the shopping experience, it is imperative to acknowledge the associated privacy and security concerns, as well as the potential for the misuse of personal data. Many jurisdictions have imposed strict regulations on the use of facial recognition technology, leading to ongoing debates about the ethical implications of such surveillance practices. Achieving a delicate balance between technological innovation and safeguarding individual privacy emerges as a pivotal challenge in the ongoing development and deployment of facial recognition and AI systems.

Big Tech companies have ascended to become global powerhouses, exerting considerable influence over the economy and society. With access to colossal amounts of data, these entities shape consumer behavior, impact the global economy, and even play a role in shaping political landscapes. As AI advances and the metaverse looms, the power of Big Tech is poised to escalate. In this evolving landscape, companies like Google, Amazon, and Meta are positioned to leverage data on an unprecedented scale, influencing public opinion, shaping government policy, and creating entirely new virtual ecosystems within the metaverse.

Metaverse

As the metaverse emerges, opportunities for Big Tech to monetize their platforms and amplify societal influence abound. The metaverse, a collective virtual shared space formed by the integration of enhanced physical reality, augmented reality (AR), and the internet, is emerging as a transformative and explosive frontier for Big Tech companies. This digital landscape not only provides innovative avenues for platform expansion but also significantly enhances their societal influence. Big Tech stands to monetize and amplify its impact through various avenues within the metaverse.

Metaverse games, for instance, offer popular virtual worlds and gameplay experiences for players. Examples include Decentraland, where you explore a decentralized virtual world, and Axie Infinity, known for its play-to-earn features. The Sandbox lets users create content and own virtual assets, while Alien Worlds provides a space-themed environment. Illuvium merges blockchain tech with gameplay, and Roblox remains a dynamic hub for user creativity. My Neighbor Alice has a charming virtual neighborhood, and Minecraft allows limitless exploration and building. Voxels and Battle Infinity also provide unique experiences. Acknowledging players' demand for autonomy, game developers have designed spaces such as Decentraland and Sandbox. These environments empower users to not just take part in interactive experiences but also to possess virtual assets, giving rise to concerns related to publicity rights, property rights, including trademarks, and the ability to mold virtual landscapes.

The metaverse's development and widespread adoption give rise to significant concerns regarding data privacy due to the extensive collection, processing, and utilization of user data within this virtual realm. Several factors contribute to these apprehensions. First, user tracking and monitoring are inherent in the metaverse experience, where activities, preferences, and behaviors are continuously observed, potentially resulting in the creation of detailed user profiles that could compromise individuals' privacy.

Furthermore, the customization of digital avatars and the incorporation of real-life elements necessitate users to divulge personal information, encompassing facial features, preferences, and even biometric data. This raises substantial worries about the security and confidentiality of such sensitive details within the metaverse.

Big Tech companies stand to monetize the metaverse through avenues like virtual real estate, digital goods, and advertising, entailing the collection and analysis of user data for targeted advertising and product recommendations. This practice raises concerns about the commodification of personal information and the potential exploitation of user data for financial gain.

The immersive and interactive nature of the metaverse introduces security risks such as hacking, identity theft, and unauthorized access to personal data. Ensuring vigilant security measures becomes imperative to protect user privacy within this digital environment, as described throughout this chapter.

Compounding these challenges is the global scale of the metaverse, making it difficult to establish standardized regulations and compliance measures for data protection. The absence of consistent privacy standards across various virtual platforms heightens the risk of varying levels of data protection for users.

Informed consent becomes a critical issue as users may not fully grasp the implications of the data they share within the metaverse. Additionally, ensuring users have control over their data, including the ability to manage and delete personal information, is essential for protecting privacy rights.

The metaverse's cross-platform nature, where users engage through various devices and platforms, raises concerns about the seamless integration of data across these channels. This integration poses potential challenges regarding how data are shared and managed, particularly when users may not be fully aware of the extent to which their information is distributed. Addressing these multifaceted data privacy concerns in a global environment necessitates a comprehensive and collaborative effort from both industry stakeholders and regulatory bodies that remains difficult to attain.

Data Breaches

A data breach occurs when unauthorized parties successfully infiltrate computer systems, networks, or databases, gaining access to sensitive and confidential information. The compromised data can range from personal details and financial records to intellectual property, leaving individuals and organizations vulnerable to various risks. The repercussions of a data breach extend beyond the immediate unauthorized access, encompassing severe financial consequences, reputational damage, legal implications, and a spectrum of harm to affected parties. The impact is not limited to individual consumers; it also extends to small businesses and major global corporations, underscoring the pervasive and indiscriminate nature of the threat. In addition to financial losses, the aftermath of a data breach may involve protracted recovery efforts, regulatory penalties, and the need for comprehensive measures to restore trust and prevent future security breaches.

While the terms *data breach* and *cyberattack* are occasionally used interchangeably, they bear separate meanings. A data breach primarily involves unauthorized access to data, such as hackers gaining entry to sensitive information like users' names, Social Security numbers, and passwords. In contrast, a cyberattack encompasses a more extensive array of malicious activities conducted by cybercriminals. This includes but is not limited to malware infections and phishing schemes specifically designed to target and compromise computer systems. Clarifying these distinctions is crucial for understanding the nuanced nature of security incidents in the digital realm and adopting appropriate measures to counteract and prevent these threats.

Chapter 3: Behind the Digital Curtains: Safeguarding Privacy in an Online World 75

Various types of data breaches present unique challenges and risks:

1. **Phishing:** Phishing attacks involve deceptive emails or messages that deceive individuals into revealing sensitive information like passwords, credit card details, or login credentials. These attacks exploit social engineering techniques, taking advantage of human trust and naivety.
2. **Malware Attacks:** Malware encompasses viruses, ransomware, spyware, and trojans designed to infiltrate systems, steal data, or disrupt operations, posing significant threats to data security.
3. **Insider Threats:** Insider threats involve individuals within an organization misusing their access privileges to intentionally or inadvertently cause a data breach. This may include employees stealing or leaking sensitive information or falling victim to phishing attacks leading to unauthorized access.
4. **Physical Breaches:** Physical breaches occur when servers, computers, or storage devices with sensitive information are stolen through theft, unauthorized entry, or improper equipment disposal without adequately erasing the data.
5. **Password Guessing:** Attackers gain unauthorized access to user accounts by attempting various password combinations, exploiting weak or easily guessable passwords.
6. **Ransomware:** Ransomware is malicious software that encrypts files or blocks access to computer systems. Victims receive a ransom message demanding payment to restore access to their files.
7. **DDoS Attack:** Distributed denial of service (DDoS) attacks aim to disrupt computer networks by overwhelming them with incoming traffic. While the objective is not unauthorized access, DDoS attacks render targeted networks unavailable to legitimate users, impacting their capacity to respond to requests. Understanding these diverse data breach types is crucial for implementing effective cybersecurity measures and safeguarding sensitive information from evolving threats.

Here is a handful of some of the most egregious data breaches suffered by big tech and social media companies.

Yahoo! experienced the largest data breach in history, with attackers infiltrating its systems and compromising around 3 billion user accounts.

The breach included unauthorized access to usernames, email addresses, passwords, and security questions. This massive security incident remained undisclosed until 2016, coinciding with Verizon's negotiations to acquire Yahoo!. The revelation of the breach led to a renegotiation of the purchase price, with Verizon reducing its initial offer by $350 million, ultimately acquiring Yahoo! for $4.48 billion.

Equifax, a major credit reporting agency in the United States, suffered a significant data breach impacting about 147 million consumers. The breach allowed attackers to access sensitive data, including Social Security numbers, birth dates, addresses, credit card numbers, and driver's license information. The fallout from the breach was severe, with Equifax facing numerous lawsuits, regulatory scrutiny, and a tarnished reputation, resulting in costs nearing $1.4 billion.

Marriott International encountered a data breach that affected roughly 500 million guests who had made reservations with its Starwood brand. The breach exposed a range of personal information, such as names, addresses, passport numbers, and payment card details. The *New York Times* reported that the breach was believed to be part of a Chinese intelligence operation aimed at collecting data on American citizens. Marriott faced fines exceeding $23 million for its failure to safeguard customer information.

In 2021, Microsoft became the target of a cyberattack on its Exchange email servers, which affected up to 60,000 companies globally. The hackers managed to gain unauthorized access to emails and, upon penetrating the servers, were capable of deploying malware, taking control of the servers, and accessing other connected systems.

LinkedIn suffered a data breach that resulted in the theft of 6.5 million encrypted passwords, which were later posted on a Russian hacker forum. However, it wasn't until 2016 that the full extent of the breach was revealed, with reports indicating that data from approximately 167 million accounts had been compromised, including emails and hashed passwords.

Facebook experienced a data breach that exposed the personal information of over 540 million users. The data, which included account names, IDs, and details about users' friends, likes, and groups, was found unprotected on Amazon's cloud computing service. This incident was one of several privacy issues that raised concerns about Facebook's data protection practices.

In early 2018, it was revealed that malicious actors had breached the world's largest ID database, Aadhaar, compromising information on over 1.1 billion Indian citizens. This extensive breach exposed details such as names, addresses, photos, phone numbers, emails, and sensitive biometric data like fingerprints and iris scans. Established by the Unique Identification Authority of India (UIDAI) in 2009, the Aadhaar database also included information about bank accounts linked to unique twelve-digit numbers, turning it into a credit breach. Notably, despite initial denials by UIDAI regarding the inclusion of such data, the breach highlighted the global nature of data vulnerabilities.

The infiltration of the Aadhaar database occurred through the website of Indane, a state-owned utility company connected to the government database via an application programming interface (API). This API allowed applications to retrieve stored data from other applications or software. Unfortunately, the lack of access controls in Indane's API left its data exposed, leading hackers to sell access to this vast trove of information for as little as $7 through a WhatsApp group. Despite warnings from security researchers and tech groups, Indian authorities took until March 23, 2018, to address the vulnerable access point and take it offline. This incident underscores the worldwide challenge of securing sensitive data and the need for robust cybersecurity measures across various global databases.

To contextualize data breaches, consider that shortly after Ben Franklin established the first US postal service, malevolent individuals devised mail fraud. Similarly, following the invention of the telegraph and telephone, criminals swiftly adopted wire fraud. The underlying message is that with each technological advancement, be it the internet or cloud computing, nefarious actors have demonstrated the capacity and inclination to partake in illicit activities.

AI, Deepfakes, and Cyberscams

Things aren't always what they appear to be, especially in the era of rapidly evolving artificial intelligence (AI) technology. This cutting-edge tech has been harnessed for a variety of purposes, some of which blur the lines between reality and fiction. Synthetic images and videos, crafted with astonishing accuracy, have featured a wide range of public figures, from celebrities like Taylor Swift and the late comedian Robin Williams and tech moguls like Mark Zuckerberg to political leaders such as President Obama, Donald Trump and Joe Biden. These creations showcase the power of AI, but they also highlight a darker side.

While many instances of AI-generated content are harmless or even entertaining, there's a growing concern over more malicious uses. Deepfake technology, for example, has been used in phishing scams, posing significant threats to personal security and privacy. But the potential for misuse doesn't stop there. Consider the implications of deepfakes in spreading misinformation during critical events, such as elections, or their use in creating fake news stories that could sway public opinion on important public policy and national security issues.

One concerning aspect is AI's role in facilitating scams by enabling scammers to create sophisticated and personalized schemes. Leveraging personal information extracted from social media profiles and various online sources, AI tailors scams to individual targets, making them more convincing and difficult to discern. In this context, scammers employ the technology to collect and replicate audio data, allowing them to clone voices, including those of children, grandchildren, or other family members. The imposter then employs tactics such as spoofing phone numbers to display a loved one's familiar number on the recipient's caller ID.

The imposter, armed with a cloned voice and convincing caller ID, initiates a call, claiming to be in dire straits and urgently requesting financial assistance. The emotional impact of hearing a familiar voice and the association with a loved one's phone number can be persuasive, prompting individuals to respond impulsively to the apparent plea for help.

In another example of deploying a deepfake phishing attack, hackers employ AI and machine learning to process diverse content, spanning images, videos, and audio clips. Using this amalgamated data, they construct a digital replica of an individual. Through the utilization of advanced neural networks, specifically autoencoders, malevolent actors can scrutinize videos, analyze images, and listen to audio recordings of targeted individuals to replicate their physical attributes effectively. A notable example is the creation of a deepfake hologram featuring Patrick Hillmann, the chief communication officer at Binance, wherein hackers synthesized content from his past interviews and media appearances. This method not only enables threat actors to convincingly mimic an individual's physical characteristics, thus deceiving human users through social engineering tactics, but it also allows them to subvert biometric authentication solutions, underscoring the multifaceted risks associated with the manipulation of AI technologies for malicious purposes.

This dual application of AI, both in tailoring scams and creating convincing impersonations, underscores the need for heightened awareness and security measures to mitigate the risks associated with the malicious use of advanced technologies. These deepfakes also cross over to interfering with a person's right of publicity.

Right of Publicity

The right of publicity serves as a crucial legal concept, empowering individuals to assert control over the commercial utilization of their name, image, likeness, or other distinctive aspects of their persona. Functioning as a property right, it grants individuals the exclusive authority to license their identity for commercial promotion. In the United States, this right is primarily safeguarded by state laws, with approximately half of the states having distinct legislation recognizing and protecting it. Rooted in both privacy and economic exploitation, the right of publicity is closely intertwined with tort law, specifically the tort of misappropriation.

The term *right of publicity* was first introduced by Judge Jerome Frank in 1953, marking the inception of a legal concept that has since evolved from a privacy interest into a nuanced amalgamation of tort law, unfair competition law, and property jurisprudence. Judge Frank's decision in *Haelan Laboratories, Inc. v. Topps Chewing Gum, Inc.* (202 F.2d 866 (2d Cir. 1953)), set precedent, establishing the right of individuals to control the commercial use of their likenesses, particularly in contexts like sports trading cards. Its historical trajectory is intricately connected to the advent initially of photography, print and broadcast media, and now the expanding use of digital media and virtual metaverse.

The First Amendment in the United States places limitations on the right of publicity, safeguarding freedom of speech and expression. Consequently, not all uses of a person's identity are considered infringing, particularly in contexts such as news reporting, commentary, and other expressive activities, such as parody.

Commercial use and misappropriation of the right of publicity often come to the forefront in advertising or merchandise, where an individual's identity is employed for commercial gain without their explicit permission. Misappropriation of a person's likeness for exploitative purposes can lead to legal liability as occurred in a case involving former basketball star Michael Jordan.

A grocery store chain in Illinois used an advertisement featuring a basketball player jumping to dunk a basketball into a hoop with the number 23, strongly resembling Michael Jordan's iconic trademarked slam dunk. The advertisement also included the text "Jewel-Osco salutes #23, thanks for the memories." During Jordan's NBA playing days his jersey number was 23.

Michael Jordan filed a lawsuit against the grocery store, arguing that they misappropriated his identity for commercial purposes without his permission. Jordan emphasized that the unauthorized use of his likeness suggested an endorsement of the grocery store and its products, leading to a false association between him and the brand. The case went to court, a federal jury ruled in favor of Michael Jordan, awarding him $8.9 million in damages for the unauthorized use of his identity in the advertisement.

In the realm of digital media, the right of publicity encounters new challenges due to the decentralized and individualized nature of digital platforms. This shift may necessitate novel approaches to protect individuals' interests, with considerations suggesting the possibility of a more open marketplace for digital media, albeit with certain restrictions, especially in cases involving commercial advertising or threats to performance values.

There are different statutory regimes relating to the right of publicity in each state. California's right of publicity statute is one of the most comprehensive in the nation and requires permission to use one's "name, voice, signature, photograph, or likeness" on products or in advertising.

The right of publicity has become a crucial legal battleground in the digital media space, as demonstrated in cases such as *Fraley v. Facebook,*

Inc. (no. 11-CV-01726 (N.D. Cal., filed April 4, 2011)). This first-of-its-kind case sheds light on the challenges arising from the unauthorized use of individuals' names and likenesses in the realm of online advertising, prompting consequential legal action. *Fraley* was a class-action lawsuit filed against Facebook alleging the misappropriation of users' names and likenesses for commercial purposes without their consent. The case centered on Facebook's "Sponsored Stories" program, which used the images and interactions of users, such as clicking the "Like" button, to create advertisements broadcast to the user's friends on the platform, effectively turning users into spokespeople for advertisers.

An out-of-court settlement was reached where Facebook agreed to pay $15 per class member, despite each person's claim being worth $750 under California state law. The settlement also required Facebook to create an opt-out mechanism for Sponsored Stories and implement "parental controls" for minors.

The Screen Actors Guild–American Federation of Television and Radio Artists (SAG-AFTRA), a major entertainment industry union, successfully lobbied for legislation in New York that expanded the state's right of publicity law to include protection against "digital replicas" of deceased celebrities like attempts to replicate the late George Carlin's creative comedic routines online for profit, and deepfake pornography of well-known celebrities. In their most recent collective bargaining negotiations, SAG-AFTRA won assurances from producers that require both consent and payment for use of AI to digitally replicate an actor's performance, though the contract did not stop studios from using a blend of performances to create "synthetic" actors.

These examples reflect the necessity for the legal system to adapt to the challenges posed by the digital age. It emphasizes the importance of clarifying and reinforcing the boundaries of the right of publicity in the context of evolving technologies and the dynamic nature of online interactions.

Summary

This chapter addresses the powerful landscape of online digital media privacy, delving into the challenges, concerns, and evolving dynamics faced by individuals, businesses, and society in the digital age. Beginning with an exploration of fundamental privacy concepts adapted from the notion of the "right to be let alone," it examines the definition of privacy in the digital context and the delicate balance between the convenience of digital services and the imperative to protect personal information. The narrative then shifts to contemporary issues and threats such as big data analytics and artificial intelligence, data breaches, cyberattacks, and the commercialization of personal information.

The evolving aspects of online digital media privacy are further examined in the context of blurred lines between personal and public information, particularly in the age of social media. Integral to the discussion is an examination of the regulatory global landscape governing online digital media privacy. As personal information becomes increasingly accessible, questions of consent, data ownership, and the right to be forgotten take center stage. The chapter outlines key privacy laws and regulations at national and international levels, emphasizing the need for ongoing efforts to adapt regulations to the rapidly evolving digital landscape and addressing challenges related to enforcement and compliance especially for multinational online businesses including websites and social media platforms.

In addition, the chapter delves into the complex and rapidly evolving landscape of publicity rights within the digital sphere. As technology advances, particularly in the realm of artificial intelligence (AI), there is a growing concern surrounding the delicate balance between an individual's right to privacy and their entitlement to control their public image.

The advent of AI, specifically in the form of chatbots capable of learning and replicating real voices and images, has ushered in a new era of challenges and opportunities. On one hand, these technologies present innovative ways for individuals to engage with their audience, creating immersive and personalized experiences. On the other hand, there is a profound risk of misuse, where AI-driven entities can mimic real voices and images for potentially harmful purposes.

In conclusion, the chapter provides a comprehensive overview of online digital media privacy, encompassing its complexities, challenges, and potential solutions. It encourages readers to critically assess their digital footprint, stay informed about privacy issues, and

Chapter 3: Behind the Digital Curtains: Safeguarding Privacy in an Online World

actively engage in the ongoing discourse surrounding the delicate balance between technological innovation and the protection of personal information.

Discussion Questions

1. How has the digital era transformed the concept of privacy, and what are the key challenges individuals face in safeguarding their personal information online?
2. In what ways do social media platforms impact user privacy, and what measures can users take to maintain control over their personal data in these environments?
3. How do data breaches and cyberattacks contribute to privacy concerns in the digital age, and what steps can organizations take to enhance cybersecurity and protect user information?
4. What ethical considerations should be considered when it comes to the collection and use of personal data by digital media companies, especially in the context of targeted advertising and personalized content?
5. How do emerging technologies such as artificial intelligence and machine learning pose challenges to privacy, and what regulatory frameworks or ethical guidelines should be in place to address these concerns?
6. If you engage in virtual gaming, does the potential fate of the personal information you disclose, with or without your explicit consent, raise any concerns for you?
7. Should the United States enact national data privacy protections instead of the current patchwork policies similar to the protections afforded citizens of the European Union?
8. In what ways do individuals willingly trade privacy for convenience in the digital era, and how can awareness and education help users make more informed decisions about their digital footprint?
9. How do cultural differences influence perceptions of privacy in the digital world, and how can global standards be established to address privacy challenges on an international scale?

10. As we move toward an increasingly digitized society, what innovative solutions and technologies can be developed to enhance privacy protection and mitigate the risks associated with the digitalization of personal information?

Works Referenced

"Artificial Intelligence and Scams," accessed at https://www.michigan.gov/consumerprotection/protect-yourself/consumer-alerts/scams/artificial-intelligence-and-scams

Berinato, Scott. "Stop Thinking about Consent: It Isn't Possible and It Isn't Right." *Harvard Business Review*, September 24, 2018, accessed at https://hbr.org/2018/09/stop-thinking-about-consent-it-isnt-possible-and-it-isnt-right

Chin, Brian X. "The Battle for Digital Privacy Is Reshaping the Internet." *The New York Times*, June 23, 2023, accessed at https://www.nytimes.com/2021/09/16/technology/digital-privacy.html

"Data Protection in the EU." European Commission, accessed at https://commission.europa.eu/law/law-topic/data-protection/data-protection-eu_en

"Deanonymization: The Thorn in the Side of Data Privacy." FasterCapital, December 7, 2023, accessed at https://fastercapital.com/content/Deanonymization--The-Thorn-in-the-Side-of-Data-Privacy.html

Fortner, Robert. *Ethics in the Digital Domain*. Rowman & Littlefield, Lanham, MD, 2021.

Grea, Francesca. "To Like or Not to Like: Fraley v. Facebook's Impact on California's Right of Publicity Statute in the Age of the Internet." *Loyola of Los Angeles Law Review*, Vol. 47, No. 3 (Spring 2014), accessed at https://digitalcommons.lmu.edu/cgi/viewcontent.cgi?article=2896&context=llr

Hill, Michael, and Swinhoe, Dan. "The 15 Biggest Data Breaches of the 21st Century." *CSO*, November 8, 2022, accessed at https://www.csoonline.com/article/534628/the-biggest-data-breaches-of-the-21st-century.html

Jones, Michael, *Art Law,* 2nd ed. Rowman & Littlefield, Lanham, MD, 2023.

Pernot-Leplay, Emanuel. "EU Influence on Data Privacy Laws: Is the U.S. Approach Converging with the EU Model?." *Colorado Technology Law Journal*, Vol. 18, No. 1 (2020), accessed at https://papers.ssrn.com/sol3/papers.cfm?abstract_id=3542730

Pop, Christina. "EU vs US: What Are the Differences between Their Data Privacy Laws?" *End Point Projector* (blog), November 1, 2023, accessed at https://www.endpointprotector.com/blog/eu-vs-us-what-are-the-differences-between-their-data-privacy-laws

Poritz, Isaiah. "AI Celebrity Fakes Clash with Web of State Publicity Laws." *Bloomberg Law*, April 14, 2023, accessed at https://news.bloomberglaw.com/ip-law/ai-celebrity-deepfakes-clash-with-web-of-state-publicity-laws

"Questions & Answers: EU-US Data Privacy Framework." European Commission, July 23, 2023, accessed at https://ec.europa.eu/commission/presscorner/detail/en/qanda_23_3752

"SAG-AFTRA Statement on Taylor Swift and George Carlin Digital Fakes." SAG-AFTRA, January 26, 2024, accessed at https://www.sagaftra.org/sag-aftra-statement-taylor-swift-and-george-carlin-digital-fakes

Smith, Brad and Browne, Carol Ann, *Tools and Weapons*. Penguin Books, New York, 2023.

"Top 10 Metaverse Games to Immerse Yourself In." Blockchain Council, accessed at https://www.blockchain-council.org/metaverse/top-10-metaverse-games

Volz, Dustin. "U.S. Spy Agencies Adopt Rules for Buying Data on Americans." *The Wall Street Journal*, May 9, 2024.

"Why Deep Fake Phishing Is a Disaster Waiting to Happen." *Games Beat*, accessed at https://venturebeat.com/security/deepfake-phishing

4

Content Control: Copyrights and the Future of Digital Distribution

Copyrights are the currency of creativity in the digital age, safeguarding the investments of creators and fostering innovation.

—AI invented quote

Intellectual property rights serve as the cornerstone of the creative component of the world, encompassing a broad spectrum of innovations spanning traditional and digital media. These rights, including patents, trademarks, copyrights, moral rights, and trade secrets, grant creators and owners exclusive control over their intellectual creations, thus incentivizing innovation and fostering economic growth.

Patents protect inventions, granting inventors exclusive rights to their discoveries for a limited period. Trademarks safeguard brands, ensuring consumers can identify the source of goods and services. Copyrights, crucial in both traditional and digital media realms, safeguard against unauthorized copying, distribution, and reproduction of original expressions of ideas. Moral rights, mostly a European concept, refers to the right of an author to prevent revision, alteration, or distortion of a person's work, regardless of who owns the work. Meanwhile, trade secrets protect confidential information, such as formulas, processes, or methods, providing a competitive advantage to businesses.

Society recognizes intellectual property rights for several reasons. First, they incentivize innovation and creativity by granting creators and inventors exclusive rights to profit from their ideas. This encourages investment in research and development, driving technological advancement and economic prosperity. Additionally, intellectual property rights facilitate the sharing of diverse experiences, perspectives, and expressions, enriching society's cultural tapestry.

The proliferation of digital platforms and online content distribution channels further complicates the enforcement of copyright laws. With the widespread dissemination of digital content across the internet, monitoring and policing potential copyright infringements become increasingly challenging. In one well-documented instance, the music industry confronted a major copyright infringement case involving YouTube, a prominent online platform for sharing content. Key record labels such as Universal Music Group, Sony Music Entertainment, and Warner Music Group took legal action against YouTube, claiming that it permitted users to upload copyrighted music without obtaining proper authorization or compensating the rights holders. Content creators must grapple with the daunting task of monitoring their intellectual property in the vast and constantly expanding digital landscape, often relying on automated tools like YouTube's Content ID, which scans uploaded videos for copyrighted material and allows rights holders to either monetize or remove the content, and algorithms to detect unauthorized use. The sheer volume of user-generated content makes it difficult to catch every infringement.

One of the primary challenges posed by digital media and artificial intelligence (AI) is the automated generation of content that may incorporate copyrighted material without proper authorization. AI algorithms can analyze and synthesize vast amounts of data, potentially reproducing or adapting copyrighted works in ways that blur the lines of originality and ownership. For instance, AI-generated articles or artworks may inadvertently incorporate elements from copyrighted sources, raising questions about the extent of permissible use and the rights of the original creators.

Additionally, the rise of nontraditional forms of digital expression, such as non-fungible tokens (NFTs), introduces novel considerations for copyright law. NFTs represent unique digital assets stored on a blockchain, often encompassing digital artworks or other creative works. The ownership and transfer of NFTs raise questions about the rights of the original creators and the potential for unauthorized exploitation or reproduction of digital content.

In light of these challenges, copyright law faces the imperative to adapt and evolve to address the complexities of digital media and AI. Legal frameworks must grapple with defining the parameters of fair use and permissible use of copyrighted material in this new technological frontier. Additionally, efforts to enhance digital rights management and establish clearer guidelines for copyright enforcement in the digital realm are essential to safeguarding the rights of content creators and owners.

Ultimately, the evolution of copyright law in response to digital media and AI underscores the ongoing need to strike a balance between fostering innovation and creativity while preserving the rights of creators and owners. By navigating these challenges thoughtfully and collaboratively, policymakers, legal experts, and stakeholders can ensure that copyright law remains relevant and effective in the digital age, supporting a thriving creative ecosystem while upholding the principles of intellectual property rights.

In addressing these complexities, stakeholders from courts to legislative bodies, cultural institutions, and developers of AI algorithms grapple with reconciling competing interests. Central to these discussions are considerations of the duration of copyright protection, innovative methods of distributing content, and the preservation of freedom of expression guaranteed by the **First Amendment**. The recent Andy Warhol Estate Supreme Court case, discussed in detail within this chapter, sheds new light on the boundaries of fair use and exemplifies the ongoing evolution of copyright law in response to media.

This chapter delves into the multifaceted approaches employed by various worldwide entities to address these evolving challenges and ensure the continued vitality of the creative arts world in the digital age. From legislative reforms to technological innovations, the landscape of intellectual property rights continues to evolve in response to the dynamic interplay of content creativity, technology, and society.

A Brief History of Copyright Law

Johannes Gutenberg, a German blacksmith, revolutionized the dissemination of knowledge with his invention of the first oil-based printing press around 1439. This invention swiftly spread throughout Europe, transforming the landscape of intellectual property rights. In England, the printing press was initially controlled by a guild of printers, or "stationers," who wielded monopoly powers over the right to print or copy materials. Notably, this control was vested in the printers rather than the authors or creators of the works.

The printers, acting as both publishers and censors, were empowered to prevent the publication of materials deemed objectionable by the English government, crown, or Church of England. Unauthorized copies produced by rival printers encroached upon the exclusive rights granted by the crown, with little consideration for the royalties or rights of the original authors.

By the late 1600s, democratic values began to take root in England, leading to the expiration of the stationers' exclusive printing powers. In response, established printers sought legislative protection against competitors, culminating in the enactment of the **Statute of Anne in 1709**. This landmark statute marked a significant shift in intellectual property law by affording protection to authors rather than solely to printers.

In 1735, England extended statutory copyright protection to include images such as prints and pictures. Meanwhile, in the United States, the Founding Fathers recognized the importance of intellectual property rights, incorporating them into the **Federal Constitution** under **Article I, section 8, clause 8**, known as the **Copyright Clause**. This clause—"To promote the Progress of Science and useful Arts, by securing for limited Times to Authors and Inventors the exclusive Right to their respective Writings and Discoveries."—granted Congress the authority to enact copyright legislation, reflecting the nation's commitment to fostering creativity and innovation while granting a limited monopoly right in the works.

One influential figure in early American copyright law was Noah Webster, who advocated for the passage of copyright laws in each of the original twelve states. Leveraging his influence, Noah Webster persuaded his cousin Daniel Webster to lobby the first Congress to enact the **Copyright Law of 1790**. This law provided copyright protection for fourteen years, renewable for another fourteen years, initially covering maps, charts, and books. Subsequent amendments expanded the scope of protected works to include etchings, engravings, photographs, drawings, sculptures, and paintings.

Chapter 4: Content Control: Copyrights and the Future of Digital Distribution

Over the years, Congress has implemented various revisions to copyright statutes, expanding the categories of protected works and enhancing artists' rights. The most significant overhaul came with the **Copyright Act of 1976**, which centralized copyright authority at the federal level and clarified the ownership of reproduction rights. This act affirmed that artists retain copyright unless explicitly transferred in writing, preventing misunderstandings and protecting the rights of creators.

An illustrative example of the importance of clarifying reproduction rights ownership occurred in a dispute between the Whistler House Museum of Art and the Guggenheim Museum. Upon discovering the unauthorized commercial use of a painting loaned to the Guggenheim, the Whistler House Museum intervened to halt reproduction and sales of notecards featuring the artwork that was displayed in Guggenheim's gift shop and online in its website. This case underscored the distinction between owning the physical work of art and possessing the copyright, highlighting the necessity of protecting artists' rights in the digital age.

The **Digital Millennium Copyright Act (DMCA)** is another landmark piece of legislation enacted in 1998 to address copyright issues arising from the rapid growth of digital technologies and the internet. One of the key provisions of the **DMCA** is the establishment of a framework for addressing copyright infringement online. The law includes provisions that shield online service providers, such as internet service providers (ISPs) and website hosts, from liability for copyright infringement committed by their users, provided they adhere to certain requirements, such as implementing a notice-and-takedown system for removing infringing content.

Today, copyright protection in the United States extends for the lifetime of the artist or author plus seventy years for works created after 1977. Works created between 1925 and 1978 are protected for ninety-five years from the date of first publication, ensuring that creative legacies are preserved for future generations. While registration of copyright is voluntary, it provides certain advantages, including the ability to initiate legal action for copyright infringement.

The evolution of copyright law has not been confined to individual nations but has also been shaped by international agreements and conventions. One such influential agreement is the **Berne Convention** for the **Protection of Literary and Artistic Work**s, established in 1886. The **Berne Convention**, which has been ratified by over 170 countries worldwide, sets forth minimum standards for copyright protection and ensures that the rights of authors and creators are recognized and upheld across borders.

Under the **Berne Convention**, signatory countries agree to provide automatic and equal protection for works originating from other member states, without the need for formalities such as registration or notice. This principle of "national treatment" ensures that creators enjoy consistent copyright protection regardless of where their works are published or distributed.

While the **Berne Convention** establishes minimum standards for copyright protection, individual countries retain the flexibility to enact their own copyright laws and regulations. As a result, copyright terms, exceptions, and enforcement mechanisms may vary significantly from one country to another. Under the **Berne Convention**, the minimum term of copyright protection is the life of the author plus fifty years.

For example, some countries may extend copyright protection for a fixed term of years after the author's death, while others may adopt a more complex system based on the date of publication or creation. Additionally, the scope of copyright protection may differ, with some countries offering broader or narrower protections for certain types of works or expressions.

A significant difference between countries adhering to the **Berne Convention** and US Copyright law lies in the concept of moral rights, which may be unfamiliar to American content creators especially visual artists. Moral rights typically encompass several key elements, including the right of attribution (acknowledgment as the author), the right to integrity (protection against derogatory treatment of the work harming the author's reputation), and sometimes the right of disclosure (control over when the work is published). In the United States, moral rights are less comprehensive than those outlined in the **Berne Convention**. The **U.S. Copyright Act** provides limited moral rights protection through the **Visual Artists Rights Act (VARA)**, specifically in **Section 106A**. **VARA** grants authors of certain visual works the limited right to claim authorship and prevent intentional distortion, mutilation, or modification of their work prejudicial to their reputation. However,

VARA does not include the right of disclosure and applies primarily to visual art such as paintings, sculptures, and drawings. Furthermore, **VARA** rights are subject to specific limitations and exceptions, unlike the broader moral rights protections found in other **Berne Convention** countries.

The diverse landscape of international copyright laws presents challenges for creators, rights holders, and content distributors operating in a globalized digital environment. In addition, the emergence of digital media and AI technologies complicates matters further, as automated processes may inadvertently infringe upon copyright protections established in different jurisdictions.

In global legal matters, "jurisdiction" means the authority a country has over copyright law within its borders. This decides which laws apply to protecting, using, and enforcing copyrights for works created or shared there. For instance, if a work is made in the United States and shared online, US copyright laws typically apply. But if it's shared in another country, their laws might also matter, especially in copyright disputes.

Jurisdictional problems come up because of the internet, which allows content to quickly spread worldwide. It can be hard to decide which country's laws should apply to online content, especially when different countries have different copyright rules. To tackle jurisdictional issues, efforts have been made to harmonize copyright laws and facilitate cross-border cooperation in copyright enforcement. International treaties and agreements, such as the **Agreement on Trade-Related Aspects of Intellectual Property Rights (TRIPS)** administered by the **World Trade Organization (WTO)**, aim to promote greater consistency and cooperation in the protection and enforcement of intellectual property rights.

Despite these efforts, significant disparities persist in the interpretation and application of copyright laws among different countries. As digital technologies continue to reshape the global landscape of intellectual property, policymakers and stakeholders must work together to address these challenges and ensure that copyright laws remain effective and relevant in the digital age. By fostering international cooperation and harmonizing legal frameworks, the global community can better protect the rights of creators and promote innovation and creativity on a global scale.

Creation, Scope, and Benefits of a Copyright

A copyright grants exclusive rights to creators of a wide array of creative works, spanning two-dimensional drawings; digitally generated prints; three-dimensional sculptures; literary compositions like novels, short stories, poems, essays, and articles; original musical compositions; motion pictures; videos, documentaries, and other audiovisual creations; unique photographic images; dance routines; choreography; architectural designs; computer programs; software applications; product designs; scripts for plays, movies, and television shows; as well as various mixed-media works. Upon creation, copyright protection automatically applies to these works, empowering creators with the authority to reproduce, create derivative works, distribute copies, and publicly display their creations, while also enabling them to prevent unauthorized use. To qualify for copyright protection, a work must meet four criteria:

1. It must be an original, not copied, work of art or authorship.
2. It must be a copyrightable subject matter—including literary works, musical works, dramatic works, pantomimes and choreographic works, pictorial-graphic-sculptural works, motion pictures and other audiovisual works, sound recordings, and architectural works.
3. It must be fixed in a tangible medium of expression—examples include woodblock prints on paper, stained glass designs, tapestries, collages on paper, watercolors on stationary, charcoal comic strips on newsprint, artwork applied to clothing, gouache and crayon on paper over canvas, murals, screen-print posters, blush pen and ink on plastic sheets, tattoos drawn on skin, and digitally saved photographs.
4. It must possess a minimum degree of creativity, produced by human input: while a selfie taken by an ape does not meet the human intellect component and thus fails the creativity test, a selfie taken by a social media influencer posted on Tik Tok shared worldwide does qualify. The creative aspect lies in framing the image, selecting the angle, and composing the shot.

These requirements for a work of art to receive copyright protection are outlined in the **Copyright Act of 1976** and are subject to administrative law and judicial interpretation.

The originality required for copyright protection doesn't demand groundbreaking creativity; rather, it necessitates a basic level of creativity that is independently conceived by the creator. This means that the work must reflect some degree of original expression, even if it's not entirely novel or unique. In essence, two identical works of art created independently can each qualify for copyright protection, as long as one wasn't copied from the other. Courts generally refrain from imposing subjective standards of what constitutes art, recognizing that creativity can manifest in various forms and degrees.

However, a landmark judicial decision, *Feist Publications, Inc. v. Rural Telephone Service Co., Inc.* (499 U.S. 340 (1991)), set a significant precedent regarding the originality required for copyright protection. In this case, the US Supreme Court ruled that an original phone directory lacked the requisite level of creativity to be protected under copyright law. The Court made two critical legal points:

First, the Court emphasized that the labor and expense involved in collecting and compiling information, often referred to as the "sweat of the brow" test, are insufficient on their own to meet the threshold of creativity required for copyright protection. In other words, mere effort and investment in assembling factual data do not automatically confer copyright protection if the work lacks original expression.

Second, the Court highlighted that the act of alphabetically listing names and phone numbers found in the public domain does not demonstrate the minimum level of creativity necessary for copyright protection. While some organizational effort may be involved, such a mechanical arrangement of information does not rise to the level of originality required under copyright law.

The *Feist Publications* ruling is crucial in the context of whether AI-generated content qualifies for copyright protection because it establishes a clear standard for what constitutes originality and creativity in copyright law. By emphasizing that copyright protection is reserved for works that exhibit a genuine spark of creativity, rather than merely labor-intensive or mechanical compilations of factual data, the decision highlights the importance of human authorship and innovation in creating copyrightable content.

When considering AI-generated content, which is created using algorithms and machine-learning systems, questions arise about whether such content can be considered sufficiently original and creative to qualify for copyright protection. While AI can produce content that is technically complex and labor intensive, the *Feist* decision suggests that mere effort and mechanical compilation of data are not enough to meet the threshold of creativity required for copyright protection.

In a controversial administrative law opinion, the US Copyright Office has ruled that works of art created by artificial intelligence without any human input cannot be copyrighted under US law. Only works with human authors are eligible for copyright protection. This was affirmed by a US district judge in Washington, DC, who agreed with the Copyright Office's rejection of an application filed by computer scientist Stephen Thaler on behalf of his AI system, DABUS. The Copyright Office has also issued guidance stating that applicants must disclose the inclusion of AI-generated content in works submitted for copyright registration.

This decision stands in contrast to rulings in the United Kingdom and Irish law permitting copyright protection of computer-generated works, with the author being the person who made the "necessary arrangements" for the creation of the work. Meanwhile, the European Union is poised to mandate that the creators of artificial intelligence technologies like ChatGPT, Google's Bard, and Perplexity would be mandated to disclose copyrighted materials used in constructing their systems.

In early 2023, the Copyright Office initiated an examination of copyright law and policy concerning artificial intelligence (AI) technology in the aftermath of the denial of AI-generated art qualifying for copyright protection. This initiative aimed to address issues such as the copyright scope for works created using AI tools and the use of copyrighted materials in AI training. The Copyright Office organized public listening sessions and webinars to gather and disseminate information about existing technologies and their implications. Subsequently, in August 2023, the Office published a notice of inquiry in the Federal Register to further explore these matters with an eye toward making recommendations to Congress related to whether, and under what circumstances, AI-generated work may qualify for copyright protection.

In a pre-AI decision that offers further precedent on the requirements for copyright protection, a notable cross-continental legal battle unfolded in a federal court in New York, shedding light on the intersection of creativity and legal considerations in the digital realm of museum and gallery art. In *Bridgeman Art Library, Ltd. v. Corel Corp* (36 F. Supp. 2d 191

Chapter 4: Content Control: Copyrights and the Future of Digital Distribution

Figure 4.1 AI-generated image not qualifying for copyright protection in the United States.

(S.D.N.Y. 1999)), Bridgeman Art Library, a British company, specialized in commercially licensing high-quality photographic reproductions of artworks in collaboration with esteemed museums and galleries. On the other hand, Corel Corporation, a Canadian firm, produced CD-ROMs containing numerous digital reproductions of public-domain works by renowned European painters.

The dispute arose when Bridgeman filed a lawsuit against Corel, alleging copyright infringement. Bridgeman claimed that Corel unlawfully used Bridgeman's transparencies of artworks from museum collections without proper authorization, incorporating them into Corel's CD-ROM without permission.

Judge Lewis Kaplan, a former Harvard Law professor with expertise in copyright law, presided over the case. He acknowledged the protectability of photographic images under copyright law, emphasizing that a photograph must exhibit more than mere technical skill to be deemed original and eligible for copyright protection. Drawing upon precedents such as *Burrow-Giles Lithographic Co. v. Sarony* (111 U.S. 53 (1884)), Judge Kaplan highlighted the requirement for sufficient originality in aspects like pose, arrangement of accessories, and lighting to warrant copyright protection.

In his ruling, Judge Kaplan emphasized that the transparencies used by Corel were exact replicas of two-dimensional paintings, which were already in the public domain due to the artists' demise. Despite Bridgeman's significant efforts in creating the transparencies, the court determined that they lacked the requisite "creative spark" essential for originality, citing the *Feist* decision.

Although initially argued under US copyright law due to the alleged infringement occurring in New York, the court agreed to reconsider the case under United Kingdom copyright law, which at that time pre-Brexit was the **Berne Convention**. Judge Kaplan ultimately concluded that Bridgeman's reproductions lacked originality and were not copyrightable under any applicable legal framework.

The *Bridgeman* decision raised questions regarding the copyrightability of photographs of three-dimensional artworks and portions of artworks in the public domain. It suggested that more creative choices in photographing three-dimensional works, such as angles, positioning, and lighting, could potentially meet the threshold for copyright protection. However, to date, no court has addressed these specific issues.

The **Copyright Act of the United States**, specifically under **17 U.S. Code § 106**, provides copyright owners with a suite of exclusive rights or benefits that are foundational to the protection and monetization of creative works. These rights are crucial for creators to control the use of their works and to benefit financially from their creativity. Let's delve into these exclusive rights with expanded examples within the US context:

Exclusive Rights

Reproduction: This right allows creators to control the copying of their works. For example, a photographer can prevent others from making unauthorized copies of their photographs. This ensures that the photographer can monetize their work through sales or licensing without the dilution of value caused by unauthorized reproductions. A software developer can restrict the copying of their software, ensuring that users must obtain a license, which can include conditions like payment or restrictions on usage, to legally use the software.

Derivative Works: Creators can produce or authorize adaptations of their works. A novelist, for instance, has the exclusive right to create a screenplay based on their book or to license others to do so. This right enables authors to explore different mediums and revenue streams from a single original work. A graphic designer can control the creation of merchandise based on their designs, such as T-shirts or posters, ensuring that any derivative products are authorized and potentially generate additional income.

Distribution: This right allows creators to control who may distribute their works and how. A musician, for example, can grant licenses to streaming platforms or record labels, choosing partners that align with their distribution goals and financial interests. An independent filmmaker can choose specific streaming services for the distribution of their film, negotiating terms that favor their financial and artistic interests, such as exclusivity periods or revenue-sharing models

Performance: Creators can control public performances of their works. A playwright can authorize specific theaters to stage their play, ensuring they receive compensation and that their work is presented in a manner consistent with their vision. A composer can grant performance rights to orchestras or ensembles, deciding on the venues and contexts in which their music is performed, and ensuring appropriate compensation for such performances.

Public Display: This right enables visual artists to control where and how their artwork is publicly displayed, such as in galleries or museums. It ensures that artists can manage the exposure of their work and receive recognition and compensation for public exhibitions. An architect can control the public display of their architectural plans or models, allowing them to be exhibited in specific contexts that respect their intellectual property and professional reputation.

These examples illustrate the breadth of control and financial opportunity afforded to creators through the exclusive rights granted by the **Copyright Act**. By leveraging these rights, creators can protect their works, negotiate favorable terms for their use, and pursue a variety of revenue-generating strategies, all of which contribute to the vibrancy and sustainability of the creative industries.

It is important to remember that ownership of a copyright, or of any of the exclusive rights under a copyright, is distinct from ownership of any material object in which the work is embodied. Transfer of ownership of any material object, including the copy or phonorecord in which the work is first fixed, does not of itself convey any rights in the copyrighted work embodied in the object; nor, in the absence of an agreement, does transfer of ownership of a copyright or of any exclusive rights under a copyright convey property rights in any material object.

Digital Copyright

Digital copyright is a form of copyright that specifically addresses intellectual property rights in the digital realm. While traditional copyright law protects works in physical forms such as books, paintings, and sculptures, digital copyright extends these protections to digital content and creations distributed and accessed through digital means. Here's how digital copyright functions as a distinct form of copyright:

1. **Protection of Digital Works**: Digital copyright safeguards various types of digital works, including software, digital music, ebooks, online articles, videos, multimedia content, and databases. It ensures that creators have control over how their works are used, distributed, and monetized in digital formats.
2. **Addressing Digital Challenges**: Digital copyright addresses unique challenges posed by the digital environment, such as digital piracy, unauthorized distribution, and technological advancements that enable easy replication and dissemination of digital content. It

provides legal mechanisms to combat copyright infringement in the digital space.
3. **Technological Protection Measures**: Digital copyright incorporates provisions for technological protection measures (TPMs) or digital rights management (DRM) systems to prevent unauthorized access, copying, or modification of digital content. These measures along with watermarks help maintain the integrity of digital works and uphold the rights of creators and rights holders.
4. **Licensing and Distribution Models**: Digital copyright facilitates the development of licensing agreements and distribution models tailored to the digital landscape. It enables creators to monetize their works through various digital platforms, subscription services, pay-per-download models, and streaming platforms while ensuring fair compensation and rights management.
5. **International Harmonization**: Digital copyright laws often reflect efforts toward international harmonization and standardization to address global challenges associated with digital content distribution and cross-border copyright enforcement. Treaties such as the **Berne Convention** and the **WIPO Copyright Treaty** provide frameworks for international cooperation in protecting digital intellectual property rights.
6. **Emerging Technologies**: Digital copyright evolves to address emerging technologies and digital innovations, such as artificial intelligence, blockchain, virtual reality, and augmented reality. It considers new modes of content creation, distribution, and consumption, ensuring that copyright protections remain relevant and effective in a rapidly changing digital landscape.

Digital copyright encompasses a wide range of digital expressions in the modern era. This extends to:

1. **Software**: Copyright law safeguards the code and structure of software programs, preventing unauthorized copying, distribution, and modification. Companies and individuals invest significant resources into software development, and copyright protection ensures that their creations are not exploited without permission.
2. **Digital Music**: With the proliferation of digital music platforms and streaming services, copyright protection is essential for musicians,

composers, and record labels. It covers original compositions, recordings, and performances, safeguarding the rights of creators and ensuring fair compensation for their work.
3. Online Articles: Writers, journalists, and publishers rely on copyright protection to safeguard their online articles and written content. This includes news articles, blog posts, opinion pieces, and other forms of digital journalism, preventing unauthorized reproduction or distribution.
4. Ebooks: Authors and publishers invest time and effort into creating digital books, and copyright protection ensures that their works are not unlawfully copied or distributed. Ebooks encompass a wide range of genres, from fiction and nonfiction to academic publications and educational materials.
5. Videos: Copyright law extends to digital videos, including movies, television shows, documentaries, and user-generated content. It protects the creative elements within videos, such as scriptwriting, cinematography, editing, and visual effects, as well as performances by actors and artists.
6. Databases: Copyright protection may also extend to certain databases that demonstrate originality and creativity in their selection, arrangement, or compilation of data. This includes databases used in research, business analytics, and information services, ensuring that the effort invested in organizing and curating data is respected and acknowledged.

Overall, digital copyright represents a specialized branch of copyright law designed to protect and regulate intellectual property rights in the digital age, safeguarding the interests of creators, rights holders, and users in the digital ecosystem.

Expression vs. Idea Dichotomy

Copyright law safeguards the unique expression of ideas or facts rather than the ideas or facts themselves, as demonstrated in various artistic and creative contexts. For instance, in a legal case involving a professional photographer's art gallery and Korea Air, the court ruled that copyright protection does not extend to ideas or subject matter choices. In this instance, the similarity between a color image of an island in a newspaper advertisement and the photographer's black and white depiction of the same island did not constitute infringement, as they represented different approaches to capturing the subject. However, had Korea Air used the photographer's image without permission, the outcome would likely have differed, affirming the creator's right to control the use of their work.

Notably, copyright protection does not extend to food creations, as they are not traditionally considered within the realm of protected artistic works. The culinary creations of individuals such as the faceless YouTube chef Babish or the more traditional host of the PBS cooking show *Ciao Italia*, Mary Ann Esposito, fall outside the scope of copyright. However, a cookbook in print or digital form featuring food photographs and related commentary by these individuals may be eligible for copyright protection.

Furthermore, utilitarian objects, geometric shapes, and typeface designs generally do not qualify for copyright protection. Nevertheless, artistic motifs or works incorporating these elements into their imagery may be protected. Examples include the iconic pop art paintings of Andy Warhol, featuring everyday objects like soup cans and Coca-Cola bottles, Keith Haring's vibrant artworks with bold geometric shapes and simplified figures, and Barbara Kruger's powerful compositions employing bold typefaces and black and white imagery to convey social and political messages frequently criticizing advertising.

Moreover, multimedia works that integrate both visual and nonvisual art elements are eligible for copyright protection. These intricate creations blend various mediums, such as computer-generated sound, video, animation, and physical art objects, to produce immersive and dynamic artistic experiences.

One notable example of digital multimedia art protected by copyright because it expresses an idea is "Gravity's Rainbow" by Refik Anadol. This immersive installation combines data visualization, machine-learning algorithms, and light projections to create a mesmerizing experience. Anadol collected and processed data from various sources, including social media interactions, weather patterns, and geopolitical events, to generate dynamic visualizations that are projected onto large-scale surfaces.

Through its use of cutting-edge technology and artistic expression, the installation challenges traditional notions of storytelling and perception, offering a compelling reflection on the digital age.

Exceptions to Ownership

The **Copyright Act of 1976** establishes that the creator of an original work of art is typically the copyright owner. However, there are important exceptions to this rule, including a specific consideration for digital media:

1. Works Made for Hire—When an employee creates a work within the scope of their employment, the employer is considered the copyright owner. The duration of copyright for works made for hire differs from that of other copyrights.
2. Pre-1978 Commissioned Works—Copyright for works commissioned by an independent contractor before 1978 usually belongs to the commissioning party.
3. Post-1978 Commissioned Works—For works commissioned after 1978, the artist retains copyright unless there is a written agreement to the contrary. This includes a statutory exception for contributions to collective works, such as an essay in an exhibition catalog.
4. Assignment—The party that purchases or is assigned the copyright from the artist becomes the copyright owner.
5. Death—Upon the death of an artist, copyright interests can be transferred to an heir or beneficiary through a will, trust, or inheritance.
6. Digital Media Exception—In the realm of digital media, the copyright may be subject to specific licensing agreements that allow for the use of the work in digital formats, such as online streaming or digital downloads, while still protecting the original copyright holder's rights.
7. Fair Use—This exception, which is discussed in detail below, allows limited use of copyrighted material without permission for purposes such as criticism, comment, news reporting, teaching, scholarship, or research.

Exclusive Reproduction and Derivative Rights

The **Copyright Act of 1976**, under **Section 106**, bestows upon the copyright owner a bundle of five distinct rights, including the exclusive right to:

- reproduce or make copies of the artwork,
- display the artwork publicly,
- perform the artwork publicly,
- sell and distribute the artwork,
- prepare derivative art works.

These provisions grant creators or assignees certain explicit rights to control the usage of their work, subject to various limitations.

An illustration of a statutory limitation pertains to the right to display art. For instance, a museum possessing a work of art or having lawfully borrowed it retains the right to display the art without requiring further permission from the copyright holder. Conversely, if the museum were to digitally replicate the art to create commercial products like posters or greeting cards for sale online, as occurred in a previous instance involving the Whistler Museum and the Guggenheim, without consent from the copyright owner, it would potentially face allegations of copyright infringement.

The "reproduction" and "sale and distribution" of images are protected activities under the statute as long as the copyright in the work has not entered the public domain. Derivative or adaptation rights extend beyond mere defense against unauthorized copying to encompass the right to create alternative versions of the original art.

For example, a company manufacturing and selling ceramic tiles by incorporating transparent images from a copyrighted art book violated the exclusive right to prepare derivative images owned by the creator's widow. Despite the tile company's argument that purchasing a copy of the book entitled them to use the works under the "first sale" doctrine, the court disagreed. While the company could sell its physical copy of the book under this doctrine, without a specific transfer of the copyright holder's exclusive right to prepare derivative works, it remained with the widow. (See: *Mirage Editions, Inc. v. Albuquerque A.R.T. Co.*, 856 F.2d 1341 (9th Cir. 1988), cert. denied, 489 U.S. 1018 (1989)).

Criticism of the court's ruling in *Mirage* has arisen from advocates who find this interpretation of artists' economic rights overly protective. Not every use of a copyrighted work constitutes the production of a derivative work; exceptions exist for libraries, archives, fair dealings, and fair use.

Balancing consumer access to copyrighted works with the recognition of content creators' rights remains complex and challenging. Digital technology offers creative tools for innovating new forms of art, such as paintings, sculptures, sounds, and movements, and facilitates their widespread distribution. However, it also introduces unforeseen intellectual property challenges, especially with the emergence of AI-generated art technologies.

For instance, online AI image generators like Stability AI and Stable Diffusion utilize AI algorithms to analyze billions of images sourced from the internet, producing near-replica works resembling those of renowned artists such as abstract artist Sam Gilliam and portrait artist Amy Sherald. These AI-generated works raise questions about copyright infringement and derivative works, highlighting the need for clear guidelines and regulations in resolving these issues.

Numerous class-action lawsuits have been filed against AI art-generating companies, alleging misappropriation of style, copyright infringement, and violation of artists' publicity rights. Getty Images sued Stability AI for allegedly utilizing over 12 million photographs from Getty's online catalog without authorization to develop its image generating software. Even Google, which previously faced copyright infringement disputes over its thumbnail images of copyrighted works, has filed lawsuits against AI companies for copyright infringement.

Artists are employing various strategies to protect their works from unauthorized use in AI models, including using metadata to detect unpermitted uses and utilizing platforms like Spawning, which enables artists to search for their works used in AI models and request removal. Additionally, AI art generators like DALL-E offer functions for artists to flag AI-generated works for biased or unauthorized use.

These ongoing legal battles underscore the evolving landscape of intellectual property rights in the era of AI and digital art, prompting discussions about the balance between artistic innovation and artists' rights protection in a digitally interconnected world. The application of intellectual property rules to these new AI and digital art tools is still in its nascent stages of litigation and remains undecided.

Infringement

Copyright infringement occurs when someone violates the exclusive rights granted to the copyright holder without their authorization. These rights typically include the right to reproduce, distribute, perform, display, or create derivative works based on the original copyrighted material. Here's a detailed expansion on copyright infringement:

1. **Violation of Exclusive Rights**: Copyright infringement entails the unauthorized use of copyrighted material. This could involve copying, distributing, displaying, performing, or creating derivative works based on the original without the copyright owner's permission.
2. **Types of Infringement**:
    - **Direct Infringement**: This occurs when someone directly violates one or more of the exclusive rights of the copyright holder. For example, reproducing a painting without permission.
    - **Indirect Infringement**: This occurs when someone contributes to or facilitates infringement by others. For instance, providing tools or services that enable others to infringe copyrights, like file-sharing websites.
3. **Determining Infringement**:
    - **Substantial Similarity**: Courts assess whether the allegedly infringing work is substantially similar to the original copyrighted work. This analysis considers both the protected elements and the expression of ideas.
    - **Access and Copying**: Evidence of access to the original work can strengthen a case of infringement, especially if there's proof that the infringer copied the copyrighted material.
4. **Legal Procedures**:
    - **Civil Cases**: Copyright infringement cases are typically handled in civil court. The copyright holder or licensee, known as the plaintiff, must demonstrate ownership of the copyright or a valid license and prove that infringement has occurred.
    - **Registration Requirement**: While copyright protection exists automatically upon creation, registration with the Copyright Office is necessary for pursuing statutory damages and attorney fees in infringement cases.

- **Statutory Remedies**: In cases of proven infringement, statutory damages and attorney fees may be awarded to the copyright holder.
5. **Defenses Against Infringement Claims**:
    - **Fair Use**: In some cases, the use of copyrighted material may be considered fair use, such as for purposes of criticism, commentary, news reporting, teaching, scholarship, or research.
    - **License or Permission**: If the alleged infringer had a valid license or permission to use the copyrighted material, they may not be liable for infringement.
6. **Penalties**:
    - **Monetary Damages**: Infringers may be required to pay damages, which could include actual damages suffered by the copyright holder or statutory damages set by law.
    - **Injunctions**: Courts may issue injunctions to stop further infringement.
    - **Criminal Penalties**: In severe cases, copyright infringement can lead to criminal charges, particularly for large-scale commercial infringement.

Copyright infringement occurs when copyrighted material is used without authorization. To establish infringement, courts assess whether there's substantial similarity between the original and the allegedly infringing works, along with evidence of access and copying. Infringement cases often consider claims of fair use as a defense. Legal consequences may include monetary damages, but only if the copyrighted work was registered with the US Copyright Office. Additionally, injunctions to halt further infringement and, in severe cases, criminal penalties may also be imposed.

Creative Commons—Granting Public Use

In the digital media era, Creative Commons (CC) has emerged as a pivotal framework for navigating the complexities of copyright law and fostering a culture of sharing and collaboration. As digital technologies have facilitated the creation, dissemination, and remixing of content on an unprecedented scale, CC licenses provide a standardized way for creators to grant permissions for the use and distribution of their works, yet still retain a level of attribution and recognition. Here are some key aspects of Creative Commons in the digital media era:

1. **Facilitating Legal Sharing and Reuse**: CC licenses enable creators to specify the conditions under which their works can be used, shared, and adapted. This is particularly crucial in the digital realm, where content can be easily copied, shared, and repurposed. By providing a clear legal framework, CC licenses make it easier for creators to share their work while retaining control over how it is used.
2. **Promoting Collaboration and Innovation**: In the digital age, collaboration and innovation thrive on the ability to build upon existing works. CC licenses facilitate this by allowing creators to grant permissions for derivative works, remixes, and adaptations. This encourages a culture of creativity and innovation, where individuals can freely build upon the work of others to create something new and meaningful.
3. **Increasing Access to Knowledge and Culture**: One of the core principles of Creative Commons is the idea of expanding access to knowledge and culture. By allowing creators to waive certain copyright restrictions, CC licenses enable wider access to educational resources, research findings, and cultural works. This is particularly important in fields such as education and research, where open access to information can have significant benefits for society as a whole.
4. **Providing Legal Clarity and Certainty**: Copyright law can be complex and confusing, especially in the digital realm. CC licenses provide a simple and standardized way for creators to communicate the permissions granted for their works. This reduces legal uncertainty and makes it easier for individuals and organizations to understand how they can use and share CC-licensed content.

Registering with Creative Commons and applying a CC license to your work involves parting with certain exclusive rights that copyright holders traditionally possess. The degree to which these rights are relinquished depends on the specific CC license chosen. Here's a breakdown of the key rights typically granted or retained when using Creative Commons licenses:

1. **Attribution (BY)**: All CC licenses require attribution, meaning that users must give appropriate credit to the original creator when using the work. This is a fundamental requirement across all CC licenses.
2. **Noncommercial Use (NC)**: Some CC licenses, such as CC BY-NC and CC BY-NC-SA, restrict the commercial use of the work. This means that others are not allowed to use the work for commercial purposes without seeking additional permission from the copyright holder.
3. **No Derivatives (ND)**: Certain CC licenses, like CC BY-ND, prohibit the creation of derivative works based on the original. This means that others cannot modify, adapt, or build upon the work in any way.
4. **Share Alike (SA)**: CC licenses such as CC BY-SA require that derivative works be shared under the same or a compatible license as the original. This ensures that subsequent works based on the original maintain the same level of openness and accessibility.

At the same time, it is important to emphasize that by choosing a Creative Commons license, copyright holders are essentially granting permissions for others to use their work under certain conditions. These permissions may include the right to reproduce, distribute, display, perform, and create derivative works, depending on the specific license terms. Additionally, CC licenses are non-revocable, meaning that once a work is licensed under a CC license, it remains available under those terms for the duration of copyright protection.

Well-known examples of organizations utilizing creative commons licenses include all images of public-domain works in the Metropolitan Museum's collection are openly available under Creative Commons Zero (CC0) and every one of Wikipedia's 55 million plus articles are shared openly and freely using a CC license.

Fair Use

Fair use, as delineated in **17 U.S. Code § 107**, is a critical doctrine within copyright law that allows for the limited use of copyrighted material without the need for permission from or payment to the copyright holder. This provision is designed to balance the interests of copyright owners

Chapter 4: Content Control: Copyrights and the Future of Digital Distribution

with the public's right to access, use, and engage with copyrighted works for purposes such as criticism, commentary, news reporting, teaching, scholarship, research, parody, appropriation art, transformative creative works, and more.

By permitting certain uses of copyrighted material under specific circumstances, fair use ensures that copyright law does not stifle creativity, hinder access to information, or impede the exchange of ideas. Determining whether a particular use qualifies as fair use often requires resolution in federal court, where judges consider four key factors to assess fair use disputes. These factors serve as guidelines that courts can adapt to specific situations on a case-by-case basis, granting judges considerable discretion in fair use determinations and making predictions about case outcomes challenging leading frequently to inconsistent decisions by different federal courts.

Under the **Copyright Act** these are the four factors that judges are required to consider:

1. **The Purpose and Character of Use**: This factor examines whether the use of copyrighted material contributes to creating something new or merely reproduces the original work verbatim. Transformative uses, where new expression or meaning is added to the original material, are generally favored in fair use analysis. Questions to consider include:
   - Has the material been transformed by adding new expressions or meaning?
   - Was value added to the original work by creating new insights or understandings? For instance, in the case of a parody, the transformation occurs by ridiculing the original work, but mere imitation does not qualify as parody.
2. **The Nature of the Copyrighted Work**: Courts consider whether the copyrighted work is factual or fictional, as well as whether it's published or unpublished. Factual works, such as biographies, allow more leeway for fair use compared to fictional works like novels. Fair use is narrower for unpublished works, as authors have the right to control the first public appearance of their expression.
3. **The Amount and Substantiality of the Portion Taken**: This factor evaluates the quantity and significance of the portion used in relation to the whole copyrighted work. Generally, using a

smaller portion increases the likelihood of fair use. However, even a small portion may not be fair use if it constitutes the "heart" of the work. Parody cases, however, permit borrowing substantial portions, even the essence of the original, to conjure up the original work.
4. **The Effect of Use on the Potential Market**: Judges assess whether the use deprives the copyright owner of income or undermines a new or potential market for the copyrighted work. If the use diminishes the market value or creates a new market that competes with the original work, it's less likely to be considered fair use.

In the digital age, the question of artistic appropriation and transformation takes on new dimensions, particularly in the realm of digital and social media. Platforms like YouTube, TikTok, and Instagram have democratized creativity, allowing individuals to remix, create a mash-up, or reinterpret existing works with unprecedented ease and accessibility.

For example, in the realm of music, digital technology has revolutionized the way musicians create and share their work. Sampling, a technique where artists incorporate snippets of prerecorded music into their own compositions, has become ubiquitous in genres like hip-hop and electronic dance music. This practice blurs the lines between original creation and derivative work, raising questions about attribution, ownership, and fair use.

Similarly, visual artists leverage digital tools to manipulate and repurpose images, videos, and memes sourced from the vast landscape of the internet. Platforms like Tumblr and Pinterest serve as virtual treasure troves of visual inspiration, where artists can freely explore, remix, and reinterpret existing imagery to create something entirely new. This process often involves collage techniques reminiscent of those pioneered by visual fine artists like Georges Braque and Pablo Picasso, albeit with a digital twist.

By the way, it was Steve Jobs who famously said in 1996 during a PBS documentary interview *Triumph of the Nerds: The Rise of Accidental Empires*: "Picasso had a saying—'good artists copy; great artists steal'—and we have always been shameless about stealing great ideas." He emphasized the importance of being inspired by existing ideas and building upon them to create something truly innovative.

Chapter 4: Content Control: Copyrights and the Future of Digital Distribution

In the realm of social media, the concept of appropriation takes on a new dimension. Memes, for instance, are a form of cultural currency that thrives on the rapid remixing and dissemination of images, videos, and text across social platforms. Memes often draw upon copyrighted material, from movie screenshots to famous artworks, to convey humor, commentary, or social critique. While some argue that memes constitute transformative fair use, others contend that they represent a form of unauthorized exploitation of copyrighted material.

One example is the "Distracted Boyfriend" meme, which originated from a stock photo of a man turning his head to look at another woman while walking with his girlfriend. The image has been widely circulated on social media with humorous captions, often referencing pop culture or current events. While the original photograph is copyrighted, the meme's transformative use has led to debates about the boundaries of fair use and the commercialization of internet culture.

Furthermore, the rise of user-generated content platforms has blurred the distinction between creator and consumer, empowering individuals to

Figure 4.2 This was one of the first popular posts using the "Distracted Boyfriend" meme on Reddit, gaining over 31,000 upvotes within twenty-four hours.

actively participate in the co-creation of culture. User-generated content platforms like YouTube and SoundCloud enable aspiring musicians, filmmakers, and artists to share their work with global audiences, often incorporating elements of popular culture into their creations.

In this digital landscape, the notion of originality becomes increasingly fluid and subjective. The line between homage and infringement, inspiration and appropriation, can be difficult to discern. As artists continue to navigate this evolving terrain, the principles of fair use and transformative creativity serve as guiding lights, helping to strike a balance between artistic freedom and copyright protection in the digital age. Ultimately, the challenge lies in fostering a creative ecosystem where innovation thrives while respecting the rights of creators and acknowledging the rich tapestry of cultural influences that shape our artistic landscape.

An example of this phenomenon is the "reaction videos," where individuals film themselves reacting to various forms of media such as music videos, movie trailers, or viral videos. While reaction videos may incorporate copyrighted material, they are often protected under fair use for purposes of commentary, criticism, or parody, demonstrating the ways in which digital technology has democratized creative expression and transformed the relationship between creators and consumers.

Leading Fair Use Cases Involving Text and New Technologies

In the landmark case of *Hustler Magazine, Inc. v. Falwell* (485 U.S. 46 (1988)), the Supreme Court of the United States delivered a pivotal decision affirming the protection of parodies targeting public figures under the **First** and **Fourteenth Amendments** to the US Constitution.

The case centered on a full-page parody advertisement published by Hustler magazine, targeting televangelist and political commentator Jerry Falwell Sr. The advertisement depicted Falwell engaging in incestuous and drunken behavior, suggesting he had a sexual encounter with his mother in an outhouse. Notably, the ad was labeled as a parody, a fair use affirmative defense to a claim for copyright infringement, and explicitly stated that it was "not to be taken seriously."

Chapter 4: Content Control: Copyrights and the Future of Digital Distribution

In the case of *Cambridge University Press v. Patton* (769 F. 3d 1232 (2014)), the Eleventh Circuit Court of Appeals grappled with the complex issue of fair use in the context of academic institutions and online education. The case arose from allegations made by Cambridge University Press and several other publishers against Georgia State University (GSU). The publishers claimed that GSU officials had committed copyright infringement by permitting professors to post unlicensed excerpts of copyrighted works on an online system for student access.

Central to the dispute was the concept of fair use, which allows for the limited use of copyrighted material without the need for permission from the copyright holder under certain circumstances. In their defense, GSU argued that the use of excerpts in the online system constituted fair use, as it was for educational purposes and did not adversely impact the market for the original works.

The Eleventh Circuit's decision in this case underscored the importance of conducting a flexible, case-by-case analysis when evaluating the four fair use factors. Rather than adhering to a rigid quantitative benchmark, such as a 10 percent standard for copying, the court emphasized the need to consider the specific facts and circumstances of each case.

In the milestone case of *Universal City Studios v. Sony Corp.* (464 U.S. 417 (1984)), commonly known as the "Betamax case," the Supreme Court delivered a decisive ruling that significantly shaped copyright law in the context of emerging technologies. The case centered on the legality of home videotaping using Betamax video cassette recorders (VCRs) and whether such practices constituted copyright infringement.

At the heart of the dispute was the practice of "time-shifting," where individuals recorded television broadcasts onto VCR tapes for later viewing at a more convenient time. Universal City Studios, along with other copyright owners, argued that this practice violated their exclusive rights to control the reproduction and distribution of their copyrighted television programs.

In its defense, Sony Corporation, the manufacturer of the Betamax VCRs, contended that home videotaping constituted fair use under copyright law. Sony argued that time-shifting was a noncommercial, personal use of the content and did not deprive copyright owners of revenue, as it did not compete with or substitute for the original broadcasts.

The Supreme Court's ruling in favor of Sony was a groundbreaking decision that established important principles regarding fair use and the rights of consumers in the digital age. The Court held that time-shifting constituted a fair use of copyrighted material, as it served the public interest by enabling individuals to enjoy television programming at their convenience without unduly harming the market for the original broadcasts.

The decision in the *Betamax* case set a precedent for the legal protection of new technologies that enable the private copying and consumption of copyrighted content. It affirmed the principle that fair use extends to innovative uses of technology that enhance personal convenience and do not significantly impact the market for copyrighted works.

Furthermore, the *Betamax* case had far-reaching implications for the development of digital technologies and consumer rights. It provided a legal framework that allowed for the proliferation of technologies such as digital video recorders (DVRs), streaming services, and other digital media platforms, enabling consumers to access and enjoy copyrighted content in new and convenient ways.

In the case of *The Author's Guild v. HathiTrust* (755 F.3d 87 (2d Cir. 2014)) the Second Circuit Court of Appeals affirmed the application of fair use principles to the creation of a full-text database by the HathiTrust Digital Library and the provision of access to disabled patrons. The lawsuit was brought by The Author's Guild and several individual authors against HathiTrust, a collaboration of academic and research institutions, including several major universities, which had digitized millions of books from their collections to create a searchable online database, an increasingly common practice.

The plaintiffs alleged that HathiTrust's digitization project constituted copyright infringement because it involved the reproduction of entire books without permission from the copyright holders. However, the Second Circuit disagreed, ruling in favor of HathiTrust and affirming the district court's decision that the project was protected by fair use.

The court's decision hinged on several key factors. First, the court recognized the transformative nature of HathiTrust's use, noting that the creation of a searchable full-text database provided significant public benefit by facilitating research, scholarship, and access to knowledge. Additionally, the court found that providing access to disabled patrons, such as individuals with visual impairments, furthered the public interest in promoting equal access to educational and cultural resources.

Chapter 4: Content Control: Copyrights and the Future of Digital Distribution

Furthermore, the court determined that the digitization project did not harm the market for the original works. Instead, it enhanced the discoverability and accessibility of the books, potentially increasing their value to copyright holders over time. The court also emphasized the limited nature of the access provided by HathiTrust, which only allowed for nonconsumptive uses such as searching, indexing, and text mining, rather than full-text reading.

Overall, the *Author's Guild* ruling exemplifies the courts' recognition of fair use principles in the digital age and their willingness to balance the rights of copyright holders with the public interest in access to knowledge and information. The decision affirmed the importance of transformative uses, such as creating searchable databases and providing access to disabled patrons, in furthering the goals of copyright law and promoting the progress of science and the useful arts.

In the case of *BMG Music v. Gonzalez* (430 F.3d 888 (7th Cir. 2005)), the court grappled with the question of whether downloading songs using peer-to-peer (P2P) file-sharing software constituted fair use under copyright law. The lawsuit was brought by BMG Music and several other music labels against Cecilia Gonzalez, an individual accused of illegally downloading and distributing copyrighted songs using P2P networks.

Gonzalez argued that her actions were protected by fair use, claiming that she was merely sampling the songs for personal use and that her downloading behavior did not harm the market for the original works. However, the court disagreed with Gonzalez's defense and ruled in favor of the music labels.

The court's decision was based on several key factors. First, the court determined that Gonzalez's use of P2P file-sharing software to download entire songs constituted a direct infringement of the music labels' exclusive rights to reproduction and distribution. Unlike other cases where sampling or excerpting portions of copyrighted works may be considered fair use, Gonzalez's actions involved the unauthorized reproduction of entire songs, which did not qualify as fair use.

Additionally, the court found that alternatives to P2P file sharing, such as legal digital music platforms like iTunes, provided legitimate means for sampling and purchasing songs without resorting to illegal downloading. These legal alternatives offered users the opportunity to listen to song previews or purchase individual tracks, thereby undermining Gonzalez's argument that her downloading behavior was necessary for sampling purposes.

Furthermore, the court considered the substantial harm inflicted on the music labels' market by widespread illegal downloading through P2P networks. The availability of copyrighted songs for free through unauthorized channels undermined the labels' ability to monetize their content and recoup their investments in music production and distribution.

Overall, *BMG Music* highlighted the limitations of the fair use defense in cases involving wholesale copying of copyrighted works through P2P file sharing. The decision underscored the importance of respecting the rights of copyright holders and promoting legal alternatives for accessing and sampling copyrighted content in the digital age.

In the case of *AIME v. Regents of the University of California* (No. CV 10-9378 CBM (MANx) (C.D. Cal. October 3, 2011)), the dispute centered on the University of California, Los Angeles (UCLA), and its practice of streaming video content without compensating the copyright holders. The lawsuit was brought by the Association for Information Media and Equipment (AIME) against the Regents of the University of California, alleging copyright infringement.

UCLA argued that its streaming of video content constituted fair use under copyright law, emphasizing the educational context in which the streaming occurred. The university contended that its use of the copyrighted materials served the public interest by furthering educational objectives and facilitating research and scholarship. In analyzing UCLA's streaming practices, the court considered several factors to determine whether fair use applied.

First, the court examined the purpose and character of the use, weighing the educational nature of UCLA's activities against the commercial interests of the copyright holders. The court recognized the important role of educational institutions in disseminating knowledge and promoting learning, which weighed in favor of fair use.

Second, the court considered the nature of the copyrighted works involved, assessing factors such as the creative expression and the degree of protection afforded to the works. In this case, the court found that while the video content was protected by copyright, its educational nature and the transformative use by UCLA favored a finding of fair use.

Chapter 4: Content Control: Copyrights and the Future of Digital Distribution 119

Third, the court evaluated the amount and substantiality of the portion used, as well as the effect of the use on the potential market for the original works. UCLA's streaming practices involved providing access to excerpts of video content for educational purposes, rather than wholesale copying of entire works. Additionally, the court found no evidence that UCLA's activities adversely affected the market for the original video content.

Ultimately, the court ruled in favor of UCLA, affirming its streaming practices as fair use under copyright law. The decision underscored the importance of considering the educational context in fair use analyses and recognized the significant public benefit derived from the dissemination of knowledge and information by educational institutions like UCLA.

In 2023, the Supreme Court decided a major fair use versus copyright infringement case in *Andy Warhol Foundation for the Visual Arts, Inc. v. Goldsmith* (598 U.S. 508 (2023)). The Court's decision represents a groundbreaking and, for many, a shocking ruling that delves deeply into the transformative nature of fair use, particularly concerning commercial purposes. At the heart of the case was Andy Warhol's iconic artwork series featuring depictions of the artist known as Prince, which he created based on a photograph taken by photographer Lynn Goldsmith.

Figure 4.3 Warhol's silkscreen magazine cover image of Prince and Goldsmith's photo of Prince.

The Court's ruling marks a significant shift in the interpretation of the first factor of the fair use test. Traditionally, courts have considered whether the use of another's work is sufficiently transformative to qualify as fair use, often focusing on whether the new work adds new expression or meaning to the original. However, the Court's holding in *Andy Warhol Foundation* emphasizes the importance of scrutinizing commercial uses of copyrighted material, even if the new work is transformative in nature, which historically has been one of the most prominent tests in determining fair use.

In its analysis, the Court held that Warhol's use of Goldsmith's photograph of Prince for a commercial purpose—creating silk screen images that appeared in a magazine thirty-five years after the original photo—did not meet the threshold for fair use. Despite Warhol's transformative reinterpretation of the photograph by exaggerating and altering the original mostly black and white colors to create a visually striking composition that emphasized the iconic status of Prince, the Court determined that the commercial nature of his artwork undermined its fair use defense. This ruling signals a heightened scrutiny of commercial uses of copyrighted material and undermines the traditional transformative test that federal courts have relied upon for years in cases involving fair use as an affirmative defense to infringement claims.

However, it is essential to note the strong dissenting language of Justice Kagan, who argued vehemently for a broader interpretation of fair use that would encompass transformative commercial uses. Justice Kagan's dissent highlights the tension between promoting creativity and innovation through transformative uses and protecting the economic interests of copyright holders. She argued that a narrow interpretation of fair use could stifle artistic expression and inhibit the evolution of culture.

This monumental ruling on copyrights could have far-reaching implications within the broader context of all media. Throughout history, creative authors, designers, and artists have drawn inspiration from existing works, blurring the line between inspiration and appropriation of copyrighted material. However, this decision introduces ambiguity, potentially deterring artists from creatively repurposing existing images. This could lead to an uptick in artists seeking licenses from original copyright holders or a surge in litigation to resolve fair use disputes.

It is vital to recognize that the primary objective of copyright law is not solely to protect the interests of artists or creators, but rather to promote the advancement of knowledge and foster progress in science and the arts. To achieve this goal, copyright grants artists a temporary monopoly over their creations, affording exclusive rights for a specified period. However, this monopoly is not absolute and is subject to limitations when it conflicts with broader public interests, such as the encouragement of new creative and intellectual works.

Digital Millennium Copyright Act and Virtual Reality

The **Digital Millennium Copyright Act (DMCA)**, enacted in 1998, aimed to tackle copyright issues arising from the rise of digital technology and the internet. It introduced critical changes to the **Copyright Act of 1976**, notably the anti-circumvention provision, which prohibits attempting to bypass mechanisms restricting copying of copyrighted works. This provision also bars the production, promotion, or sale of products or services intended to circumvent such measures, such as digital rights management systems (DRMs). While certain exemptions exist for entities like nonprofit libraries, museum archives, and educational institutions, which may need to override DRMs to safeguard their collections, the statute also prohibits falsification of copyright management information and distribution of works containing false copyright information.

Another key change was limiting Internet Service Provider (ISP) liability for primary or secondary copyright activities. The safe harbor provision enables ISPs to avoid liability for transient routing or connecting copyright-infringing material flowing through their networks. ISPs aren't held accountable for storing infringing material if promptly removed upon request from the copyright holder or licensee. Additionally, ISPs are relieved from liability when inadvertently linking to sites containing copyright-infringing works. However, how ISPs consider the fair use affirmative defense when receiving takedown requests for alleged copyright infringement remains unclear.

Civil remedies under the **DMCA** include statutory copyright damages, actual damages, and injunctive relief. Willful violations for personal or financial gain can lead to criminal charges and up to ten years of imprisonment.

Google's "Images" feature, introduced over two decades ago, has faced copyright litigation, notably regarding the display of thumbnails in search results. Courts ruled thumbnails as fair use, considering search engines passive participants, with end users potentially infringing on copyright. Despite concerns, technological advancements have enhanced art accessibility, exemplified by the Google Art Project. This platform showcases artworks from over 150 museums globally, offering high-resolution images. While most displayed artwork is either in the public domain or licensed for online exhibition, some works have been removed due to copyright complaints.

Subsequently, Google launched Google Arts & Culture, a more comprehensive initiative aiming to make art and culture accessible through online exhibitions, virtual tours, and educational resources. Collaborating with museums, cultural institutions, and artists, it offers diverse online content, including artworks, cultural artifacts, historical sites, and performing arts.

The growth of virtual museums and the emergence of the metaverse present significant copyright concerns as the boundaries between physical and digital realms blur. While these technologies offer exciting opportunities for cultural exploration and engagement, they also raise questions about ownership, reproduction, and distribution of digital artworks and cultural artifacts.

One major concern is the unauthorized replication and distribution of copyrighted material within virtual environments. As virtual museums expand, there's a risk of artworks being scanned, replicated, and shared without proper authorization from the copyright holders. For example, if a virtual museum includes digital representations of paintings, sculptures, or other artworks protected by copyright, reproducing these works in the virtual space without permission could constitute copyright infringement.

Moreover, the metaverse introduces new challenges for copyright enforcement due to its decentralized nature and user-generated content. In virtual worlds where users can create and manipulate digital assets, monitoring and regulating copyright infringement becomes more complex. For instance, if users recreate copyrighted artworks within a metaverse platform without permission, it may be difficult to enforce copyright laws and hold individuals accountable for infringement.

Additionally, issues may arise regarding the ownership and control of virtual spaces where copyrighted material is displayed. In some cases, virtual museums or metaverse platforms may claim ownership or exclusive rights over the digital representations of artworks, potentially conflicting with the rights of the original copyright holders.

Examples of copyright concerns in virtual environments include instances where virtual replicas of real-world artworks are created and distributed without authorization. For instance, if a virtual museum includes unauthorized digital copies of famous paintings or sculptures, it could undermine the market value and rights of the original artists or their estates. Similarly, if users in a metaverse platform reproduce copyrighted characters, logos, or designs without permission, it could lead to legal disputes over intellectual property rights.

To address these concerns, virtual museums and metaverse platforms need to implement vigorous copyright policies and mechanisms for obtaining proper licenses and permissions for digital content. Additionally, copyright holders must remain vigilant in monitoring and enforcing their rights in virtual environments, collaborating with platform operators to ensure compliance with copyright laws.

Overall, while virtual museums and the metaverse offer exciting possibilities for cultural engagement, it's essential to navigate these spaces responsibly and ethically to protect the rights of creators and copyright holders.

International Dimensions to Copyright

The implementation of the **EU Directive on Copyright in the Digital Single Market**, known as the **Copyright Directive**, has brought about significant changes and debates in European copyright law, particularly concerning digital media and online content sharing. It is important to note the relationship between the **Copyright Directive** and the **Berne Convention**. While the **Berne Convention** provides the foundational framework for copyright protection internationally, the **EU Copyright Directive** seeks to address specific challenges that have emerged with digital distribution and the internet, which were not envisioned when the **Berne Convention** was established. The **Directive** can be seen as a regional implementation that complements and expands upon the **Berne Convention's** objectives, tailoring copyright protections to the realities of the digital single market. It operates within the broader framework set by the **Berne Convention** but focuses on the nuances of digital copyright issues, aiming to harmonize copyright laws across EU member states in a way that supports the digital economy and cultural diversity.

Here are some key aspects of the **Copyright Directive** and examples illustrating their implications:

1. **Article 17 (formerly Article 13)**:
   - **Article 17** mandates that online platforms obtain licenses from copyright holders for content shared on their platforms. If licensing isn't feasible, platforms must implement effective measures like filters to prevent unauthorized uploads of copyrighted material.
   - Example: The implementation of **Article 17** has led to the development of upload filters by platforms like YouTube. However, these filters have faced criticism for their potential to over-block legitimate content due to their inability to accurately distinguish between infringing and non-infringing uses.
2. **Fair Use and Fair Dealing**:
   - Concerns have been raised about the compatibility of the **Copyright Directive** with fair use and fair dealing principles. While the EU's approach includes exceptions for parody, caricature, and pastiche, it's seen as less flexible than the fair use doctrine in the United States.
   - Example: In the case of parody or satire, the interpretation of the EU's exceptions may vary, leading to uncertainty for creators and platforms. For instance, a platform may be unsure whether a particular use qualifies as parody or caricature under EU law, potentially leading to over-cautious content removal.
3. **Impact on Freedom of Expression and Creativity**:
   - Critics argue that the strict requirements of **Article 17** and the lack of fair use provisions like those found in the United States could stifle freedom of expression and creativity online.
   - Example: Artists, content creators, and internet users fear that the implementation of upload filters and stringent copyright

Chapter 4: Content Control: Copyrights and the Future of Digital Distribution 125

enforcement measures may limit their ability to engage in transformative and creative activities online, hindering innovation and cultural expression.
4. **Challenges for Platforms and Users**:
   ○ The **Copyright Directive** poses challenges for both online platforms and users, who must navigate complex copyright regulations and enforcement mechanisms.
   ○ Example: Online platforms face the daunting task of developing and implementing effective content filtering systems to comply with **Article 17**, while users may encounter difficulties in understanding and adhering to copyright restrictions, potentially leading to unintended infringement.

The European standards aimed at safeguarding the exclusive rights of copyright holders are notably stricter compared to those in the United States by imposing heavier obligations on social media platforms.

In a case law development clarifying these new initiatives, the European Court of Justice ruled in 2021 that online platforms such as Google's YouTube are not automatically liable for copyright-infringing uploads by users. The court clarified that platforms are not engaged in illegal communication to the public of copyrighted content uploaded by users unless they possess specific knowledge of infringing material and fail to promptly remove or block it. Once an online platform knows that certain content is available illegally, it needs to swiftly remove it or risk copyright infringement proceedings. This ruling came amid broader copyright reforms in the European Union aimed at adapting rules to the digital age, including controversial requirements for platforms to install filters to prevent the sharing of copyrighted material.

The **Copyright, Designs and Patents Act 1988** in the United Kingdom serves as a legal framework to safeguard the rights of creators and copyright owners. Under this legislation, various forms of copyright infringement are criminalized, including unauthorized copying of a work, issuing copies to the public without permission, and communicating a work to the public without proper authorization.

Criminal liability under the **Act** typically arises when infringing acts are conducted "in the course of a business" or when they cause "substantial loss" to the copyright owner. This means that individuals or entities engaged in commercial activities or those whose actions result in significant financial harm to copyright holders may face criminal prosecution for copyright infringement.

Instances of criminal prosecution under the **Copyright, Designs and Patents Act 1988** have occurred, demonstrating the seriousness with which copyright infringement is treated under UK law. For example, not long ago, a UK man received a significant prison sentence of thirty-three months for illegally streaming copyrighted content online. This high-profile case served as a stark reminder of the severe consequences of engaging in copyright infringement and sent a clear message about the importance of respecting intellectual property rights in the digital age.

Overall, the **Act** plays a crucial role in deterring and penalizing copyright infringement in the United Kingdom, ensuring that creators and copyright owners are protected and fairly compensated for their work. By imposing criminal liability for serious breaches of copyright law, the legislation aims to uphold the integrity of the creative industries and promote a culture of respect for intellectual property rights within society.

Summary

In the contemporary digital landscape, copyright's significance is magnified, especially within the expansive realms of digital and social media. This chapter thoroughly explores the intricate domain of copyright law within the online sphere, shedding light on fundamental principles, emerging trends, and pragmatic considerations for all stakeholders involved, be it content creators, users, or platforms.

At its inception, the chapter outlines the core tenets of copyright law, underscoring the pivotal need to grasp concepts such as originality, fixation, and ownership in the context of digital content creation and dissemination. It traces the evolution of copyright legislation, spotlighting pivotal moments and international agreements designed to fortify intellectual property rights within the digital milieu.

Subsequently, the chapter delves into the distinctive hurdles posed by social media platforms, where the instantaneous dissemination and viral propagation of content often blur traditional boundaries of copyright ownership and enforcement. Key topics explored include user-generated content, fair use doctrines, and the evolving role of platforms in mediating

Chapter 4: Content Control: Copyrights and the Future of Digital Distribution   127

copyrighted material, shedding light on the intricate legal and ethical dilemmas.

Moreover, the narrative extends to examine the surge in digital content monetization and its reverberations on copyright holders and content creators. Robust strategies for safeguarding intellectual property rights in the digital marketplace, encompassing tactics like watermarking, licensing agreements, and digital rights management tools, are examined.

The chapter further explores the transformative impact of emergent technologies like artificial intelligence and virtual reality on copyright law and enforcement mechanisms. It discerns the myriad challenges and opportunities engendered by these innovations, advocating for adaptive legal frameworks and proactive measures to uphold creators' rights in the digital epoch.

Real-world case studies and exemplars punctuate the discourse, illuminating the tangible implications of copyright law within digital and social media milieus. From landmark infringement litigations to pioneering content-sharing endeavors and contentious fair use disputes, these case studies offer invaluable insights into the evolving tapestry of copyright in the digital era.

Ultimately, the chapter underscores the paramount importance of a studious comprehension of copyright law in investigating the intricate landscapes of digital and social media, transcending geographical boundaries. By cultivating a keen awareness of legal principles, embracing optimal practices in content creation and dissemination, and judiciously harnessing technological innovations, individuals and entities can efficaciously safeguard and manage their intellectual property rights within the dynamic contours of today's digital realm.

Discussion Questions

1. How have advancements in digital technologies transformed the landscape of copyright law and enforcement?
2. What are the key principles of fair use, and how do they apply to the use of copyrighted material in digital media?
3. Can you provide examples of recent copyright infringement cases in the context of digital media, and what were the outcomes?

4. How do emerging technologies such as artificial intelligence and virtual reality present challenges and opportunities for copyright enforcement?
5. What are some strategies for content creators and copyright holders to protect their intellectual property rights in the digital age?
6. How do social media platforms navigate copyright issues, particularly concerning user-generated content?
7. What role do licensing agreements and digital rights management tools play in managing copyrighted material online?
8. How have international agreements and treaties influenced the development of copyright law in the digital era?
9. What ethical considerations should be taken into account when using copyrighted material in digital media?
10. How do copyright laws balance the interests of content creators, copyright holders, and the public in an increasingly digitized society?

Works Referenced

Adams, Stan. "Why the EU Copyright Directive Is a Threat to Fair Use." Center for Democracy & Technology, March 1, 2019, accessed at https://cdt.org/insights/why-the-eu-copyright-directive-is-a-threat-to-fair-use

Bertuzzi, Luca, and Killeen, Molly. "EU Court Ruling Clarifies Online Platforms' Responsibility for Copyright Infringements." EuRACTIV, June 23, 2021, accessed at https://www.euractiv.com/section/copyright/news/eu-court-ruling-clarifies-online-platforms-responsibility-for-copyright-infringements

"Better Sharing. Brighter Future." Creative Commons, accessed at https://creativecommons.org

"Copyright Registration Guidance: Works Containing Material Generated by Artificial Intelligence: A Rule by the Copyright Office, Library of Congress." Federal Register, March 16, 2023, accessed at https://www.federalregister.gov/documents/2023/03/16/2023-05321/copyright-registration-guidance-works-containing-material-generated-by-artificial-intelligence

"How Copyright Works with Social Media." liveabout.com, accessed at https://www.liveabout.com/copyrights-and-social-media-issues-397821

Jondal, Manish. "What Is Digital Copyright?" Bytes Care, December 5, 2023, accessed at https://bytescare.com/blog/what-is-digital-copyright

Jones, Michael, *Art Law*, 2nd ed. Rowman & Littlefield, Lanham, MD, 2023.

Kaplan, Benjamin. *An Unhurried View of Copyright*. Clark, NJ, The Law Book Exchange, 2008. (Originally published by Columbia University Press, 1967.)

Kramarsky, Stephen M., and Millson, John. "Court Reviews Fair Use Protection for Publishers Embedding Social Media Posts." *New York Law Journal*, January 13, 2023, accessed at https://www.law.com/newyorklawjournal/2023/01/13/court-reviews-fair-use-protection-for-publishers-embedding-social-media-posts

Peroff, M., and Saunders, D. "Apparel Design and Creation: What to Do When Copyright Trolls Are Lurking." Tech Transformation, October 22, 2018, accessed at https://risnews.com/apparel-design-and-creation-what-do-when-copyright-trolls-are-lurking

Schechter, Sam. "EU Extends Content Law to AI." *The Wall Street Journal*, April 28, 2023.

"17 U.S Code § 106—Exclusive Rights in Copyrighted Works." Cornell Law School, Legal Information Institute, accessed at https://www.law.cornell.edu/uscode/text/17/106

"Summaries of Fair Use Cases." Stanford Libraries, accessed at https://fairuse.stanford.edu/overview/fair-use/cases

5
Brand Protection in Pixels: Managing Trademarks and Online Identities

Trademarks help distinguish products and services, both in terms of quality and source.

—Justice Sonia Sotomayor (*Matal v. Tam*, 582 U.S. 218 (2017))

In the ever-evolving landscape of digital media, intellectual property (IP) rights stand as the guardians of creativity and innovation. From the birth of an idea to its fruition in the digital realm, the protection of creations, inventions, and brand identities becomes paramount. At the heart of this protection lies trademarks, trade secrets, trade dress, and service marks—cornerstones of IP law designed to fortify the integrity of digital assets and safeguard the interests of individuals and businesses alike.

Distinct from copyrights, which protect original works of authorship such as literary, artistic, and musical creations, trademarks serve as identifiers of the source of goods or services, distinguishing one entity's offerings from those of others in the marketplace. Unlike patents, which safeguard novel inventions and processes, trademarks focus on protecting the distinctive signs, symbols, and designs that consumers associate with particular brands. Furthermore, trademarks differ from trade secrets, which safeguard confidential information crucial to a company's competitive advantage, and trade dress, which protects the distinctive visual appearance of a product or its packaging. Together, these various forms of IP rights constitute a comprehensive framework for safeguarding creativity, innovation, and brand integrity in the digital age.

One notable contrast between copyrights and trademarks lies in their duration. Copyrights last for the life of the creator plus seventy years, whereas trademarks in the United States operate on a distinct timeline. Initially, trademarks are registered for a period of ten years. However, to maintain their validity, trademarks must undergo renewal. This renewal process requires demonstrating continued use of the mark in interstate commerce or submitting a declaration of continued use.

This chapter will delve into the meaning and benefits of trademark registration in the context of digital media, examining leading cases and examples in a consumer-oriented environment with global implications. We will explore how trademark registration serves as a crucial tool for businesses to establish and protect their brand identities in the digital sphere. By analyzing landmark cases and real-world scenarios, we will uncover the strategic significance of trademark registration in fostering consumer trust, preventing brand dilution, and combating online infringement. Moreover, we will highlight the international dimensions of trademark protection in the digital age, considering the challenges and opportunities presented by the global marketplace. Through a comprehensive examination of trademark law and its application in digital media, readers will gain valuable insights into navigating the complexities of brand management and IP protection in an increasingly interconnected world.

The Origins of Trademark Law

In the annals of legal history, the evolution of trademark law represents a fascinating journey from ancient symbols of craftsmanship to modern-day symbols of brand identity in the digital realm.

The genesis of marking goods for identification traces back to ancient practices aimed at distinguishing ownership, a necessity in burgeoning agricultural and commercial societies. Initially, these marks primarily served agrarian purposes, aiding farmers, ranchers, and landholders in

Chapter 5: Brand Protection in Pixels: Managing Trademarks and Online Identities 133

distinguishing their livestock and produce. However, as commerce evolved from localized exchanges to expansive trade networks, the significance and utility of such marks proliferated.

The origins of trademarks can be traced back to long-ago civilizations where rudimentary forms of branding were employed to signify the origin and quality of goods. In China, dating back to around 5000 BCE, pottery makers began inscribing the emperor's name and other manufacturing details onto their creations. These markings not only served as a form of identification but also conveyed information about the product's quality and authenticity. Furthermore, in Mesopotamia, cylinder seals were used to imprint distinctive designs onto clay tablets, serving as a form of authentication for transactions and contracts.

The historical tapestry reveals glimpses of early marking practices across civilizations. Egyptian edifices dating back to 4000 BCE bear witness to the use of quarry marks and stonecutters' insignia, attesting to the early application of marks in construction and craftsmanship. Similarly, artifacts from diverse cultures manifest symbols carved for religious, superstitious, and identification purposes.

The Greco-Roman epochs unveiled the emergence of "potters marks," etched into pottery to signify the artisan responsible for its creation, thereby laying the foundation for artisanal branding. Roman signboards unearthed amid the ruins of Pompeii provide insights into commercial signage, reflecting an early form of brand identity. These symbols on goods circulated within ancient Rome and adjacent regions foreshadow the trademarks that are now ubiquitous in contemporary commerce.

The utilitarian aspect of marks extended beyond mere identification, assuming crucial roles in facilitating commerce and governance. In medieval England, swordsmiths inscribed identifying marks to trace defective weapons back to their origins, ensuring accountability and quality control. Royal privileges sanctioned the marking of swans' beaks to denote ownership, exemplifying the intersection of marks with legal frameworks.

During the medieval period in Europe spanning nearly one thousand years starting around 476 CE, guilds played a crucial role in regulating trade and craftsmanship. Guild members were required to affix specific marks or symbols onto their products, serving as a guarantee of quality and authenticity. These marks, often referred to as guild marks, not only distinguished the products of guild members from those of nonmembers but also provided assurance to consumers of the goods' craftsmanship and adherence to established standards.

Guilds imposed strict regulations regarding the use of these marks, ensuring that only qualified artisans could display them on their products. This system not only protected consumers from inferior goods but also fostered a sense of trust and reliability in the marketplace. Additionally, guild marks served as a form of advertising, as they became associated with quality and prestige. monarchs began granting royal charters, allowing certain individuals or groups exclusive rights to produce and sell particular goods. These proprietary marks evolved in response to the exigencies of maritime trade, offering recourse to merchants grappling with the uncertainties of sea voyages.

Legal frameworks evolved in tandem with commercial practices, culminating in the formulation of trademark laws in thirteenth-century England. These laws aimed to safeguard commercial interests by preventing unauthorized replication of products, laying the groundwork for modern intellectual property regimes.

The ascent of merchant and craft guilds during the fourteenth and fifteenth centuries heralded a new chapter in marking practices. Guilds, synonymous with artisanal excellence, employed distinct symbols and logos to signify quality and authenticate their products. These marks, emblematic of guild membership, underscored the symbiotic relationship between marks and collective reputational capital.

Development of Modern Trademark Law

In 1857, France established a pioneering milestone in the realm of intellectual property with the enactment of the first comprehensive trademark system in the world. This groundbreaking legislation represented a pivotal moment in the evolution of trademark law, laying the foundation for modern-day practices and principles that govern brand protection and commercial identity.

The French trademark system emerged against the backdrop of a rapidly industrializing society, where the proliferation of goods and services necessitated robust mechanisms for distinguishing products and safeguarding consumer interests. Recognizing the imperative of providing legal recourse for brand owners, the French government took decisive action to codify trademark rights, setting a precedent that would reverberate across the globe.

At its core, the French trademark system introduced a formalized framework for the registration and protection of trademarks, granting owners exclusive rights to their marks and empowering them to take legal action against infringement. This landmark legislation represented a paradigm shift, signaling society's recognition of the intrinsic value of brands and the need to afford them legal recognition and protection.

The establishment of the French trademark system not only facilitated greater clarity, transparency, and protection in commercial transactions but also fostered a culture of innovation and entrepreneurship. By providing a secure legal environment for brand owners to invest in and develop their trademarks, the legislation spurred economic growth and incentivized creativity and differentiation in the marketplace.

Moreover, the influence of the French trademark system extended far beyond its national borders, serving as a model for other countries seeking to enact their own trademark laws. The principles and practices enshrined in the 1857 legislation laid the groundwork for the harmonization of trademark regimes on a global scale, contributing to the development of international treaties and conventions aimed at promoting cooperation and standardization in intellectual property protection.

Under the framework of English common law, the perpetration of fraud and the illicit appropriation of marks, commonly known as "passing off," constituted actionable offenses, for which legal remedies were available and continue to be upheld today. While common law provided a foundation for protecting intellectual property rights, it was not until 1905 that England established a comprehensive statutory regime for trademark protection, lagging nearly half a century behind France's pioneering efforts.

Prior to the landmark 1905 Act, England enacted the Merchandise Marks Act of 1862, aimed at combating deceptive practices in trade, followed by the **Trade Mark Registration Act of 1875**, which laid the groundwork for formal trademark registration. The subsequent **1905 Trademark Act** underwent amendments in 1919 and 1937, culminating in the enactment of a new Trademark Act in 1938. This seminal legislation marked a watershed moment, introducing groundbreaking provisions that propelled England's trademark regime to the forefront of international standards.

The **1938 Trademark Act** introduced innovative concepts such as "associated trademarks," which allowed for the grouping of related marks under a single registration, fostering administrative efficiency and clarity in trademark management. Additionally, it established a consent-to-use system, enabling parties to authorize the use of their marks by others under specified conditions, thereby promoting flexibility in trademark licensing arrangements. Moreover, the Act introduced a defensive mark system, empowering trademark owners to preemptively register marks to ward off potential infringements and protect their brand integrity.

A notable departure from prevailing US trademark law norms was the provision allowing registration based on a "bona fide intent to use," irrespective of actual usage, thus affording prospective trademark holders greater flexibility and foresight in securing their rights. However, unlike the stringent registration systems in Japan and Germany, English registrations conferred only a presumption of trademark ownership, lacking the unequivocal establishment of a "fixed right."

The evolution of England's trademark landscape continued with the incorporation of a service mark registration system in 1986, aligning its practices with international standards and enhancing protection for service-oriented businesses. By 1995, major industrialized nations including the United States, Germany, France, and Japan adopted similar service mark registration frameworks, solidifying the emergence of a global standard.

In response to evolving market dynamics and harmonization efforts within the European Union (EU), England expanded the scope of its trademark subject matter in 1994, aligning its requirements with EU directives and modernizing its legal framework to accommodate emerging forms of intellectual property. This legislative overhaul saw the abolition of outdated provisions such as the associated trademarks system and the defensive mark system, streamlining trademark administration and bolstering legal clarity and efficacy in trademark enforcement. England has continued to follow this framework even after it exited the EU (Brexit).

History of Trademark Law in the United States

Although trademarks represent the oldest form of intellectual property rights, their formal protection under federal statute in the United States was a belated development, with infringement cases remaining scarce until the late nineteenth century.

The imperative for federal trademark legislation became evident in the wake of the Civil War, as the nation entered a period of rapid industrialization and burgeoning trade. Manufacturers clamored for legal mechanisms to safeguard their brands and identities amid a burgeoning marketplace. Consequently, the first federal trademark law was enacted in 1870, marking a pivotal step toward formalizing trademark protection. However, this initial legislation faced judicial scrutiny and was ultimately invalidated by the Supreme Court citing constitutional limitations on Congress's authority.

Undeterred by this setback, Congress swiftly responded with the **Trademark Act of 1881**, anchored on the **Commerce Clause** of the US Constitution. This legislation aimed to regulate trademarks employed in interstate commerce, reflecting the expanding reach of American trade networks. Nevertheless, the evolving dynamics of the economy necessitated subsequent revisions, culminating in a major amendment in 1905 and periodic partial revisions in ensuing years.

The post–Second World War economic boom heralded a new era of trademark proliferation, necessitating heightened public awareness and legal clarity. In response, the landmark **Lanham Act** was enacted in 1946, marking a watershed moment in American trademark law. Named after Congressman Howard W. Lanham, a staunch advocate for its enactment, the Lanham Act elevated American trademark law to the stature of its European counterparts.

The Lanham Act embraced principles of use-based trademark protection, mirroring the foundational tenets of English trademark law. However, it introduced a more stringent requirement for registration, mandating actual use of the mark as opposed to mere intention, thereby bolstering the integrity and reliability of registered trademarks. This emphasis on use as a prerequisite for registration reflected the Act's commitment to fostering a robust and competitive marketplace.

In subsequent years, international harmonization efforts prompted adjustments to the Lanham Act aligning American trademark practices with global standards that are described in more detail within this chapter. These amendments underscored the dynamism and adaptability of American trademark law in response to evolving economic and legal landscapes.

The Lanham Act, a cornerstone of American trademark law, establishes a comprehensive framework for the federal registration and protection of trademarks. Trademarks meeting specific criteria can attain coveted placement on the Principal Register, entailing a host of benefits and enhanced legal protections. Alternatively, trademarks not meeting all requirements for Principal Register listing may find placement on the Supplemental Register, providing a pathway for registration of marks from foreign jurisdictions or descriptive marks lacking distinctiveness.

While federal registration is not mandatory, trademarks listed on the Principal Register enjoy robust legal safeguards, bolstering their enforceability in federal court proceedings. Notably, trademarks must be in use by the owner in interstate commerce to qualify for federal registration, aligning with the Act's emphasis on regulating commercial activities spanning state lines.

Federal registration overseen by the United States Patent and Trademark Office (USPTO) entails stringent eligibility criteria, historically including prohibitions against immoral, deceptive, or scandalous marks, as well as marks that may disparage or falsely suggest a connection with certain entities or geographic locations. However, two recent rulings by the US Supreme Court have significantly altered the landscape of trademark registration.

In the first case, the Court determined that a provision of trademark law prohibiting disparaging terms—exemplified by "Slants" as the name of an Asian American musical band that sought trademark registration but was denied because it was deemed racially offensive—infringed upon the **First Amendment's** protections of free speech. The Court argued that the government cannot suppress expression simply because it is offensive (*Matal v. Tam*, 137 S. Ct. 1744 (2017)).

In the second case, the Court addressed the federal government's rejection of trademarks deemed "immoral" or "scandalous," to wit, the term *fuct*. The Court concluded that such refusal also violated the free speech clause of the First Amendment, thereby allowing for the registration

Figure 5.1 "Fuct" trademark registered by Brunetti.

of trademarks that may be perceived as vulgar or offensive, provided they are not unlawfully used (*Iancu v. Brunetti*, 139 S. Ct. 2294 (2019)).

Overall, these two decisions have liberalized the criteria for trademark registration in the United States, providing greater protection for free speech rights in the realm of branding and intellectual property. As a result, individuals and businesses have more flexibility in selecting and registering trademarks, even if they may be unconventional or controversial.

Additionally, trademarks deemed merely descriptive, deceptively misdescriptive, primarily geographically misdescriptive, primarily merely surnames, or functional are ineligible for registration under the Lanham Act.

In tandem with federal registration, each US state maintains its own trademark registration system, providing an additional avenue for trademark protection. While state registration is not compulsory, it offers supplementary legal recourse and reinforces trademark rights within state jurisdictions.

Noteworthy symbols, such as ® for federally registered trademarks and ™ or SM for unregistered or state-registered marks, serve to notify third parties of trademark ownership and potential infringement risks.

The proliferation of television during the 1950s spurred heightened consumer awareness and a surge in trademark applications, prompting the establishment of the Trademark Trial and Appeal Board (TTAB) in 1958 to address burgeoning appeals and disputes. Subsequent amendments to the Lanham Act in 1962 broadened the "likelihood of confusion" test, enhancing clarity in trademark infringement determinations. In 1975, Congress amended the Lanham Act to authorize the award of attorneys' fees in exceptional cases.

The rampant proliferation of trademark counterfeiting prompted the passage of the **Trademark Counterfeiting Act of 1984**, introducing stringent civil remedies to combat infringement. The **Trademark Clarification Act** of the same year addressed ambiguities arising from court decisions, clarifying the determination of generic terms and safeguarding trademark integrity. Further amendments, including the **Trademark Law Revision Act of 1988** and the **Dilution Act of 1996**, aimed to align US trademark law with global standards and fortify protections against trademark dilution and infringement.

With the rise of e-commerce, social media, and online advertising, businesses face unique challenges in protecting their trademarks ensuring brand identity and consumer trust against infringement and dilution. Digital media has reshaped trademark enforcement strategies with the adoption of legislation such as the **Anticybersquatting Consumer Protection Act (ACPA) of 1999.**

The ACPA stands as a pivotal piece of legislation strategically crafted to address the increasingly prevalent issue of cybersquatting also known as cyberpiracy. Cybersquatting, at its core, involves the registration, trafficking, or utilization of an internet domain name with the malicious intent of capitalizing on the established goodwill associated with another entity's trademark.

A classic online example is the case of *Panavision International, L.P. v. Toeppen*. In this case, Christopher Toeppen registered the domain name "panavision.com" with the intention of selling it to Panavision, a renowned camera and lens manufacturer, at an inflated price. Despite not using the domain for any legitimate purpose related to Panavision's business, Toeppen demanded a substantial sum for its transfer. Panavision filed suit under the ACPA, arguing that Toeppen's actions constituted cybersquatting. The court ruled in favor of Panavision, establishing an important precedent under the ACPA that registering a domain name identical or confusingly similar to a trademark, with the intent to profit from it, is considered cybersquatting and is prohibited by law.

In response to the challenges presented by technological advancements and the digital landscape, the United States has enacted several other trademark laws. The **Trademark Modernization Act (TMA) of 2020** stands as a significant reform, introducing measures to modernize the trademark system generally on expedited procedural process grounds. These include provisions aimed at combating fraudulent trademark filings, streamlining trademark cancellation proceedings, and facilitating the removal of unused trademarks from the register.

Chapter 5: Brand Protection in Pixels: Managing Trademarks and Online Identities

A brand example in the digital media space that has faced challenges related to trademark infringement and abuse is Nike, a globally recognized brand in the sportswear industry. It has encountered numerous instances of counterfeit products being sold on online platforms like Amazon, eBay, and Shopify. Fraudulent trademark filings have been used by individuals or entities to register trademarks that mimic Nike's iconic logos, designs, and brand elements, with the intention of deceiving consumers into purchasing counterfeit goods.

These counterfeit products not only infringe on Nike's intellectual property rights but also pose significant risks to consumers who may unknowingly purchase inferior quality or potentially harmful items. The proliferation of such counterfeit goods on online commerce platforms has been a persistent issue for Nike and other reputable brands, undermining their brand reputation and eroding consumer trust.

To combat these challenges, Nike has actively employed legal strategies, including monitoring online marketplaces for trademark infringement, filing cease-and-desist notices against sellers of counterfeit goods, and collaborating with authorities to take legal action against perpetrators of trademark abuse.

Although the **Consumer Review Fairness Act (CRFA) of 2016** does not center explicitly on trademarks, it safeguards consumers' ability to post honest online reviews of products and services without fear of reprisal, indirectly supporting trademark owners by preserving consumer trust and fostering transparent feedback mechanisms. Some businesses have been known to include gag clauses in their contracts or terms of service agreements, prohibiting consumers from posting negative reviews online. For example, the Federal Trade Commission (FTC) settled a case with a company called Roca Labs, which sold weight-loss supplements. Roca Labs had inserted clauses in its customer contracts that fined customers for posting negative reviews about its products. The FTC deemed these clauses as violations of the **CRFA**.

Furthermore, the **Stop Counterfeiting in Manufactured Goods Act (SCMGA)** strengthens penalties for trafficking counterfeit goods and bolsters enforcement mechanisms, indirectly benefiting trademark owners by deterring infringement and counterfeit activities. Numerous SCMGA cases have arisen involving counterfeit automotive parts sold online. In various instances, law enforcement agencies have seized counterfeit automotive components, such as brake pads, airbags, and wheel bearings, which were falsely branded with trademarks of reputable manufacturers. These counterfeit parts not only infringe on intellectual property rights but also pose significant safety risks to consumers. The SCMGA was designed to combat such trafficking of counterfeit products by making it illegal to knowingly use a counterfeit mark.

Similarly, the **Fight Online Sex Trafficking Act (FOSTA)** and **Stop Enabling Sex Traffickers Act (SESTA) of 2018**, aimed primarily at combating online sex trafficking, also address issues of online platforms' liability for facilitating illegal activities, including trademark infringement and counterfeit sales. One of the most significant impacts of FOSTA-SESTA was the seizure of Backpage.com by federal authorities. Backpage was a large online platform for buying and selling commercial sex, and it had been accused of facilitating sex trafficking, including child sex trafficking. The seizure occurred just days before FOSTA was enacted into law.

These legislative endeavors underscore the US government's acknowledgment of the evolving challenges posed by digital technologies and its commitment to updating trademark laws to safeguard intellectual property rights in the digital age. Some of the most recent changes to the Lanham Act include the USPTO mandating electronic filing for trademark applications and introduced identity verification for account holders using the Trademark Electronic Application System (TEAS). The USPTO also has transitioned to the electronic issuance of Trademark Registrations replacing paper registrations with digital certificates.

In the context of the digital environment, trademark law is also being challenged and shaped by the emergence of the metaverse and non-fungible tokens (NFTs). Brand owners are raising legal concerns about possible infringement and inappropriate use in the metaverse, and the USPTO has been dealing with a significant rise in trademark applications related to virtual goods and services.

In a groundbreaking legal ruling, a New York court determined that First Amendment protections did not extend to a digital project that blurred the boundaries between art and commerce. Luxury fashion brand Hermès emerged victorious in a trademark lawsuit against Mason Rothschild, the creator of MetaBirkins, a non-fungible token (NFT) collection.

A jury ordered Rothschild to pay $110,000 for trademark infringement and an additional $23,000 for cybersquatting due to the use of a domain name resembling Hermès's. The lawsuit centered on Rothschild's creation

Chapter 5: Brand Protection in Pixels: Managing Trademarks and Online Identities 143

Figure 5.2 Examples of MetaBirkins: The NFTs sold online by Mason Rothschild for $450 apiece.

of MetaBirkins, a collection featuring digital renditions of Hermès Birkin bags, which sold for approximately $790,000 in cryptocurrency.

Rothschild's defense attempted to argue that his work was protected under the First Amendment as expressive speech, drawing parallels to Andy Warhol's art. However, Hermès successfully contended that MetaBirkins impeded their potential entry into the NFT market and caused consumer confusion, further supported by misleading news reports linking MetaBirkins to Hermès.

Despite Rothschild's assertion that the inclusion of "Meta" distinguished his work, Hermès maintained that it was a trademark violation. The court applied the Rogers Test (See: *Rogers v. Grimaldi*, 875 F.2d 994 (2d Cir. 1989)), assessing whether the NFTs constituted artistic expression or consumer deception. While the test suggested artistic intent, the jury determined that confusion persisted, bolstered by evidence suggesting Rothschild viewed MetaBirkins as a lucrative venture.

These legislative efforts underscore the evolving nature of trademark law in attempting to adapt to technological advancements and global market dynamics, reaffirming its pivotal role in safeguarding intellectual property rights and fostering commercial innovation within the digital media space.

Trademark Law: The Foundation of Brand Identity

As described earlier, prior to the introduction of the Lanham Act, trademark safeguarding in the United States predominantly adhered to common law principles and state statutes. This decentralized methodology resulted in a fragmented assortment of inconsistent regulations, creating complexities in ensuring that brand protection transcended state lines. The inception of the Lanham Act aimed to rectify this issue by instituting a standardized federal mechanism for both trademark registration and protection.

Trademark protection is available for brands, slogans, and other indicators that meet certain requirements. The eligibility for trademark protection is typically assessed based on the distinctiveness of the mark. Trademarks are categorized based on their distinctiveness in several categories, each with varying levels of protection. Here are the main categories:

Fanciful Marks: Fanciful marks are invented or coined terms that have no prior meaning in the language. These marks are inherently distinctive and receive the strongest level of protection. Examples include "Google" for online search engines, "Zynga" for online gaming or "Accenture" for management consulting and professional services.

Arbitrary Marks: Arbitrary marks consist of common words or symbols that have no direct connection to the goods or services they represent. While these marks have meanings in everyday language, they are used in a context unrelated to their ordinary meaning. Arbitrary marks are also considered inherently distinctive and receive strong protection. Examples include "Apple" for computers, "Amazon" for online retail, or "Adobe" for software products.

Suggestive Marks: Suggestive marks indirectly suggest qualities or characteristics of the goods or services they represent, requiring consumers to use their imagination or perception to understand the connection. These marks are considered inherently distinctive and are afforded a high level of protection. Examples include "Netflix" for streaming services, "Pinterest" for social media platform (suggests collecting and organizing ideas or interests), "Under Armour" for athletic apparel and gear (suggests protection and performance) or "Coppertone" for sunblock.

Descriptive Marks: Descriptive marks directly describe a characteristic, quality, or feature of the goods or services they represent. Initially, descriptive marks are **not** eligible for trademark protection **unless** they acquire secondary meaning, which occurs when consumers associate the mark with a specific source. Descriptive marks can only be registered after they have acquired secondary meaning. Examples include "All-Bran" for cereal, "Whole Foods Market" for organic and natural grocery stores, "Budget Rent a Car" for car rental services or "Bank of America" for banking and financial services.

Generic Terms: Generic terms consist of common names or terms that refer to the general category of goods or services. These terms are not eligible for trademark protection because they are incapable of identifying a specific source. Examples include "Computer" for computers, "Coffee Shop" for a place that sells coffee and related beverages, or "Car" for automobiles.

To be eligible for trademark protection, a brand or slogan must fall within one of the first three categories (fanciful, arbitrary, or suggestive). Descriptive marks may be eligible if they have acquired secondary meaning, while generic terms cannot be protected as trademarks. It's important to conduct a comprehensive trademark search at uspto.gov website to determine the eligibility and strength of a mark before seeking registration.

It is possible for trademarked brands to lose their protection. This is referred to as genericization or genericide. This happens when a trademarked brand name becomes so commonly used that it is no longer capable of identifying and distinguishing the goods or services of one particular source. Essentially, the trademark becomes synonymous with the general product or service itself, rather than specifically identifying a source.

Examples of genericization include:

1. **Aspirin:** Originally trademarked by Bayer, "Aspirin" was once a brand name for acetylsalicylic acid, a pain reliever and fever reducer. However, the term became so widely used to refer to any similar product that it lost its trademark protection in many countries, including the United States.

2. **Escalator:** Originally a trademark of Otis Elevator Company, "Escalator" was used to describe moving staircases. The term became so commonly used to refer to any moving staircase that it lost its trademark protection in the United States and other countries.
3. **Zipper:** The term "Zipper" was once a trademark of the B.F. Goodrich Company for a particular type of fastening device. Over time, the term became genericized and is now commonly used to refer to any similar device for closing garments or bags.
4. **Yo-Yo:** Originally a trademark of Duncan Toys Company, "Yo-Yo" was used to describe a particular type of toy consisting of a spool attached to a string that is wound and unwound. The term became genericized and is now used to refer to similar toys produced by various manufacturers.
5. **Thermos:** "Thermos" was once a trademark of Thermos LLC for insulated beverage containers. The term became genericized and is now commonly used to refer to any vacuum-insulated container for keeping beverages hot or cold.

Well-known digital related terms such as Bitcoin, blockchain, cryptocurrency, decentralized finance (DeFi), smart contracts, open source, and peer-to-peer (P2P) have gained widespread recognition without securing exclusive trademark protection. This is because creators express reluctance to register these terms as brands, while the open-source community of creators encourages their use to foster greater innovation. Consequently, these terms remain available for other entities or individuals to use, as they lack legal safeguards against unauthorized use. They share a similar legal status to familiar brand names that have lost trademark protection and entered the public domain because they have become so widely used that they refer to an entire class of similar products or services.

Trademark Infringement, Dilution, and Unfair Competition

In addition to the before-mentioned protections afforded trademark holders against cybersquatting or cyberpiracy and counterfeiting goods

Chapter 5: Brand Protection in Pixels: Managing Trademarks and Online Identities

or services online, the **Lanham Act** establishes procedures for addressing trademark infringement, dilution, and false advertising claims.

Infringement: Trademark infringement occurs when an individual or entity employs a trademark belonging to another party, or a comparable mark, in a manner that is liable to cause confusion among the public regarding the origin or endorsement of their goods or services. This type of infringement represents one of the most prevalent forms of trademark violations and serves to uphold the fundamental aim of trademarks, which is to prevent consumer confusion. Infringement cases can be litigated in federal court, with potential remedies including injunctions, damages, and attorney's fees.

A prominent case illustrating trademark infringement in the digital media domain is *Tiffany (NJ) Inc. v. eBay Inc.* (600 F.3d 93 (2010)). In this case, Tiffany, the renowned jewelry retailer, sued eBay, the online marketplace, alleging that eBay facilitated the sale of counterfeit Tiffany products on its platform. The court held that while eBay was not directly liable for trademark infringement, it had a duty to take reasonable steps to prevent the sale of counterfeit goods on its platform. This case highlights the importance of online platforms in policing trademark infringement and the responsibility they bear in ensuring the authenticity of goods sold through their services.

Another notable example is *Google LLC v. American Blind & Wallpaper Factory, Inc.* (No. 5:2003cv05340—Document 302 (N.D. Cal. 2007)), where American Blind & Wallpaper Factory, a retailer of window blinds, sued Google for trademark infringement, claiming that Google's AdWords program allowed competitors to bid on American Blind's trademarks as keywords, leading to ads for competing products appearing in search results. The court ruled in favor of Google, stating that the use of trademarks as keywords did not constitute infringement because there was no likelihood of confusion among consumers. This case established important precedent regarding the use of trademarks in online advertising.

Instances of digital space infringement claims can arise from various scenarios. For instance, when Meta rebranded from Facebook, it encountered intellectual property challenges. Trademark lawsuits were filed against Meta by investment firm Metacapital and virtual reality company MetaX, and Meta also settled another lawsuit related to its new infinity-symbol logo. The decision by billionaire Elon Musk to rename Twitter as X could potentially lead to legal complications. This is because companies like Meta and Microsoft already hold intellectual property rights to the letter X.

The letter X is a common element in US trademarks, with nearly 900 active registrations incorporating it across various sectors. This prevalence suggests that Elon Musk's use of the letter X in his trademarks—for instance, in the software and social media category for "X" and for "XAI" for computer software platforms that employ machine learning and artificial intelligence for tasks like data labeling, modeling, and analytics—could potentially lead to legal challenges. If companies believe that Twitter's use of the X or XAI branding undermines the value associated with their own trademarks featuring the letter X, they might consider pursuing infringement claims.

For example, Microsoft has held an X trademark since 2003, specifically related to communications about its Xbox video game system. Additionally, Meta Platforms, with its Threads platform posing as a Twitter rival, owns a federal trademark registered in 2019 for a blue-and-white letter "X," covering software and social media fields.

A continuous illustration of joint trademark holders, which is somewhat rare among brand companies, collaborating to uphold their trademark rights is demonstrated by DC Comics and Marvel concerning the term *superhero*. While the trademark for "superhero" was obtained in 1979 for a line of Halloween costumes featuring characters from both DC Comics and Marvel, its validity has been questioned because it does not explicitly designate the source or origin of the product or service in the marketplace. Despite their rivalry, DC Comics and Marvel have recognized the mutual benefit of cooperating as joint owners of the "superhero" trademark. This collaboration stemmed from the realization that neither company would succeed in obtaining a more general trademark over the other's objection.

Figure 5.3 Xbox series X logo vs. Twitter X logo vs. Musk's XAI logo.

Chapter 5: Brand Protection in Pixels: Managing Trademarks and Online Identities 149

DC Comics' and Marvel's co-ownership of the "superhero" trademark primarily pertains to publications, but they have extended their challenges to other uses of the term. Instances include a Chicago ice cream parlor receiving a cease-and-desist letter for a shield shape resembling the Superman crest, and warnings issued to a Kentucky creamery and a T-shirt factory for using the term *superhero*. Legal experts suggest that the companies have avoided pursuing legal challenges to their end in court due to apprehensions about setting a precedent judgment against them.

The document below, Figure 5.4, shows the various broadening of goods and services trademark and service mark registrations by DC Comics and Marvel since the initial registration with the USPTO.

One notable case that exemplifies the challenges to their trademark enforcement efforts involved British businessman and law student Graham Jules, who intended to publish a self-help book titled "Business Zero to Superhero." In response, DC Comics and Marvel issued a joint cease-and-desist letter. However, Jules contested this, arguing that the term had become part of the public lexicon. Despite attempts to settle, Jules refused, prompting DC Comics and Marvel to withdraw their opposition just before a hearing, citing "commercial reasons." Legal experts suggest that DC Comics and Marvel have not pursued a legal challenge to its end in court due to the fear of a precedent judgment against them.

Dilution: Trademark dilution occurs when a renowned trademark is used in a manner that could diminish its ability to uniquely identify the owner's goods or services, or potentially tarnish the mark's reputation. Unlike typical trademark infringement cases, the trademark owner doesn't need to prove consumer confusion, and dilution can occur even if the goods or services involved are entirely different from those of the trademark owner. Consequently, it's generally not advised to name a blog "Multi-touch Insider" or "Fortnight Times" unless the content is directly related to Multi-touch (Apple Inc.) or Fortnight (Epic Games) (in which case, careful consideration of trademark usage guidelines is warranted).

In a 2023 decision with global implications, Louis Vuitton Malletier S.A., a renowned French luxury brand known for its leather goods and accessories, pursued legal action against Louis Vuitton Dak, a South Korean fried chicken restaurant, for its name and logo resembling Louis Vuitton's trademarks. Despite operating in different sectors, the restaurant's branding raised concerns about customer confusion and trademark dilution. Louis Vuitton Dak was ordered to change its name and logo and

Mark	Reg. No.	Date of Reg.	Goods/Services
SUPER HEROES	1,179,067	11/24/81	publications, particularly comic books and magazines and stories in illustrated form; notebooks and stamp albums
SUPER HEROES	1,140,452	10/14/80	toy figures
SUPER HEROES	3,674,448	8/25/09	t-shirts
MARVEL SUPER HERO ISLAND	2,276,421	9/7/99	amusement park services
COMPUTER SUPER HEROES	3,419,713	4/29/08	computer service, namely, acting as an application service provider in the field of knowledge management to host computer application software for creating searchable databases of information and data; an application service provider in the field of knowledge management to host computer application software for searching and retrieving information from databases and computer networks; an application service provider in the field of knowledge management to host computer application software for the collection, editing, organizing, modifying, book marking, transmission, storage and sharing of data and information; creating and maintaining web sites for others; data recovery services; designing and implementing network web pages for others; designing and implementing web sites for others; namely creating indexes of information, sites and other resources available on computer networks; managing web sites for others; computer site design; software consultation; computer software design for others; computer software development; computer systems analysis; and computerized

Mark	Reg. No.	Date of Reg.	Goods/Services
			database management

Each of these registrations (copies of which are attached hereto as Exhibit "A") issued prior to Applicant's filing date, and consequently there is no question of priority of rights, such priority clearly belonging to Opposer. Moreover, these registrations are incontestable under 15 U.S.C. § 1065.

6. Through Opposer's activities, and through the extensive promotion and advertising of Opposer and its licensees connected therewith, the public and trade have come to associate the trademark and service mark "SUPER HEROES" and variations thereof with Opposer, and with its products and services.

7. By virtue of its prior use in commerce of "SUPER HEROES" and variations thereof, Opposer is entitled to hold itself out to the public and trade as having the exclusive right to use "SUPER HEROES" and its variations thereof as trademarks and service marks for its products and services. Registration of the applied-for mark would be inconsistent with such right of Opposer.

Figure 5.4 Document from a US Trademark Notice of Opposition filed by DC Comics and Marvel over the use of the terms *Superman* and *Batman*.

pay $14.5 million for noncompliance after initially attempting a name change deemed insufficient by the court.

The case highlights the complexities of trademark dilution, where even similar but nonidentical marks can potentially damage a brand's reputation. They also demonstrate the evolving legal landscape surrounding trademark protection, with courts balancing the interests of brand owners and the right of others to use similar names without causing undue confusion or harm.

False Advertising

The advent of social media has revolutionized the way businesses advertise their products and services. However, this digital transformation has also led to an increase in deceptive advertising practices. False advertising on social media is a significant legal issue that involves the dissemination of misleading information to consumers. The regulation of such practices is critical to protect consumers and maintain fair competition among businesses.

False advertising, governed by the Lanham Act, stands as a substantial concern in the digital age, where businesses leverage various platforms for promotion. The Lanham Act, particularly **Section 43(a)**, acts as a legal bulwark against deceptive or misleading statements made by companies regarding their products or services. It establishes grounds for civil action against entities disseminating false or misleading information that could potentially deceive consumers. In the digital space, where information spreads rapidly, this legislation becomes even more critical in ensuring fair competition and safeguarding consumer interests.

To initiate a claim for false advertising under the Lanham Act, several pivotal elements must be demonstrated by the plaintiff, each vital in substantiating the allegation. First, there must be a presentation of false or misleading statements made either about the defendant's own offerings or those of another entity. This requirement extends to digital platforms and social media, where companies often engage in comparative advertising or make claims about their products' superiority especially with the prevalence of social media influencers and digital influencers. Notably, cases such as *Pom Wonderful LLC v. Coca-Cola Co.* (573 U.S. 102 (2014)) highlight instances where false or misleading statements in digital advertising were litigated at the behest of a competitive company who alleged unfair competition under the Lanham Act in conjunction with other federal regulatory agencies.

Second, evidence of actual deception or at least a tendency to deceive a substantial portion of the intended online audience is necessary. With the prevalence of social media influencers and digital influencers, the assessment of audience perception becomes intricate. Cases like *Fleischer Studios, Inc. v. A.V.E.L.A., Inc.* (654 F.3d 958 (9th Cir. 2011)) examine the complexities of audience interpretation in the digital realm. In this case, Fleischer Studios Inc., the company behind the beloved cartoon character Betty Boop, sued A.V.E.L.A. Inc., for selling merchandise featuring Betty Boop images. They claimed that A.V.E.L.A.'s use of these images infringed on their trademark rights and constituted unfair competition.

The key legal question was whether A.V.E.L.A.'s use of Betty Boop images would confuse consumers about the merchandise's origin. The court had to assess how audiences interpreted these images and whether they associated them with Fleischer Studios or mistakenly believed the merchandise was officially licensed by the studio.

Ultimately, the Ninth Circuit ruled in favor of A.V.E.L.A., stating that the Betty Boop images used were unlikely to confuse consumers into thinking the merchandise was endorsed by Fleischer Studios. The court noted that the images had entered the public domain and were used by A.V.E.L.A. as functional images on merchandise rather than trademarks so did not constitute false advertising.

Furthermore, the deception must be material, meaning it has the potential to influence purchasing decisions. This aspect is particularly pertinent in the context of online reviews and testimonials, where consumers heavily rely on digital feedback. Case law, such as *Federal Trade Commission v. Devumi LLC* (18-cv-03282 (S.D.N.Y. 2019)), provides insights into cases involving the materiality of false advertising claims in the digital space.

In this New York decision, the crucial issues regarding false online advertising and the sale of fake social media influence were brought to light. Devumi, LLC faced accusations from the Federal Trade Commission (FTC) that they were allegedly selling fake social media indicators like followers, subscribers, views, and likes across platforms such as LinkedIn, Twitter, YouTube, Pinterest, Vine, and SoundCloud. These actions allowed Devumi's clients to misrepresent their online influence and credibility to

Chapter 5: Brand Protection in Pixels: Managing Trademarks and Online Identities 153

potential clients, partners, and the public. The order banned Devumi from selling or assisting others in selling social media influence indicators and making false representations about social media influence. This case marked the first time the FTC challenged the sale of fake social media influence.

Additionally, for a false advertising claim to be actionable under the Lanham Act, the advertised goods or services must engage in interstate commerce, reflecting the interconnected nature of digital commerce. In terms of remedies, successful plaintiffs in false advertising cases under the Lanham Act may be entitled to injunctive relief, damages (potentially trebled for willful violations), corrective advertising, and attorneys' fees. In the digital sphere, where misinformation can proliferate rapidly, injunctive relief becomes particularly crucial in halting the dissemination of false advertising.

However, it is important to remember, not all claims related to advertising in the digital space are actionable under the Lanham Act. Puffery, which entails exaggerated claims that no reasonable person would take literally, and opinions, as well as truthful but negative statements, are generally not grounds for a false advertising claim. Within the digital landscape, distinguishing between puffery and actionable claims becomes paramount.

The case of *Kimzey v. Yelp! Inc.* (836 F.3d 1263 (9th Cir. 2016)) involves a related issue of whether a social media platform is liable for posted negative reviews within the context of false advertising litigation. Douglas Kimzey, the plaintiff, sued Yelp! Inc. over a negative review posted on its platform, alleging harm to his business. Kimzey argued that Yelp! should be held accountable for the user-generated review's content, claiming that its star-rating system and review management made it akin to a content creator. Yelp!'s defense was that it was shielded from online liability for third-party content.

The central legal question revolved around whether Yelp! could be held accountable for user-generated content under the Communications Decency Act (CDA), specifically **Section 230**, which shields online platforms from liability for third-party content. Douglas Kimzey argued that Yelp! should be considered a content creator due to its review management, while Yelp! asserted it operated as a service provider. The Ninth Circuit Court of Appeals ruled in favor of Yelp!, affirming its immunity under Section 230 and emphasizing that online platforms are generally not liable for user-generated content.

However, it's important to note a key distinction: while Section 230 and the **Digital Millennium Copyright Act** provide "safe harbors" for online platforms, they typically do not protect against trademark claims as they are not listed as exceptions.

While the Lanham Act primarily involves private litigation between businesses, the FTC, as observed in the fake social media influence case above, plays a crucial role in enforcing laws and regulations related to false advertising, including those applicable to online advertising. The FTC has provided detailed guidelines for social media advertising, emphasizing the need for disclosures to be close to the claims they modify, easily visible, and readable in terms of font size and color. For example, on X, the use of "#ad" or "Ad:" at the beginning of a tweet is recommended to identify sponsored content.

It is clear that companies using video streaming platforms and social media for marketing must swim through a complex legal landscape. Posts from corporate accounts can be used to support claims of libel, defamation, trademark infringement, and deceptive or false advertising. Social media marketing is subject to oversight by various regulatory bodies besides the FTC, including the Securities and Exchange Commission (SEC), Food and Drug Administration (FDA), and **Health Insurance Portability and Accountability Act (HIPAA)**.

Boundaries of Fair Trademark Use

Determining the boundaries of fair trademark use can be complex, particularly regarding commentary, parody, or criticism. Courts must navigate these gray areas, balancing trademark protection with free speech rights. As described earlier in the *Brunetti* and *Tam* cases, certain provisions of the Lanham Act have faced First Amendment challenges, particularly regarding restrictions on trademark registration based on content or viewpoint.

Trademark parody, which involves using well-known trademarks in a humorous or critical manner, has been a contentious issue leading to numerous legal disputes. The landmark case of *Jack Daniel's Properties, Inc. v. VIP Products LLC* (599 U.S. 140 (*2023*)) has notably influenced the legal landscape, particularly by limiting the defenses available in parody cases, especially when parodies serve as source identifiers for the parodist's own goods or services without receiving heightened First Amendment protection.

Before the recent landmark Jack Daniel's Supreme Court case, courts had recognized several instances of acceptable trademark parody. Among these examples, two stand out prominently. In the case of *Haute Diggity Dog, LLC v. Hartman* (507 F.3d 252 (2007)) the court ruled in favor of Haute Diggity Dog, a company manufacturing plush dog toys resembling high-end fashion accessories. Notably, one of their products, titled "Chewy Vuiton," parodied the Louis Vuitton brand. The court determined that the Chewy Vuiton toys were unmistakably intended as humorous parodies and did not lead to consumer confusion regarding the origin of the products. Consequently, they were deemed permissible under trademark law. Similarly, in *Mattel, Inc. v. MCA Records, Inc.* (296 F.3d 894 (9th Cir. 2002)) the court addressed the song "Barbie Girl" by the band Aqua, which satirized the Barbie doll and its associated lifestyle. Despite Mattel's assertions of trademark infringement, the court upheld that the song constituted protected speech under the First Amendment. The parody was deemed transformative and distinctly separate from the Barbie trademark, thus falling within the realm of acceptable parody.

The case between Jack Daniel's Properties and VIP Products LLC centered on a dog toy resembling a Jack Daniel's bottle called "Bad Spaniels." The Supreme Court's ruling narrowed the defenses available for parody cases, suggesting that parodies used as source identifiers for the parodist's own goods or services no longer enjoy heightened **First Amendment** protection. This decision represents a significant shift in how courts may approach parody trademarks, prioritizing commercial interests over creative expression in certain contexts.

Historically, courts considered several factors when determining whether a parody trademark constitutes infringement, including the likelihood of consumer confusion, the intent behind the parody, and potential harm to the original trademark owner's reputation. The transformative nature of the parody, its impact on the trademark's commercial value, and whether it clearly mocks and criticizes the brand are also crucial considerations. Evaluating these factors is challenging, requiring careful consideration of intellectual property protection and creative freedom, as viewed in the Court's Jack Daniels' decision. As courts continue to refine their approach to parody trademarks, both the

Figure 5.5 Jack Daniel's vs. parody Jack Daniels.

legal community and creators must remain vigilant in understanding the implications of these changes for trademark protection and creative freedom.

International Trademark Law

J. K. Rowling, the creator of the Harry Potter universe, offers a compelling case study on the intricacies of global trademark law and brand protection. Despite birthing the enchanting world of Harry Potter,

Chapter 5: Brand Protection in Pixels: Managing Trademarks and Online Identities

Rowling does not hold trademark rights to the brand; instead, Warner Bros. Entertainment (now Warner Bros Discovery International) retains registrations in multiple jurisdictions including the United States and European Union for various aspects of the series, notably the renowned "Harry Potter" name. However, Rowling maintains trademarks for her own name and "J.K. Rowling's Wizarding World," particularly concerning film distribution. The jointly owned "Wizarding World" trademark, shared by Rowling and Warner Bros, encompasses materials from both the Harry Potter and "Fantastic Beasts and Where to Find Them" films. Warner Bros. serves as the primary trademark holder for the Harry Potter brand, securing registrations across merchandise categories and entertainment services. Co-ownership of the rights to produce movies and plays inspired by the Harry Potter series exists between Warner Bros. and J. K. Rowling, with unauthorized usage potentially constituting copyright and trademark infringement. Despite legal nuances such as fair use, Rowling and Warner Bros jointly wield significant trademark protections over various elements of the series, ensuring control over its commercial exploitation. Crucially, the Harry Potter trademark extends to digital assets and rights, empowering Warner Bros to govern the digital representation and distribution of Harry Potter content, including motion picture films and digital audio tapes. This authority encompasses the production of movies and plays derived from the Harry Potter series, thus incorporating digital rights associated with their distribution, streaming, and digital marketing endeavors. Additionally, the co-owned "Wizarding World" trademark extends to digital content linked to these movies, including online promotional materials, digital downloads, and streaming services.

In comparing and contrasting trademark laws between the United States and the European Union, several notable differences emerge, impacting the acquisition, registration process, use requirements, and other aspects of trademark protection.

First, the basis for acquiring trademark rights differs significantly. In the United States, trademark rights can be obtained through both registration and first use in commerce. This means that even without formally registering a trademark, using it in commerce can afford certain legal protections. Conversely, in the European Union, trademark rights are exclusively acquired through registration, meaning that the act of using a mark in commerce does not automatically grant legal protection. Instead, individuals or businesses must formally register their trademarks with the appropriate trademark office, such as the European Union Intellectual Property Office (EUIPO). Once registered, the trademark owner obtains exclusive rights to use the mark for the goods or services specified in the registration within the territory of the European Union.

Second, the registration process itself varies between the two jurisdictions. US trademark registration provides nationwide protection. The process considers prior use and examines whether the proposed mark is confusingly similar to existing ones. On the other hand, EU trademark registration offers a streamlined process whereby a single registration grants protection across all member states. This means that a trademark owner doesn't need to file separate applications in each individual EU member state to secure protection throughout the entire European Union.

One of the primary considerations during the EU trademark registration process is whether the mark is inherently distinctive. Inherently distinctive marks are those that are unique and capable of distinguishing the goods or services of one entity from those of others. Marks that are descriptive or lacking in distinctiveness may face challenges during the registration process.

For example, a company seeking to register a brand name for its clothing line would want to choose a distinctive and memorable name that doesn't simply describe the product (e.g., "Cozy Clothes" would likely be considered descriptive and lacking in distinctiveness). Instead, a more creative and unique name (e.g., "Zephyr Apparel") would have a better chance of being accepted for registration.

Additionally, once a trademark application is published by the EUIPO, third parties have an opportunity to oppose the registration if they believe it conflicts with their existing rights. This opposition period allows interested parties to challenge the registration of a trademark that they believe infringes upon their own rights or conflicts with prior trademarks.

For instance, if another clothing company already holds a registered trademark for the name "Zephyr" for clothing, they may file an opposition against the registration of "Zephyr Apparel" if they believe it would create confusion among consumers or dilute the distinctiveness of their own mark.

Regarding use requirements, the US system places emphasis on the benefits of registration in strengthening rights, but even unregistered trademarks enjoy some protection if actively used in commerce. In

Chapter 5: Brand Protection in Pixels: Managing Trademarks and Online Identities

contrast, the European Union does not have a strict "use it or lose it" requirement, but prolonged nonuse can weaken trademark rights and render them susceptible to cancellation.

A case that exemplifies the importance of use requirements in trademark law is the dispute between Louboutin and Van Haren in the European Union. Louboutin, a renowned luxury footwear brand, holds a trademark for its distinctive red sole shoes. A Dutch shoe retailer Van Haren began selling high-heeled shoes with red soles in its stores in the Netherlands, prompting Louboutin to file a lawsuit for trademark infringement.

Louboutin argued that Van Haren's use of red-soled shoes constituted trademark infringement, as it diluted the distinctiveness of Louboutin's trademark. However, Van Haren countered that Louboutin's trademark registration should be canceled because the mark had not been put to genuine use within the European Union for a continuous period of five years, as required by EU trademark law.

The case ultimately reached the European Court of Justice (ECJ) (Case C-163/16), which ruled in favor of Louboutin. The ECJ held that Louboutin's red sole mark had acquired distinctiveness through use and had become a recognizable sign associated with the brand. As a result, the mark was deemed valid, and Van Haren's use of similar, red-soled shoes was found to infringe upon Louboutin's trademark rights.

This case highlights the significance of use requirements in the EU trademark system. While the European Union does not have a strict "use it or lose it" requirement like the United States, prolonged nonuse of a trademark can weaken its distinctiveness and render it susceptible to cancellation. However, if a trademark owner can demonstrate that the mark has acquired distinctiveness through genuine use in commerce, they may still be able to enforce their rights against infringing parties.

Additional disparities include the types of marks eligible for protection. The European Union allows for a broader range of marks to be registered, including sounds and shapes, while the United States tends to be more restrictive in this regard. Moreover, the renewal process differs; the US mandates renewal every ten years, while the European Union requires renewal every ten years after the initial ten-year registration period.

These disparities underscore the variations between US and EU trademark laws, highlighting the significance of understanding the specific regulations and requirements governing trademark protection in each jurisdiction.

Global trademark treaties and laws, overseen by institutions such as the **World Intellectual Property Organization (WIPO)** and the **Agreement on Trade-Related Aspects of Intellectual Property Rights (TRIPS)**, serve as crucial components of international intellectual property (IP) law, establishing a unified framework for safeguarding and enforcing trademark rights worldwide. Within WIPO's jurisdiction, a comprehensive array of treaties is administered, spanning various categories to ensure robust IP protection on a global scale. These treaties encompass basic standards of IP protection, global protection systems, and classification structures aimed at facilitating efficient trademark management and accessibility.

A prime example of WIPO's impact is the **Madrid System**, which streamlines the international registration of trademarks by enabling applicants to file a single application, valid across more than 120 member countries. This mechanism significantly simplifies the complexities associated with securing trademark protection in multiple jurisdictions, reducing administrative burdens and costs for businesses operating on a global scale.

Complementing WIPO's efforts, the **TRIPS** Agreement, under the auspices of the **World Trade Organization (WTO)**, establishes minimum standards for IP protection among member nations, encouraging robust trademark regimes while affording flexibility for countries to extend greater protection if desired. Key provisions within the TRIPS Agreement mandate minimum trademark protection durations, grant trademark owners' exclusive rights to prevent unauthorized use of their marks, and recognize the significance of well-known marks, irrespective of registration or usage within a particular country.

Beyond setting minimum standards, these global treaties aim to harmonize trademark protection worldwide, fostering an environment conducive to international trade and innovation. By adhering to principles such as national treatment and most-favored-nation treatment, these frameworks ensure equitable treatment for trademark owners across borders, promoting predictability and security in the global marketplace.

Moreover, WIPO's involvement extends beyond trademarks to encompass copyright protection, as demonstrated by the **WIPO Copyright Treaty (WCT)**. This treaty addresses the challenges of the digital age, extending traditional copyright principles to digital works and authors' rights, thereby ensuring the continued relevance and protection of creative works in an increasingly digitalized world.

Leading trademark infringement cases under the purview of the WIPO and the TRIPS illuminate the complexities of global IP enforcement and set important precedents. These cases often span multiple jurisdictions and industries, offering insights into the interpretation and application of intellectual property laws on an international scale. Here are some notable examples derived from WIPO arbitration cases and TRIPS principles:

WIPO Arbitration Examples:

1. **European Luxury Goods vs. Asian Manufacturer**: This case involved a dispute between a European luxury goods company and an Asian manufacturer selling fashion products under a similar trademark. Despite administrative cancellation proceedings in Europe, the conflict persisted, leading to WIPO expedited arbitration. The resolution resulted in a trademark coexistence agreement. However, subsequent infringements underscored the challenges of enforcing such agreements across borders, highlighting the complexities of global IP enforcement.
2. **US Technology Licensing Agreement**: In another instance, a German company terminated a technology licensing agreement with a US counterpart, alleging trademark infringement and breach of trade secrets. The inclusion of a WIPO Arbitration clause in the agreement underscored the importance of clear contractual terms in cross-border transactions and the potential for legal disputes arising from international licensing agreements.
3. **North American Software Developer vs. Computer Hardware Manufacturer**: This case centered on a dispute over nearly identical trademarks used for communication software and computer hardware in the United States and Canada. Legal proceedings across various jurisdictions highlighted the difficulties of protecting trademarks in a global market, where overlapping jurisdictions and differing legal standards pose significant challenges.

TRIPS Agreement and Well-Known Marks

The TRIPS Agreement, which sets minimum standards for intellectual property protection among member countries, extends specific protections to well-known marks. **Article 16.3** of TRIPS mandates that member countries protect well-known marks, even if used on unrelated goods, if such use indicates a connection to the owner and is likely to cause damage. This principle is mirrored in national laws like the Lanham Act, which safeguards well-known marks from infringement or unauthorized registration, emphasizing the importance of brand recognition and the prevention of consumer confusion.

These cases and principles underscore the intricate nature of global trademark enforcement and the vital role of international frameworks like WIPO and TRIPS in harmonizing intellectual property protection across borders. They highlight the imperfections and challenges businesses face in traversing cross-border digital marketing and emphasize the importance of clear contractual agreements and robust trademark protection strategies in the global marketplace.

Summary

In considering trademark law in the digital era, it's crucial to acknowledge its rich history and development. Over time, trademark law has evolved to encompass a broad spectrum of protections and considerations, including safeguards against infringement and the preservation of First Amendment rights. The Lanham Act, enacted in 1946, serves as the cornerstone of modern trademark law in the United States, providing a framework for the registration, protection, and enforcement of trademarks. Under the First Amendment, there are protections against restrictions on both the infringement and registration of trademarks that may impede freedom of expression. However, these protections are not absolute and must be balanced against the rights of trademark owners to protect their intellectual property.

Infringement of trademarks occurs when unauthorized use of a mark creates a likelihood of confusion among consumers regarding the source of goods or services. This can include a wide range of activities, from counterfeiting and cybersquatting to unauthorized use of trademarks in advertising or product packaging. Parody, a form of expressive speech that humorously or critically comments on well-known trademarks, presents a unique challenge in trademark law. While parody is generally protected under the First Amendment, determining when a parody crosses the line into actionable infringement requires careful consideration of factors such as the likelihood of consumer confusion and the transformative nature of the parody.

Chapter 5: Brand Protection in Pixels: Managing Trademarks and Online Identities

In the digital era, the proliferation of online platforms, e-commerce, social media, and user-generated content has significantly altered the trademark landscape. The global nature of the internet has expanded the reach and scope of trademarks, creating new challenges for enforcement and protection. Additionally, the rise of AI-generated content and virtual environments introduces novel complexities that require innovative approaches to trademark law.

To address these challenges and opportunities effectively, stakeholders must collaborate to develop adaptable legal frameworks that strike a delicate balance between protecting intellectual property rights and fostering innovation, creativity, and freedom of expression. By leveraging technology, collaboration, and evolving legal doctrines, policymakers, legal practitioners, businesses, and creators can ensure the continued relevance and efficacy of trademark protection in an ever-evolving digital landscape.

Discussion Questions

1. How has the Lanham Act evolved to address trademark issues in the digital space and social media era?
2. What are the key considerations when determining whether a trademark infringement has occurred in online contexts such as social media platforms?
3. How do courts balance First Amendment protections with trademark rights when evaluating parody in digital spaces?
4. What are the challenges and opportunities presented by the global nature of the internet for trademark enforcement and protection?
5. How does the rise of user-generated content on social media platforms impact trademark infringement and enforcement?
6. Can AI-generated content pose unique challenges for trademark law and enforcement in the digital space? If so, how?
7. What role does consumer confusion play in determining trademark infringement in digital and social media environments?
8. How do companies utilize social media platforms to protect their trademarks and enforce their intellectual property rights?
9. How have recent legal developments, such as landmark cases or legislative changes, influenced the landscape of trademark law in the digital era?

10. What strategies can businesses employ to balance trademark protection with fostering creativity and freedom of expression on social media platforms?

Works Referenced

Brittain, Blake. "Meta, Microsoft, Hundreds More Own Trademarks to New Twitter Name." Reuters, July 25, 2023, accessed at https://www.reuters.com/technology/problem-with-x-meta-microsoft-hundreds-more-own-trademarks-new-twitter-name-2023-07-25

Federal Trade Commission. "Devumi, Owner and CEO Settle FTC Charges They Sold Fake Indicators of Social Media Influence: Cosmetics Firm Sunday Riley, CEO Settle FTC Charges that Employees Posted Fake Online Reviews at CEO's Direction." October 21, 2019, accessed at https://www.ftc.gov/news-events/news/press-releases/2019/10/devumi-owner-ceo-settle-ftc-charges-they-sold-fake-indicators-social-media-influence-cosmetics-firm

Feagle, Chelsea R. "Fighting the Faceless Foe Known as the Online Trademark Counterfeiter: Forum Shopping Tactics in the Digital Age." *Journal of Intellectual Property Law,* Vol. 26, No. 2 (2020), accessed at https://digitalcommons.law.uga.edu/cgi/viewcontent.cgi?article=1447&context=jipl

Fondo, Grant P., and Burns., Emily F. "Counterfeits: Beyond the Knockoff." *The National Law Journal,* October 16, 2006, accessed at https://www.law.com/nationallawjournal/almID/1160730320483

Jones, Michael, *Art Law*, 2nd ed. Rowman & Littlefield, Lanham, MD, 2023.

Keller, Bruce P. "It Keeps Going and Going and Going": The Expansion of False Advertising Litigation under the Lanham Act." Duke Law, accessed at https://scholarship.law.duke.edu/cgi/viewcontent.cgi?article=4325&context=lcp

"Louis Vuitton v. Louis Vuitton dak." IPR Studio, accessed at http://iprstudio.com/trademark-infringement-case-study-2

"Meta v. Meta—Battle over Name and Logo in Digital Space." Hodgson Russ, July 21, 2022, accessed at https://www.hodgsonruss.com/newsroom-publications-13830.html

Morales, Xavier. "Harry Potter Trademarks." Secure Your Trademark, January 27, 2022, accessed at https://secureyourtrademark.com/blog/harry-potter-trademarks

Peek, Sean. "Apple vs. Apple: 6 Trademark Cases and What You Should Learn from Them." business.com, updated, October 31, 2023, accessed at https://www.business.com/articles/5-trademark-cases-and-what-you-should-learn-from-them

Pronk, Alec. "Hermès Wins Landmark MetaBirkins NFT Trademark Trial." IP Watchdog, February 9, 2023, accessed at https://ipwatchdog.com/2023/02/09/hermes-wins-landmark-metabirkins-nft-trademark-trial/id=156364

Romoser, James. "Justices Fetch New Case on Trademark Law and Parody." *SCOTUSblog*, November 21, 2022, accessed at https://www.scotusblog.com/2022/11/justices-fetch-new-case-on-trademark-law-and-parody

"Sex Trafficking: Online Platforms and Federal Prosecutions." US Government Accountability Office, June 21, 2021, accessed at https://www.gao.gov/products/gao-21-385

Small, Zachery. "Hermès Wins MetaBirkins Lawsuit: Jurors Not Convinced NFTs Are Art." *The New York Times*, February 23, 2023, accessed at https://www.nytimes.com/2023/02/08/arts/hermes-metabirkins-lawsuit-verdict.html

Stewart, D. G. "The 'Superhero' Trademark: How the Name of a Genre Came to Be Owned by DC and Marvel, and How They Enforce It." *World Comic Book Review*, June 1, 2017, accessed at https://worldcomicbookreview.com/2017/06/01/superhero-trademark-name-genre-came-owned-dc-marvel-enforce

Tabberone. "The History of Trademark Law." Tabbers Temptations, accessed at http://www.tabberone.com/Trademarks/TrademarkLaw/History/History.shtml

"Trademark Basics." United States Patent and Trademark Office, accessed at https://www.uspto.gov/trademarks/basics

"WIPO Arbitration Cases." WIPO, accessed at https://www.wipo.int/amc/en/arbitration/case-example.html

6

Defamation, Deceit, and Disparagement in the Digital Age

> *Where the Internet provides an easy, inexpensive, and almost anonymous way to target reputations, a potential plaintiff, armed only with his computer, can inflict significant reputational—and, thus, financial—harm.*
> —Judge Alex Kozinski in *Roommates.Com, LLC v. Fair Housing Council of San Fernando Valley*

The transition from the analog to the digital world has fundamentally altered the nature of communication and information dissemination, bringing to the forefront new challenges in the realm of defamation and other legal liabilities. The digital age, characterized by the rapid proliferation of digital platforms and social media, has not only expanded the reach of individuals' voices but has also magnified the potential for reputational harm through the spread of false information. This chapter delves into the intricacies of defamation law as it adapts to the digital landscape, exploring the nuances of libel and slander in an era where the line between publisher and platform is increasingly blurred.

Defamation law serves to protect individuals and entities from unwarranted harm to their reputation caused by false statements. The primary interests that defamation seeks to protect are the dignity, reputation, and privacy of individuals, alongside the economic impacts that defamation can have on businesses. By holding individuals accountable for spreading false information, defamation law aims to maintain a level of trust and truth in public discourse, which is essential for the functioning of society.

Brief History of Defamation Law

The roots of defamation law can be traced back to early English common law, where it was divided into two categories: libel and slander. Libel referred to written defamation, while slander was spoken defamation. The distinction was significant due to the permanence and thus perceived greater harm of written statements. As societies and their legal systems evolved, the principles of defamation law adapted to new forms of communication, including broadcast media and, more recently, digital platforms.

The historical evolution of defamation law across England, Europe, and the United States mirrors broader shifts in societal values concerning honor, reputation, and freedom of expression. From its roots in the medieval courts of Europe and England to the sophisticated legal debates of today, defamation law has continually adapted to new challenges posed by changes in communication methods and social norms.

In medieval Europe, the significance of honor and reputation was paramount, with local and manorial courts addressing cases of slander, and the church viewing defamation as a sin impacting one's moral standing. England, by the thirteenth century, enacted the "Scandalum Magnatum" statute to protect the nobility from defamatory attacks, underscoring the intertwining of defamation law with social hierarchy and the protection of status.

The development of the common law system in the sixteenth century marked a pivotal moment for English defamation law, establishing the crucial distinction between libel (written) and slander (spoken), with the former considered more egregious due to its enduring nature. This era saw English law increasingly safeguard individual honor and social standing, albeit sometimes at the cost of free speech. Notable statutes like the Star Chamber's decree against libel in the early seventeenth century exemplify this trend, where defamation law served not only to protect individual reputations but also to maintain public order and the social fabric.

The American colonies, infused with Enlightenment ideals, placed a higher emphasis on the value of free speech, leading to a more restrained approach to defamation law in comparison to English practices. The evolution of early US defamation law at the state level highlighted a fundamental shift, notably incorporating truth as a defense—a stark departure from English law, where defendants bore the burden of proving the veracity of their statements.

The twentieth century witnessed the United States moving toward a more balanced approach between protecting reputations and facilitating public discourse on matters of interest. Conversely, England's defamation law continued to be critiqued for favoring reputation over free expression until the enactment of the Defamation Act 2013. This Act introduced reforms intended to better balance these interests, such as requiring claimants to show substantial harm and strengthening defenses like "truth" and "honest opinion," reflecting a significant shift toward protecting speech.

State vs. Federal Law

The landscape of defamation law in the United States is indeed characterized by a complex and intriguing interplay between state-specific statutes and overarching federal constitutional principles. Each state has developed its own body of defamation law, which includes statutes and case law that define what constitutes defamation, the defenses against a defamation claim, and the types of damages that can be awarded. These variations reflect the diverse legal traditions and policy preferences of the states.

For instance, in California, plaintiffs in defamation lawsuits must prove that the statement was false and caused damage, reflecting the state's prioritization of free speech but also the protection of individuals against harmful falsehoods. New York, on the other hand, has a unique provision under its Civil Rights Law that provides for the use of a person's name, portrait, picture, or voice for advertising or trade purposes without written consent as a type of defamation, showcasing a blend of defamation law with privacy rights.

Texas has the Defamation Mitigation Act, which requires plaintiffs to provide a request for a retraction or correction to the defendant before proceeding with a defamation lawsuit for certain claims. This reflects an interest in resolving disputes outside of court. In contrast, Florida does not have such a requirement, illustrating a different approach to pre-litigation dispute resolution.

The statute of limitations for bringing a defamation lawsuit also varies significantly. For example, Ohio and Illinois have a one-year statute of limitations for defamation claims, emphasizing a swift resolution to such disputes. Meanwhile, Massachusetts allows up to three years, providing more time for potential plaintiffs to consider their legal options.

Despite this variability at the state level, federal constitutional principles, particularly those enshrined in the First Amendment regarding freedom of speech and press, serve as a critical unifying layer that influences and, in some cases, limits state defamation laws. The US Supreme Court has played a central role in shaping these principles through landmark decisions such as *New York Times Co. v. Sullivan* (376 U.S. 254 (1964)), which established the "actual malice" standard for defamation claims involving public figures. This standard requires that the plaintiff, if a public figure, must prove that the statement was made with knowledge of its falsity or with reckless disregard for the truth. The rationale behind this higher standard is to protect the robust discussion and criticism that is fundamental to a democratic society, especially when it concerns individuals who have more significant influence on public life.

This historic US Supreme Court decision significantly influenced state defamation law, particularly concerning public officials and figures. Responding to a 1960 full-page ad in *The New York Times* that aimed to highlight the civil rights movement's challenges without directly naming L. B. Sullivan, the police commissioner of Montgomery, Alabama, Sullivan claimed the ad defamed him by inaccurately portraying the police department's actions under his leadership. The pivotal legal question was whether the First Amendment's freedom of speech protections could defend a news outlet from defamation liability for inaccuracies about public officials without proving the publication was made with "actual malice"—knowingly or with reckless disregard for the truth.

The Supreme Court's unanimous ruling in favor of *The New York Times* established the "actual malice" standard for defamation cases involving public officials, stating that the First Amendment protects all statements about public officials' conduct unless made with actual malice. This monumental decision underscored the importance of free speech and a free press in democratic societies, emphasizing that public issue debates should be "uninhibited, robust, and wide-open," even at the risk of including harsh criticisms of government and public officials.

The legacy of *New York Times Co. v. Sullivan* in shaping defamation law was notably expanded through subsequent Supreme Court rulings, particularly through *Curtis Publishing Co. v. Butts* (388 U.S. 88 (1967)) and *Gertz v. Robert Welch, Inc.* (418 U.S. 323 (1979)). These decisions further developed a complex legal framework that discerns among public officials, public figures, and private individuals when addressing defamation disputes.

Curtis Publishing Co. involved a defamation claim by Wally Butts, the former athletic director of the University of Georgia, against *The Saturday Evening Post* for publishing an article that alleged he conspired to fix a college football game. The Supreme Court's decision to extend the Sullivan decision's actual malice requirement to public figures like Butts acknowledged that individuals who have prominence in public life, by virtue of their positions or their influence on societal matters, are similarly vulnerable to the dissemination of harmful falsehoods as are public officials. This ruling underscored the need for a heightened standard of proof in defamation cases involving individuals who play a significant role in public discourse, such as prominent entrepreneurs, tech CEOs, professional athletes, Hollywood celebrities, and social media influencers, thereby broadening the scope of protected speech under the First Amendment.

Following this, *Gertz v. Robert Welch, Inc.* involved Elmer Gertz, a private individual and an attorney, who was falsely accused by a publication of being part of a conspiracy to frame a police officer. This case adjusted the legal equilibrium by providing greater protections for private individuals in defamation cases. The Supreme Court ruled that while private individuals do not need to demonstrate actual malice to win defamation suits, there must at least be proof of negligence on the part of the publisher. This distinction recognized the comparatively limited avenues available to private individuals for countering false public narratives, thereby enhancing their protection against defamation while also ensuring the preservation of free speech by not imposing too stringent a standard that could chill public discourse.

Together, *Curtis Publishing Co. v. Butts* and *Gertz v. Robert Welch, Inc.* significantly contributed to the Supreme Court's efforts in safeguarding free expression, while also carefully weighing the potential harm caused by defamatory statements. This jurisprudence fosters a legal environment that supports vigorous public debate as well as respect for individual dignity and reputation, demonstrating the nuanced approach required to balance these often-competing interests in a democratic society.

The tension between state defamation laws and federal constitutional principles highlights the delicate balance between protecting individuals' reputations and ensuring freedom of expression. Federal principles act as a check on state laws, ensuring that the right to free speech, particularly on matters of public concern, is not unduly stifled by defamation claims. However, the specifics of how defamation cases are adjudicated, including the evidence required and the damages awarded, can still vary significantly depending on state law.

This dual system underscores the importance of navigating both state statutes and federal constitutional jurisprudence when dealing with defamation issues. For individuals and entities involved in defamation disputes, understanding the interplay between state and federal law is crucial for assessing the strength of a claim or defense and for strategizing effectively within the legal process.

Understanding Defamation in the Digital Age

Defamation law, traditionally aimed at balancing freedom of speech with the protection of individual reputation, faces unique challenges in the digital realm. The core elements of a defamation claim—publication, falsity, harm, and fault—remain the same, but their application becomes complicated in a space where content can go viral in seconds, and the sources of information are often nebulous. The digital age demands a reevaluation of what constitutes "publication" and mental intent, and how harm is assessed when false statements can reach a global audience instantaneously.

Interests Protected by Defamation Law

Reputation: The core interest protected by defamation law is the reputation of individuals and entities. A good reputation is considered a valuable asset, crucial for personal relationships, professional opportunities, and social standing.

Privacy: Defamation law intersects with privacy interests by protecting individuals from unwarranted public scrutiny based on falsehoods.

Freedom of Expression: Although seemingly paradoxical, defamation law also protects freedom of expression. By delineating the boundaries of acceptable speech (i.e., not allowing false and damaging statements), it ensures that truthful and constructive discourse thrives.

Economic Interests: For businesses and professionals, defamation can have serious economic consequences, affecting their ability to attract customers or clients and maintain partnerships.

The evolving landscape of defamation in the digital age is underscored by an intriguing case involving entrepreneur, inventor and angel investor Elon Musk, cofounder of companies like PayPal, Space X, Tesla, OpenAI, and XAI. One of his noteworthy online controversies began after Vernon Unsworth, a British cave diver who played a key role in the rescue of twelve boys and their soccer coach trapped in a flooded cave in Thailand, criticized Musk's proposal to use a mini-submarine to assist in the rescue efforts. Unsworth dismissed the idea as a "PR stunt" in a CNN interview, suggesting it had no chance of working and telling Musk he could "stick his submarine where it hurts."

In response, Elon Musk took to Twitter, now X, where he made several statements about Unsworth, including a now-infamous tweet in which he referred to Unsworth as "pedo guy," a baseless and derogatory accusation implying that Unsworth was a pedophile. Musk did not provide any evidence to support this claim, and it was widely condemned as defamatory. Despite later deleting the tweet and issuing an apology to Unsworth, the damage was already done.

Unsworth filed a defamation lawsuit against Musk seeking compensatory and punitive damages for the harm Musk's tweet had caused to his reputation. The case raised important questions about the responsibility of public figures in their use of social media and the implications of their online conduct.

The trial was closely watched as a test of how defamation law applies to statements made on social media platforms by high-profile individuals. During the trial, Musk's defense argued that his tweet was not meant to be taken literally and was merely an insult precipitated by Unsworth's critique of the submarine rescue proposal. They contended that "pedo guy" was a common insult used in South Africa, where Musk grew up, and did not imply an accusation of pedophilia in a factual sense.

Ultimately, the jury found that Musk's tweet did not meet the legal definition of defamation. They concluded that the plaintiff, Vernon Unsworth, had not proven that Musk made the statement with actual malice—that is, with knowledge that it was false or with reckless disregard for its truthfulness. As a result, Musk was not held liable for defamation, and Unsworth was not awarded damages.

Another prominent celebrity was on the opposite side of a digital media defamation charge. The Grammy-nominated American rapper, social media personality, and former reality star Cardi B filed a lawsuit against YouTuber Tasha K, whose real name is Latasha Kebe. The facts of the case were rooted in a series of videos posted on Kebe's YouTube channel, where Kebe made various unsubstantiated claims about Cardi B. These allegations included accusations of drug use, prostitution, and contracting sexually transmitted diseases, among others. Cardi B argued that these claims were not only false but also harmful to her reputation, causing her distress and embarrassment.

The case went to trial in 2022. Throughout the trial, Cardi B's legal team presented evidence that Kebe's statements were not only baseless but had been made maliciously, aiming to profit from the increased viewership that controversy tends to attract. Kebe's defense, on the other hand, argued that her comments were protected under the First Amendment as freedom of speech.

The jury, however, sided with Cardi B, finding Kebe liable for defamation, invasion of privacy through false light portrayal, and intentional infliction of emotional distress. The court awarded Cardi B $1.25 million in general damages for the harm to her reputation and the distress she endured. Subsequently, additional punitive damages and legal costs brought the total award to over $4 million. This ruling underscored the message that freedom of speech does not extend to making defamatory statements without facing legal consequences.

The resolutions of these prominent social media defamation cases underline the dual-edged nature of the digital era: it is a realm that champions free speech yet demands responsibility, particularly when such expressions inflict harm. These cases serve as pivotal junctions, delineating the boundaries of celebrity rights within the expansive influence of digital media, and establishing firm limits on the liberties individuals may take when levying public allegations without substantiation. They illuminate the intricacies of adapting age-old defamation laws to the modern context of digital and social media, particularly when the statements originate from highly visible figures.

These legal battles spotlight the stringent criteria required to establish defamation, including the necessity of proving actual malice, thereby crafting a roadmap for navigating similar disputes in the future. More than just legal disputes, these cases cast a light on the tangible effects of defamation, underscoring how it can tarnish reputations and inflict emotional suffering. The experiences of those who have pursued justice in the face of defamation underscore the profound, lasting effects such actions can have on personal well-being, extending far beyond the confines of the courtroom.

Defenses to Defamation Claims

Understanding the defenses against a defamation complaint in digital media is critical for those accused of making potentially defamatory statements, as well as for plaintiffs seeking redress for damage to their reputation. These defenses play a pivotal role in shaping the outcome of defamation litigation. The cornerstone defense is the truth of the statement in question; proving the statement to be true or substantially true negates defamation claims, reflecting the legal system's reluctance to penalize individuals for truthful statements, even if they are damaging to someone's reputation.

Another key defense is categorizing the statement as an opinion rather than a fact, given that opinions are inherently subjective and not subject to verification of their truthfulness. This principle is vividly demonstrated in the legal battle of *Sandals Resorts International Ltd. v. Google, Inc.* (862 A.D. 32 (2011)). Sandals Resorts pursued legal action to identify an anonymous individual who circulated emails critiquing the company's employment practices, suggesting they were discriminatory. The company contended that these communications were defamatory and sought to initiate a libel lawsuit against the email's author. However, the New York appellate court concluded that the content of the email was a nonactionable opinion rather than a defamatory statement. The court observed that the email's critique of Sandals' employment strategies, including its implications about the exploitation of Jamaican labor, fell into the category of protected opinion under the First Amendment, especially given the anonymous nature of the email, which, according to the court, would lead reasonable readers to approach its claims with skepticism rather than as factual allegations. Keep in mind, however, this defense has limitations, especially if the opinion implies unfounded defamatory facts.

Privileges, both absolute (see: Speech or Debate Clause of the US Constitution, Article I, Section 6) and qualified, offer protection for statements made in certain contexts where freedom of speech is deemed paramount, such as legislative discussions or within judicial reports, or in situations where statements are made in good faith with a relevant interest, like employer references. Consent from the plaintiff to publish the statement effectively nullifies defamation claims, as it removes the wrongful nature of the publication. Additionally, the statute of limitations serves as a defense by enforcing a timeframe within which defamation claims must be filed, varying by state but typically set between one to three years.

Specific statutory defenses also exist, including protections under Section 230 of the Communications Decency Act for internet service providers hosting third-party content, and Anti-SLAPP (Strategic Lawsuit Against Public Participation) statutes designed to prevent lawsuits that aim to suppress public participation. Other, less commonly invoked defenses include the wire service defense, which protects entities that republish content from reputable news services in good faith, and the libel-proof plaintiff doctrine, applicable to individuals whose reputations are deemed already so damaged that further defamation is deemed impossible.

Anti-SLAPP statutes are pivotal in safeguarding individuals and entities from litigation aimed at curtailing their freedom of speech on matters of public interest. California's Anti-SLAPP law stands out as one of the strongest in the nation, enabling early dismissal of lawsuits that challenge free speech activities related to public issues, barring unlawful speech.

A compelling case that underscores the application of Anti-SLAPP statutes within digital media is the lawsuit filed by former US Congressman

Devin Nunes against Twitter (now X), political strategist Liz Mair, and two parody Twitter accounts, "Devin Nunes' Cow" and "Devin Nunes' Mom." Nunes launched a legal battle in Virginia, seeking $250 million in damages for alleged defamation stemming from tweets by the parody accounts and criticisms from Mair.

The defendants, including Mair and the operators behind the parody accounts, moved to dismiss Nunes's lawsuit under Virginia's Anti-SLAPP statute, arguing their tweets constituted protected speech about a public figure on issues of public concern. The essence of Anti-SLAPP statutes is to thwart the weaponization of legal systems to intimidate or silence individuals participating in protected speech, acknowledging the critical role of free expression on matters of public interest. These statutes aim to quickly end baseless lawsuits, deterring plaintiffs from engaging in legal intimidation to suppress opposition or criticism. The quick dismissal of the defamation claim serves as a critical example of the legal mechanisms in place to protect the dynamics of digital discourse and the expression of political satire and criticism against attempts to stifle such expressions through litigation.

Grasping the subtle differences of these defenses is crucial for anyone involved in defamation lawsuits. The choice and impact of a particular defense can vary greatly, influenced by the specific details of each case. Moreover, each state's defamation laws and judicial precedents can differ, further affecting how defenses are selected and their eventual success.

Legal Framework and Challenges in Digital Media

The legal debates surrounding Section 230 of the Communications Decency Act (CDA) and its immunity for internet service providers and intermediaries have significantly shaped the protections against defamation liability online. The California Supreme Court's decision in *Barrett v. Rosenthal* (146 P.3d 150 (2006)) is an eminent case highlighting these protections. The court reversed a lower court's ruling, affirming Section 230. This ruling removed the distinction between active and passive use of internet services, thereby providing broad statutory protection for internet service providers (ISPs), social media platforms, and forums against defamation claims for content reposted by third-party users.

The rationale behind the court's decision aligns with Congress's original intent for the CDA—to foster a free exchange of ideas and information on the internet without imposing the burden of publisher liability on service providers or users. The decision to protect individuals and platforms from defamation liability for third-party content has significantly contributed to the expansion of online forums for public discourse, fostering a dynamic and open environment for internet communication. This legal shield encourages a flourishing exchange of ideas by reducing the fear of litigation over user-generated content. Nevertheless, this approach has also faced criticism and sparked controversy, as it raises concerns about accountability and the responsibility of platforms in moderating harmful or misleading content.

This backdrop of legal protection for online speech is further supported by other pivotal cases. *Cubby v. CompuServe* (776 F, Supp. 135 (2006)) established that online service providers acting as distributors rather than publishers of content are not liable for defamation without actual knowledge of defamatory content. In contrast, *Stratton Oakmont v. Prodigy* (23 Media L. Rep. 1794 (N.Y. Sup. Ct. 1995)), which held Prodigy liable for its editorial control over content, was effectively nullified by the CDA. Moreover, *Zeran v. America Online* (129 F.3d 327 (4th Cir. 1997)) reinforced Section 230's broad immunity, ruling that internet service providers cannot be held liable for third-party defamatory content, even if they are notified and fail to remove it.

While Section 230 provides legal immunity to online platforms for content created entirely by third-party users. As described above in current case law, this means that if a user posts something defamatory on a platform like Facebook, the individual who posted could be held liable, but Facebook itself would be protected under Section 230. However, this protection does not extend to content that the platform has created, either wholly or in part. For example, if Facebook were to host a section of its website featuring news articles authored by its employees, Facebook could then be held accountable in defamation lawsuits related to those articles.

The evolving legal framework aimed at safeguarding online speech and platform moderation practices has indeed been shaped significantly through various court rulings. These decisions have carved out important legal precedents that underscore the judiciary's understanding of defamation in the context of digital communication, ensuring the internet remains a vibrant space for the exchange of ideas. However, this journey toward establishing a balanced approach to free speech and content moderation online has encountered its share of criticisms.

Critiques often revolve around the perceived broad protections afforded to digital platforms under laws like Section 230. Some argue that these protections enable platforms to shirk responsibility for the spread of harmful content, including misinformation (spreading false information without malicious intent), disinformation (deliberately spreading false information), hate speech, and defamation, without adequate accountability. Concerns have been raised about the potential for these platforms to influence public discourse and societal norms negatively, prompting calls for more stringent regulatory measures.

In response to these criticisms, it's widely acknowledged that Congress holds the responsibility for addressing the evolving concerns related to digital platforms and the scope of their legal immunities. As the legislative body that originally enacted Section 230, Congress is seen as the appropriate authority to reevaluate and amend the law to better align with the current digital landscape. This may involve refining the language to narrow the scope of immunity especially when the harm affects minors, imposing additional requirements for content moderation, or introducing mechanisms that increase platform accountability for the content they host or amplify.

Alex Jones and Infowars

The lawsuit against Alex Jones by the families of the Sandy Hook Elementary School shooting victims stands as a critical example of defamation within digital media and its negative impact on families. This case revolved around Jones's persistent promotion of the baseless assertion that the 2012 Newtown, Connecticut, massacre was a fabricated event, with the bereaved families labeled as actors in a supposed government scheme aimed at restricting gun rights. Alex Jones, known for his conspiracy theories and as the host of *Infowars*, had repeatedly broadcasted claims that the tragic shooting, which resulted in the deaths of twenty-six people, was a hoax. These unfounded statements led to prolonged harassment and threats directed at the victims' families by Jones's followers.

The legal battle culminated in significant verdicts against Jones, with a Texas jury in August 2022 awarding $49.3 million in damages to the parents of one victim, followed by a Connecticut jury's 2022 decision to order Jones to pay nearly $1 billion to a group of families affected by the tragedy. Jones faced a default judgment for his failure to comply with court orders, including the provision of crucial documents for the trial. Testimonies from the families during the Connecticut trial highlighted the deepened anguish caused by Jones's conspiracy theories.

These verdicts are notably among the highest financial penalties ever awarded in a defamation case, underscoring the severity of Jones's actions. The legal proceedings against Jones have brought to light the dire repercussions of disseminating falsehoods and established a significant precedent for holding individuals responsible for the tangible effects of their online speech, particularly when it inflicts widespread harm.

Despite the monumental awards, the enforceability of the judgments remains uncertain due to Jones's and his company's subsequent bankruptcy filings. Nonetheless, the families have voiced their determination to pursue the enforcement of the verdicts, although Jones's financial strategies and the bankruptcy cases might complicate these efforts.

In essence, the defamation suits against Alex Jones mark a critical moment in addressing the repercussions of false statements and their real-world impacts. This case reaffirms the value of truth and accountability in public discourse and signifies a potential shift in the legal approach to tackling defamation, especially in the era of digital media where conspiracy theories and misinformation can rapidly spread. Yet Jones continues to have a public forum on media broadcasts like "Tucker (Carlson) on X" and Joe Rogan's podcasts found on Spotify. However, the outcomes of these trials serve as a cautionary tale, illustrating the potential legal consequences for those who engage in defamatory speech, setting a precedent that may influence future legal actions against similar forms of harmful discourse.

Business Trade Libel

The intricacies of defamation law, particularly when it pertains to businesses, stem from the necessity to establish not only the inaccuracy of the contentious statement but also the intent of the issuer and the resultant

Chapter 6: Defamation, Deceit, and Disparagement in the Digital Age

damage. In the realm of US law, "trade libel" or "product disparagement" holds significant relevance for businesses. This legal domain zeros in on untrue declarations about a company's goods or services that lead to financial loss. A successful trade libel claim necessitates proving the falsehood of the statement about the product or services, its dissemination to a third party, the defendant's malice or reckless disregard for truth, and direct financial harm suffered by the business due to the statement.

The standard of "actual malice" becomes pivotal for public entities and businesses, especially in disputes touching on public interest. This criterion, solidified by the previously discussed Supreme Court decision in *New York Times Co. v. Sullivan*, mandates that the claimant proves the defamatory statement was made with knowledge of its falsity or with reckless indifference to its truthfulness. These stringent standards safeguard free expression while offering a recourse for addressing injurious falsehoods that can be particularly harmful to the reputation of businesses where news, falsehoods, and rumors travel quickly on social media.

In a case that marked a dramatic moment in legal history, Dominion Voting Systems, a manufacturer of voting machines, accused Fox News of broadcasting unfounded allegations during the 2020 US presidential election that its machines and software were manipulated to alter votes from Donald Trump to Joe Biden, feeding into wider conspiracy theories about election fraud. The lawsuit culminated in a $787 million settlement in favor of Dominion, a figure that underscores the severity of the claims and the potential damage to Dominion's business. Tucker Carlson, a prominent Fox News host now hosting *Tucker on X*, was suddenly fired from the network days after it settled the defamation lawsuit. This settlement was reached on the eve of what promised to be a contentious and highly publicized trial, sparing Fox News from further public scrutiny.

At the heart of Dominion's lawsuit were claims that Fox News had recklessly promoted baseless conspiracy theories, thus tarnishing Dominion's reputation. Evidence suggested that despite internal doubts among Fox News executives and on-air personalities about the truthfulness of these allegations, the network continued to air them. The lawsuit challenged the "actual malice" legal standard, a formidable defense for news outlets, requiring that plaintiffs prove the defendant knew the statements were false or exhibited a reckless disregard for the truth.

The outcome of this lawsuit carries broader implications for the media landscape, highlighting the fine line between freedom of the press and the necessity for responsible journalism. The hefty settlement serves as a cautionary tale for media entities regarding the repercussions of spreading misinformation. While Fox News acknowledged the inaccuracy of certain claims post-settlement, the absence of a formal apology leaves a lingering question about media accountability. Comments by Dominion's CEO underscored that no monetary compensation could fully rectify the harm inflicted by these falsehoods.

The digital media era as exemplified by the *Dominion v. Fox News* saga has introduced unprecedented challenges to maintaining accuracy in reporting. Several factors contribute to these challenges:

Speed over Accuracy: The rapid pace of digital media often prioritizes speed over accuracy, with outlets racing to publish stories first. This rush can lead to insufficient fact-checking or reliance on unverified sources, increasing the risk of disseminating false information.

Volume of Information: The sheer volume of information available online makes it difficult for both journalists and audiences to discern accurate reporting from misinformation. The abundance of sources, including social media, blogs, and traditional news outlets, complicates the verification process.

Echo Chambers and Confirmation Bias: Digital platforms often serve as echo chambers, where users are exposed to information that reinforces their preexisting beliefs. This environment can perpetuate misinformation, as false claims are shared and amplified within like-minded communities without critical scrutiny.

Anonymity and Lack of Accountability: The anonymity afforded by the internet allows individuals to spread false information without facing direct consequences. This lack of accountability can encourage the dissemination of defamatory content, as seen in the accusations against Dominion Voting Systems.

Economic Incentives: Digital media platforms and outlets often rely on advertising revenue, which can be driven by clicks and engagement. Sensational or controversial content, regardless of its accuracy, can attract more views, incentivizing outlets to prioritize engagement over truth.

Legal and Ethical Standards: The legal protections for freedom of speech, particularly in the United States, create a high threshold for proving defamation. This legal framework, while protecting the press and encouraging open debate, can also make it challenging to hold outlets accountable for spreading false information. The *Dominion v. Fox News* case highlighted the complexities of proving "actual malice" in defamation lawsuits, underscoring the delicate balance between protecting reputations and upholding free speech.

Manipulation and Propaganda: State actors and organized groups can exploit digital platforms to spread propaganda and manipulate public opinion. The global reach and accessibility of digital media make it an effective tool for influencing elections, public policy, and societal norms, further complicating the task of maintaining accurate reporting.

The manipulation of public opinion through digital platforms and AI by state or nation actors, especially in the context of influencing elections and shaping public policy, has been increasingly prevalent beyond reputational defamation concerns. Among the notable examples, Russia's Internet Research Agency (IRA) stands out for its efforts during US presidential elections. The IRA leverages social media to disseminate disinformation, create divisive content, organize political rallies, and exacerbate social and political tensions in the United States.

China's engagement in public opinion manipulation employs AI technologies both domestically and internationally to control the narrative. AI-driven bots on social media platforms are used to amplify pro-government narratives and suppress dissent. Additionally, the "Great Firewall" exemplifies China's use of AI to censor information and manage the digital environment within its borders, showcasing the government's commitment to controlling the public discourse.

In Venezuela, AI-generated propaganda has taken a novel form with state media outlets producing deepfake videos of news anchors to spread pro-government messages. These videos, created using technologies provided by companies like Synthesia, highlight the advanced capabilities of AI in generating realistic and persuasive propaganda content, blurring the lines between reality and fabrication.

Iran's contribution to the landscape of digital manipulation involves disinformation campaigns targeted at the United States and other nations. Through the creation of fake news websites and social media accounts, Iran aims to sow discord and manipulate public perception, contributing to the global challenge of combating online disinformation.

The role of AI in eroding trust in information is a significant concern. The emergence of AI-generated content, including deepfakes and synthetic media, has led to a phenomenon known as the "liar's dividend," where the proliferation of false information makes it harder for people to distinguish between what is true and what is not, especially during critical times such as crises or political conflicts. The ease with which disinformation can be created and spread via AI technologies poses a significant challenge to democratic processes and the integrity of public discourse.

In another highly reported business defamation case, Tesla Motors filed a lawsuit against the BBC's "Top Gear" for libel and malicious falsehood, alleging the show falsely depicted its Roadster vehicle as running out of power during test laps, which Tesla claimed was misleading and detrimental to its business reputation. The court ultimately dismissed Tesla's lawsuit, determining that no reasonable viewer would equate the car's performance on a racetrack with its real-world capabilities, thereby siding with the defense of creative freedom and journalistic expression.

Conversely, Beef Product's Inc.'s (BPI's) lawsuit against ABC News involved a staggering claim of $1.9 billion over the network's coverage of its lean finely textured beef product, which ABC News labeled as "pink slime." BPI contended that such coverage misled consumers and inflicted severe financial damage on the company. The settlement of $177 million in favor of BPI underscores the profound impact media coverage can have on a business's reputation and the financial ramifications of defamation claims.

Defamation litigation involving businesses navigates the fine line between protecting the company's reputation and upholding the principle of free speech. The actual malice requirement for cases involving matters of public interest introduces additional complexity, underscoring the imperative for unequivocal evidence of intent. Overall, while US defamation law furnishes businesses with a mechanism to confront false and harmful assertions, the elevated proof burden and the imperative to harmonize free speech rights render these cases multifaceted and fraught with challenges.

Consumer Protection in Digital Media

Consumer protection in the digital media landscape has become an increasingly pressing issue, particularly as businesses gather and exploit consumer data more extensively. Regulatory agencies like the Federal

Trade Commission (FTC) play a crucial role in safeguarding consumers against deceptive practices, false advertising, and violations of data privacy.

One emblematic case that brought the issues of consumer privacy and consent to the forefront involved Vizio, a smart TV manufacturer now owned by Walmart. Recently, the FTC took significant action against Vizio for covertly collecting data on viewers' watching habits and selling this information to advertisers without consumer knowledge or consent. The FTC's complaint highlighted that Vizio's data collection on 11 million consumer TVs constituted unfair and deceptive practices under the Federal Trade Commission Act. The settlement with Vizio necessitated a $2.2 million payment to address the charges, underscoring the paramount importance of transparency and consumer consent in data collection practices.

This incident with Vizio serves as a critical reminder of the essential need for companies to obtain clear consumer consent before gathering and disseminating personal data. The FTC's enforcement actions have sent a strong message to the industry about the necessity for transparent data practices and securing consumer consent upfront.

The scrutiny over digital media platforms and online services' practices has only intensified. For instance, in 2023, the FTC issued orders to eight major social media and video streaming platforms to provide information on their methods for monitoring and curbing deceptive or fraudulent advertising. This move came in response to a significant increase in consumer financial losses to fraud on social media, which exceeded $1.2 billion in the last year reported.

The case of *FTC v. Devumi* represents a monumental moment in the regulation of digital commerce and the ethics of social media marketing. In 2019, the FTC settled its inaugural complaint against the deceptive sale of fabricated indicators of social media influence, marking a significant enforcement action against digital fraud. Devumi, LLC, and its owner were at the heart of this legal action, accused of engaging in the sale of fake social media metrics, including followers, subscribers, views, and likes across various platforms.

Devumi's business model was built on providing clients—a mix of celebrities, politicians, businesses, and other entities—with artificial means to boost their online presence and influence. By selling these fake indicators, Devumi offered its customers a shortcut to digital prominence, essentially allowing them to purchase an appearance of greater popularity and credibility than they actually possessed. This practice not only misled consumers who believed these indicators reflected genuine public engagement but also distorted the competitive landscape by elevating the standing of individuals and businesses through deceptive means.

The FTC's complaint highlighted several critical concerns, including the undermining of trust in digital platforms and the deceptive practices that could mislead consumers and distort market realities. By acting against Devumi, the FTC sent a clear message about the illegality of such practices and the importance of authenticity in digital interactions.

The settlement with Devumi required the company and its owner to cease all fraudulent activities related to the sale of social media influence indicators. Although financial penalties were limited due to Devumi's insolvency at the time of the settlement, the case set a precedent for future regulatory actions against similar deceptive practices online.

Moreover, the Consumer Financial Protection Bureau (CFPB) has also been active in this domain, issuing warnings that digital marketing providers must adhere to federal consumer finance protections. The CFPB has made it clear that digital marketing providers can be held liable for unfair, deceptive, or abusive acts or practices (UDAAPs) under the Consumer Financial Protection Act (CFPA) when they are materially involved in the development of content strategy for marketing financial products or services. The interpretive rule specifically targets digital marketing practices that go beyond merely providing time or space for advertisements. When digital marketers engage in activities such as identifying or selecting prospective customers, or selecting or placing content to affect consumer engagement, they are providing a material service and are therefore considered service providers subject to the CFPA. This includes situations where digital marketers use behavioral analytics and sophisticated targeting techniques to deliver highly personalized advertisements.

The "meme stock" phenomenon, particularly highlighted by the dramatic price surges of companies like GameStop and AMC, has drawn scrutiny from regulatory bodies such as the Securities and Exchange Commission (SEC) for potential market manipulation and fraud. This event was largely fueled by retail investors and traders congregating on online platforms, notably Reddit's WallStreetBets forum, where they coordinated buying efforts to drive up the stock prices of these companies. This activity not only resulted in significant volatility in the stock prices of the companies involved but also posed substantial losses to hedge funds and institutional investors that had short positions on these stocks, betting that their prices would fall.

Platforms like Reddit, Indeed, X, Twitter, and Discord have become influential spaces where individual investors can share insights, strategies, and coordinate actions. In 2022, the US Securities and Exchange Commission (SEC)'s securities brought fraud charges against several social media influencers who allegedly were involved in a scheme to manipulate stock prices, resulting in approximately $100 million in illegal gains. They falsely claimed to be investing in certain stocks to their followers, only to sell their shares for a profit once the stock prices rose, without disclosing their real intentions to sell.

Even high-profile celebrities have not been immune to entanglements with regulatory authorities over questionable social media investment promotions. Notably, Kim Kardashian was prohibited by the SEC from promoting any cryptocurrencies for three years and was fined $1 million. This action came after she was charged with recommending a crypto security to her 330 million Instagram followers without disclosing that she received payment for the endorsement. Similarly, actor Steven Seagal found himself in hot water with the SEC and agreed to a settlement requiring him to pay over $300,000. This agreement also included a three-year ban on promoting investments, stemming from charges related to undisclosed compensation for online investment endorsements. The pattern of such regulatory actions continued from earlier instances, such as when professional boxer Floyd Mayweather Jr. and music producer DJ Khaled settled with the SEC. They faced charges for not disclosing payments received for promoting investments in digital currency, illustrating the broader issue of undisclosed promotional activities by celebrities across various entertainment sectors.

The concerted efforts of the FTC, CFPB, and SEC highlight their commitment to enforcing consumer protection laws in the evolving digital sphere. These regulatory actions, from the Vizio case to the broader scrutiny of digital platforms' practices and the role of social media influencers, underscore the ongoing challenges and necessities for businesses and individuals in the digital media industry to engage in lawful, transparent practices that prioritize consumer privacy, fairness, integrity, and consent. As the digital landscape continues to develop with new technologies, the importance of adhering to consumer protection laws remains paramount, signaling a continuing trend toward greater accountability and protection in the digital economy by government regulators.

Global Perspectives

Defamation laws vary significantly across the globe, often reflecting a country's legal traditions, values concerning free speech, and the status of public figures. Unlike in the United States, where defamation is predominantly treated as a civil matter, requiring the plaintiff to prove "actual malice" in cases involving public figures, many countries incorporate criminal penalties for defamation, especially when it involves monarchs, heads of state, or public officials.

In the United Kingdom, a significant shift occurred in 2009 with the abolition of most criminal prosecution for defamation offenses. This move was motivated by the understanding that such archaic offenses could be used to justify restrictions on free speech in other countries. In New Zealand and Australia, defamation remains largely a civil offense, with New Zealand having abolished criminal defamation back in 1993. Yet specific forms of defamation, like spreading knowingly false information to influence voters or causing serious emotional distress online, can lead to criminal prosecution in New Zealand.

Conversely despite recommendations from international rights organizations, criminal defamation laws persist, and these laws are often more severe when the victim is a public official or figure, a stance that contravenes international standards. Japan provides a notable example where criminal defamation laws were tightened in 2022 following the suicide of Hana Kimura, a professional wrestler and reality television star whose death was attributed to severe online harassment and cyberbullying.

Kimura's death ignited a nationwide call for enhanced legal measures to combat defamation and bullying online. The legislative amendments enacted aim to deter cyberbullying by introducing the possibility of up to one year in prison or fines for offenders, marking a significant escalation from previous sanctions.

Under the Japanese legal system, defamation is subject to both criminal and civil proceedings. The Criminal Code's Article 230-1 stipulates penalties for publicly defaming someone by alleging facts, with potential imprisonment of up to three years or substantial fines, irrespective of the veracity of the claims. An exception exists for defamation concerning matters of public interest aimed at benefiting the public; here, if the alleged facts are proven true, no punishment is issued.

Japan's Civil Code, through Articles 709 and 710, provides for lawsuits based on tort, allowing courts to mandate measures for reputation restoration alongside or instead of awarding damages. A statute of limitations applies, expiring three years from when the victim became aware of the damage and the identity of the perpetrator, or twenty years from the tortious act.

Despite these provisions, enforcing defamation laws in Japan faces challenges, especially in the digital age. Victims often prefer criminal prosecution to civil lawsuits, attributed to relatively low damages awarded in civil cases (typically up to $50,000) and the proactive role of police in addressing criminal libel. This has led to the arrest of hundreds annually for criminal libel, underscoring Japan's stringent stance against defamation especially toward authority figures.

In Southeast Asia, nations such as Pakistan and Bangladesh have established defamation laws that enable both civil and criminal proceedings, including specific regulations that target actions perceived as diminishing the authority or the institutions of the state. These laws have sparked significant debate due to their implications on freedom of expression and press freedom.

In Pakistan, civil cases typically seek reparations for damages to reputation, whereas the criminal approach may result in incarceration and monetary fines. A particularly controversial element of Pakistan's defamation laws is the proposed legislation that aims to criminalize "ridiculing" or "scandalizing" the military or judiciary. This proposal advocates for penalties of up to five years in prison and significant fines for those found guilty of such offenses.

Recent cases and discussions around defamation laws in Pakistan have shown a trend toward using these laws in various contexts, including potentially to silence victims of sexual harassment or to curb dissent and criticism. The Women's Action Forum (WAF) and other activist organizations have expressed concerns about the misuse of criminal defamation laws as a deterrent against individuals seeking relief or speaking out on sensitive issues like sexual assault and abuse by prominent figures.

Similarly, Bangladesh enforces strict penalties for online defamation through its Information Technology (IT) law, positioning itself at a critical juncture between protecting reputations and ensuring the right to free speech in an increasingly digital world. The law stipulates severe criminal consequences for publishing material online deemed to be false and defamatory. The law covers a wide range of subjective offenses, including publishing information that is "fake and obscene," "deteriorates law and order," "prejudices the image of the state or a person," or "hurts or may hurt religious belief or instigate against any person or organization" without adequately defining any of these terms.

An example of the application of Bangladesh's defamation law occurred when Abdul Latif Morol, a journalist from Bangladesh, was arrested after posting a satirical comment about the demise of a goat, a gift from a state minister. The situation surrounding Morol and other journalists exemplifies the potential for defamation laws to be wielded in a manner that seems excessively punitive relative to the accused conduct. Furthermore, it highlights ongoing concerns regarding the abuse of authority and the intimidatory impact such actions may have on the freedom of speech.

In China, defamation laws are multifaceted, including both civil and criminal components, and are frequently employed against those who critique the government or partake in activities seen as critical of the state. Civilly, defamation falls under tort law, safeguarding individuals' rights to reputation, honor, and privacy. Violations of these rights necessitate the offender to assume tort liability, with potential remedies encompassing the cessation of infringement, reputation restoration, effect elimination, apologies, and mental harm compensation.

Criminally, defamation becomes prosecutable under Article 246 of the Criminal Law when it poses a serious risk to public order, such as protesting against the Chinese government in Tiananmen Square, particularly in remembrance of the 1989 Tiananmen Square massacre by China against its own protesting citizens, or the national interest, targeting acts of written or oral defamation or libel that damage an individual's reputation, unauthorized disclosure of personal details causing reputational harm, or inaccurate news reporting leading to reputational damage.

Furthermore, in China, attempts to search for terms associated with "4 June Tiananmen Square" on the internet often lead to censored outcomes or can even trigger temporary disruptions in internet connectivity. The censorship apparatus meticulously filters web pages containing certain keywords and entirely blocks access to sites that promote the Chinese democracy movement from abroad.

The application of these laws has extended to the suppression of dissent and narrative control over sensitive issues. Notable instances include the imprisonment of Qiu Ziming, a well-known blogger, for questioning China's casualty figures in a border skirmish with India, under laws that penalize defamation against "heroes and martyrs" with up to three years in prison for severe offenses. Similarly, Luo Changping faced arrest for comments deemed insulting to the People's Volunteer Army on Weibo—a popular Chinese microblogging platform, often compared to Twitter, that allows users to post short messages, images, and videos. A woman surnamed Xu was sentenced to seven months in prison after making online remarks that were construed as derogatory toward Dong Cunrui, a revered historical figure in China. Dong Cunrui is celebrated for his sacrifice during the Chinese Civil War, and Xu's comments, which compared him unfavorably to fictional and negative characters, were seen as an insult to his memory and, by extension, to the values of the Communist Party.

Ai Weiwei, a renowned Chinese artist and activist, chose to leave China due to the country's repressive policies on freedom of speech and expression, including restrictions on visual art. His bold and provocative work, often critical of the Chinese government's stance on human rights, democracy, and freedom of expression, led to his increased surveillance, harassment, and eventual detention by Chinese authorities. Seeking a space where he could freely express his art and opinions without fear of government reprisal, Ai Weiwei relocated to countries that offered him the liberty to continue his work and advocacy, living in places like Germany, Great Britain, and the United States.

These examples underline the broad and politically motivated interpretation of defamation laws in China, used to curb criticism and manage public discourse, drawing international scrutiny. The implementation of these laws, particularly in political and historical contexts, has sparked concerns over their stifling effect on freedom of expression and the Chinese Communist Party's use of such legislation to maintain a specific narrative and suppress dissent. Hence, while ostensibly aimed at protecting reputational rights, China's defamation laws have been leveraged to penalize government criticism and control the flow of dissenting opinions, raising significant concerns about the infringement on the freedom of speech and the right to political dissent.

In the African nation of Nigeria, defamation is acknowledged as both a civil wrong and a criminal offense, encompassing libel and slander with significant potential repercussions for the accused. Civil defamation in Nigeria is actionable without the need to prove actual damages, with examples including false accusations of a punishable crime, false statements about communicable diseases like HIV/AIDS, or professional conduct that could harm one's reputation. Conversely, criminal defamation, as defined in Section 373 of the Nigerian Criminal Code, involves acts that could injure someone's reputation, exposing them to contempt or ridicule or harming their professional standing. There have been instances where these laws were used against online journalists and critics. Well-known cases include the arrest of bloggers and digital publishers for reporting on governmental figures misusing funds or engaging in criminal activities, highlighting the laws' misuse. Defenses against defamation charges in Nigeria include mistake of fact, mere vulgar abuse, comments on public interest, and innocent dissemination. Despite the legal frameworks in place to protect against defamation, the application of these laws, especially against media members, indicates a contentious aspect of Nigeria's legal landscape regarding freedom of expression and press freedom.

In Russia, the legal landscape regarding defamation has evolved to increasingly target government critics, particularly those voicing opposition to the war in Ukraine. The nation's defamation laws criminalize libel and the insult of public officials, with recent amendments extending these provisions to include acts perceived as defaming or "discrediting" the military and its volunteers. These legislative changes, under the leadership of President Vladimir Putin, form part of a wider initiative to control the narrative surrounding Russia's military engagements, notably its involvement in Ukraine.

A marked development occurred recently when President Putin enacted legislation penalizing the defamation or "discrediting" of military volunteers, reinforcing efforts to monitor and shape public discourse on Russia's military actions. Further tightening the noose, in 2024, the Russian parliament deliberated on a bill aimed at enabling the state to confiscate the property of individuals convicted of defaming the security forces or making public calls against state security. This proposed legislation specifically targets those criticizing the war in Ukraine, including expatriates with property holdings in Russia, illustrating a strategic move to penalize dissent and curb freedom of speech.

The repercussions of these legislative changes on freedom of expression in Russia are profound. By leveraging laws against defamation and the discrediting of military activities, the state effectively muzzles dissent and restricts public discourse regarding the Ukraine conflict. High-profile cases, such as the charges against renowned novelist Boris Akunin for discrediting the military and the sentencing in absentia of writer Dmitry Glukhovsky to eight years for disseminating "false information" about the armed forces, underscore the legal system's role in suppressing opposition voices.

International observers and human rights organizations have expressed alarm over the application of defamation laws to stifle freedom of expression and debate in Russia. The evolution of the internet and digital communication platforms, while amplifying challenges in reputation management, has also served as a pretext for the enactment of stringent legal measures curtailing online freedom and the right to dissent. Despite global concerns, the Russian government has persisted in augmenting its defamation statutes, particularly concerning criticisms of the Ukraine war, raising significant concerns about the future of open discourse and democratic freedoms in Russia.

The global status of defamation laws encapsulates the delicate uneasy equilibrium between safeguarding individuals' reputations and ensuring the freedom of expression. This balance is influenced by diverse legal and cultural frameworks that range from initiatives to decriminalize defamation, aligning with international human rights standards, to the implementation of severe criminal penalties, especially in cases implicating public figures or state entities. Within the sphere of international human rights, defamation is navigated with consideration to the protection against "unlawful attacks" on one's "honor and reputation," as delineated in Article 17 of the International Covenant on Civil and Political Rights (ICCPR). However, the application of defamation laws has often been critiqued for suppressing freedom of expression and dissent, highlighting the challenge of striking a fair balance between reputation protection and speech freedom. The trend in more democratic nations toward decriminalization acknowledges the disproportionate impact of criminal penalties on free speech, yet the digital age introduces complexities with the rise of online defamation in an era of hate speech and deepfakes, and the ambiguity in applying traditional laws to the internet.

International jurisprudence, including rulings from the European Court of Human Rights and the United Nations Human Rights Committee, underscores the necessity of balancing reputation protection with free speech assurance, often critiquing criminal defamation laws and advocating for civil remedies. Despite these international inclinations, some nations like China and Russia persist in using strict defamation laws politically to silence dissenters and critics. The ongoing global dialogue on defamation laws continues to confront the challenges of online defamation, the potential misuse of laws to stifle dissent, and the efficacy of legal reforms in genuinely promoting free speech, underscoring the continuing debate over protecting reputation without unduly curtailing the right to free expression in an increasingly digital world where many nations seek to stifle any dissent.

AI and Defamation

In the emerging legal digital media landscape, the question of whether artificial intelligence (AI) can bear legal responsibility for defamatory statements is increasingly pertinent. A remarkable case that dives into this issue involves OpenAI, the organization behind the AI language model ChatGPT, illustrating the complexities of defamation claims in the context of AI-generated content.

In 2023, radio host Mark Walters initiated a legal battle against OpenAI in a Georgia state court, centering on allegations that ChatGPT had generated and disseminated a summary with false and defamatory content about him. The contested summary, which was provided to a journalist, erroneously implicated Walters in embezzlement activities from a nonprofit organization, a claim Walters staunchly denied, asserting the complete falsehood of every alleged fact concerning him presented by the AI.

OpenAI's defense strategy to seek dismissal of the case hinged on the argument that Walters's claim failed to meet the foundational requirements of a defamation lawsuit. The defense underscored the terms of use of ChatGPT, which caution users about the potential inaccuracies in the content generated by the AI, indicating that users should critically assess the veracity of any information produced. This stance posits that users, and not OpenAI, bear the ultimate responsibility for any content released into the public domain.

The legal dispute brings to the forefront critical considerations regarding the accountability of AI systems and their developers for defamatory content. Traditional defamation laws necessitate that the aggrieved party demonstrate that the defendant knowingly disseminated false information to a third party, causing harm. Applying these established legal principles to AI-generated materials introduces novel hurdles, such as the applicability of intent or malice to an AI's actions and the extent of responsibility that should be attributed to AI developers or users for the output generated.

The broader policy ramifications of this case are profound, signaling a pivotal moment as AI technologies become increasingly woven into the fabric of daily life. The potential for AI systems to fabricate or "hallucinate" misinformation underscores urgent concerns about the propagation of unfounded claims and the subsequent damage to individuals' reputations, and not insignificantly how to seek redress for the harm done to one's reputation. Consequently, the legal domain is now challenged with adapting traditional defamation doctrines to address the unique dynamics presented by AI entities.

The resolution of the *Walters v. OpenAI* case is poised to establish important legal precedents for handling defamation claims involving AI-generated content. Should OpenAI be held accountable for the defamatory statements produced by ChatGPT, it could significantly influence the future development and utilization of AI technologies. Alternatively, a decision absolving the AI developer from liability might catalyze more rigorous regulatory measures aimed at mitigating the risks associated with AI outputs.

In essence, the *Walters v. OpenAI* lawsuit serves as a first-of-its-kind case, testing the limits of defamation law in an era increasingly dominated by artificial intelligence. The principles and regulatory frameworks that emerge from this legal inquiry will likely shape the treatment of AI-induced falsehoods and the accountability mechanisms for technology firms behind AI innovations, marking a decisive moment in the intersection of law, ethics, and technology.

Summary

The advent of digital media has transformed the landscape of communication, bringing with it new challenges and complexities in the realm of defamation law. Noteworthy legal cases, such as *Barrett v. Rosenthal*, *Dominion v. Fox*, *Elon Musk*, and *Alex Jones* have been instrumental in shaping the understanding of intent, intermediary liability and even the responsibilities of digital platforms in moderating content. These cases highlight the evolving legal interpretations of defamation in the context of social media and other online forums, setting precedents that influence how future disputes are resolved.

At the heart of many of these legal battles is Section 230 of the Communications Decency Act (CDA) of 1996, a foundational law of the digital age that insulates online platforms from lawsuits for content posted by their users. This legal provision has created a regime of nonregulation in the United States, allowing digital platforms to operate with minimal restraint in online publishing. Unlike traditional publishers, which can be held liable for false assertions causing injury, Section 230 protects platforms such as X, Facebook, and Instagram from defamation claims. This broad immunity has opened doors for both the dissemination of misinformation and disinformation, and the potential for harm, as platforms can profit from audience reach while enjoying protection from legal repercussions.

The "meme stock" phenomenon, where users of online platforms like Reddit's WallStreetBets influenced the stock prices of companies like GameStop and AMC, serves as an illustrative example of the potential for digital media to impact financial markets. This event prompted scrutiny from the Securities and Exchange Commission (SEC) for potential manipulation and fraud, underscoring the challenges regulatory bodies face in monitoring digital platforms.

Social media platforms serve as fertile ground for the spread of false information especially when exploited by foreign adversaries, exponentially increasing the potential for defamation, and undermining democratic norms and policies. The dynamics of social media defamation, characterized by rapid dissemination and anonymization of sources, present new challenges for identifying perpetrators and holding them accountable. The legal landscape must adapt to address the multifaceted nature of online activities and the legal and ethical challenges they pose, encompassing both civil and criminal charges.

The digital media era has ushered in a new legal frontier for defamation, requiring a delicate balance between protecting free speech and ensuring accountability for false and damaging statements. The integration of AI raises pressing questions about the origin of defamatory content and the extent to which creators of AI, alongside users and platforms, can be held responsible. As digital platforms continue to play a central role in how information is disseminated and consumed, regulatory bodies and the legal system must navigate the complexities of this evolving landscape to uphold the principles of justice and fairness in the digital age.

Discussion Questions

1. How do artificial intelligence (AI) and deepfake technologies challenge the current legal definitions of defamation in digital media?
2. In what ways can international cooperation and harmonization of legal standards effectively address cross-border defamation in the digital age?
3. What ethical considerations should guide the development and use of AI-driven tools in detecting and mitigating the spread of digital misinformation?
4. How does Section 230 of the Communications Decency Act balance the need for freedom of expression with the protection against digital defamation? Should it be reformed, and if so, how?
5. What are the implications of applying traditional defamation defenses, such as truth, opinion, and privilege, in the context of digital media?
6. How do varying global approaches to defamation involving public officials reflect on the principles of free speech and democracy?
7. What role do digital platforms have in preventing the spread of defamatory content without infringing on users' rights to free speech?
8. How can legal frameworks adapt to the rapid technological advancements in digital media to protect individuals from reputational harm?

9. Discuss the potential consequences of criminalizing speech about public figures in certain jurisdictions compared to others that offer broad protections for such speech.
10. In what ways can public education and awareness about the risks and realities of digital defamation contribute to a more informed and respectful online discourse?

Works Referenced

"AI and Manipulation on Social and Digital Media." Rathenau Institute, June 3, 2022, accessed at https://www.rathenau.nl/en/digitalisering/ai-and-manipulation-social-and-digital-media

Aral, Sinan. "What Digital Advertising Gets Wrong." *Harvard Business Review*, February 19, 2021, accessed at https://hbr.org/2021/02/what-digital-advertising-gets-wrong

Bauder, David, Chase, Randall, and Mulvihill, Geoff. "Fox, Dominion Reach $787M Settlement over Election Claims." AP News, April 18, 2023, accessed at https://apnews.com/article/fox-news-dominion-lawsuit-trial-trump-2020-0ac71f75acfacc52ea80b3e747fb0afe

"Comparing U.S. Libel Laws with Other Nations." Radford University Comm Law and Ethics 400 accessed at https://revolutionsincommunication.com/law/intl-libel/

Conway, Danielle M. "Defamation in the Digital Age: Liability in Chat Rooms, on Electronic Bulletin Boards, and in the Blogosphere." *ALI-ABA Bus. L. Course Materials J*, 17 (2005).

"CFPB Warns that Digital Marketing Providers Must Comply with Federal Consumer Finance Protections." Consumer Financial Protection Bureau, August 10, 2022, accessed at https://www.consumerfinance.gov/about-us/newsroom/cfpb-warns-that-digital-marketing-providers-must-comply-with-federal-consumer-finance-protections

Gans, Jared. "US Government Charges Social Media Influencers with Securities Fraud." *The Hill*, December 14, 2022, accessed at https://thehill.com/business/3774945-us-government-charges-social-media-influencers-with-securities-fraud

Greiner, Thomas, "United States Legal Perspective on AI Defamation." *Media Laws*, November 23, 2023, accessed at https://www.medialaws.eu/united-states-legal-perspective-on-ai-defamation

Johnson, Vincent R. "Comparative Defamation Law: England and the United States." *University of Miami International and Comparative Law Review,* Vol. 24, No. 1 (Fall 2016), Article 3, 8-28-2017.

Jones, Michael, *Art Law,* 2nd ed. Rowman & Littlefield, Lanham, MD, 2023.

Kong, Sasha. "China: Where a Post Can Land You in Prison." *FairPlanet,* February 21, 2022 accessed at https://www.fairplanet.org/story/china-where-a-post-can-land-you-in-prison

Nord, James. "ABC Settles Pink Slime Defamation Suit for More than $177 Million." *Chicago Tribune,* August 10, 2018, accessed at https://www.chicagotribune.com/2017/08/10/abc-settled-pink-slime-defamation-suit-for-more-than-177-million

Online Defamation Law, Electronic Freedom Foundation, 2014, accessed at https://www.eff.org/issues/bloggers/legal/liability/defamation

Poritz, Isaiah. "First ChatGPT Defamation Lawsuit to Test AI's Legal Liability." *Bloomberg Law,* June 12, 2023, accessed at https://news.bloomberglaw.com/ip-law/first-chatgpt-defamation-lawsuit-to-test-ais-legal-liability

Socha, Michael. "Double Standard: A Comparison of British and American Defamation Law." *Penn State International Law Review,* Vol. 23, No. 2, Article 9, 10-1-2004

"What Are the Defamation Laws around the World?" *Times of India,* March 24, 2023, accessed at https://timesofindia.indiatimes.com/india/what-are-the-defamation-laws-around-the-world/articleshow/98951867.cms

7

Data Protection, National Security, and Hacking: Defending the Digital Frontier

Data and its exploration can be endless. We cannot know everything but sometimes everything we know is enough.

—Anonymous

Former FBI director James Comey once starkly observed, "There are two kinds of companies in the United States. There are those who've been hacked by the Chinese, and those who don't know they've been hacked by the Chinese." This chapter looks into the complex issues at the forefront of data protection, national security, and the swift pace of the digital era, using Comey's statement to underscore the pervasive threat of cyberattacks in our current digital landscape.

The increase in data breaches, unauthorized access to critical information, and the exploitation of digital platforms have escalated into significant global concerns. What were once considered secure digital boundaries are now easily penetrated by hackers, leading to substantial leaks of confidential data and, in some instances, endangering national security. Moreover, the digital media space, previously lauded for its potential for innovation, has transformed into a battleground where privacy rights, freedom of expression, and state security interests frequently clash. This chapter aims to outline the legal frameworks developed to confront these challenges and critically evaluate their efficacy. Through a detailed analysis, we endeavor to survey the complex terrain of digital media law, spotlighting the continuous effort to protect our digital ecosystem from the risks of unauthorized access and cyberattacks.

The chapter material includes examples of significant breaches within the digital media landscape, such as the Facebook-Cambridge Analytica scandal that raised serious concerns about privacy, consent, and the ethical handling of user data, leading to stricter data protection laws like the **General Data Protection Regulation (GDPR)**. The 2020 SolarWinds cyber espionage case underscored the national security risks of digital breaches, with malicious actors accessing sensitive information through a widespread software compromise. In 2024, thousands of Roku user accounts were obtained by "unauthorized individuals" who in some cases sought to purchase streaming subscriptions via the hack. A few years back the names, addresses, phone numbers, birth dates, email addresses and encrypted credit card details of nearly 500 million Marriott customers were stolen including the travel histories and passport numbers of a smaller number of hotel guests.

In the most recently reported year in the United States, more than 350 million individuals, or nearly every person living in America, were affected by data breaches, leakage and exposure. Data breaches, which involve unauthorized access to private and sensitive information, present a multifaceted threat for entities across the board, including businesses, governments, and individuals. The repercussions of such incidents are far-reaching, encompassing not only substantial financial losses but also lasting damage to an organization's or individual's reputation, alongside potential legal consequences. The spectrum of breaches spans from the tangible—such as the physical theft of devices carrying sensitive data, including laptops and smartphones—to the digital realm, where sophisticated cyberattacks like ransomware, phishing, and malware infections prevail.

Ransomware attacks have become particularly notorious, with cybercriminals encrypting victims' data and demanding hefty ransoms for the decryption keys. Yet paying these ransoms offers no guarantee of data recovery, leaving affected entities in a precarious position. Equally concerning are attacks that hinge on password compromise, where attackers deploy brute force or dictionary attacks to unlock unauthorized access to systems. This highlights the vulnerability of weak or reused passwords—a seemingly simple oversight that can open the floodgates to significant breaches.

The list of prevalent breach methods extends to keylogging and phishing attacks, which stealthily harvest sensitive information, and malware or virus infections that compromise system integrity from within. Distributed Denial of Service (DDoS) attacks, while not directly aimed at stealing data, incapacitate services, often serving as a smokescreen for more insidious breaches. Similarly, malvertising introduces malware through corrupted digital ads, silently infecting users' devices. On a broader scale, supply chain attacks target vulnerabilities in third-party vendors and service providers, exploiting these connections to infiltrate multiple organizations simultaneously. Insider threats, whether malicious or negligent, underscore the risk posed by those with authorized access exploiting their privileges, while DNS tunneling offers attackers a covert channel to siphon off data undetected. Data poisoning is the latest form of data breach related to the surge of AI advancements. In this instance, data are not merely hacked but also manipulated by bad actors.

In response to these incidents, governments, industry stakeholders, privacy advocacy groups, and international organizations have introduced regulatory frameworks aimed at attempting to enhance personal data protection and securing digital platforms. This chapter will peruse key pieces of legislation, such as the GDPR, the **California Consumer Privacy Act (CCPA)** and the **Cybersecurity Information Sharing Act (CISA)**, scrutinizing their impacts and the extent to which they have succeeded in mitigating the risks associated with digital media breaches. Through case studies, legal analysis, and policy review, we aim to offer a thorough overview of the current state of digital media law and the ongoing efforts to protect the digital ecosystem from unauthorized access and cyber threats.

What Constitutes Data and Why Is Protection Important

In the digital media era, the meaning of the term *data* encompasses a vast array of information ranging from personal identifiers like names and email addresses to more sensitive details such as financial data, DNA, purchasing habits, and health records. This era is marked by an unparalleled surge in data creation and storage, propelled by the ubiquity of internet-connected devices and the digital transformation of traditional business models. Data, in this context, emerge not just as a by-product of digital activity but as a cornerstone of organizational strategy, fueling everything from operational decisions to the personalized experiences that have become the hallmark of digital platforms. However, this extensive reliance on data has ushered in significant privacy and security challenges, catalyzing a global push toward enacting more robust data protection and privacy measures.

Data protection strategies are designed to shield data from unauthorized access, corruption, or loss, emphasizing the privacy, integrity, and availability of data. These measures range from encryption and access controls to comprehensive data backup and recovery plans, and adherence to government regulations. Conversely, data privacy, as discussed in an earlier chapter, zeros in on the rights of individuals over their personal data, advocating for ethical usage and stringent consent mechanisms that empower users to control their data footprint.

The imperative for demanding data protection and privacy practices is underscored by the repercussions of data breaches, which can lead to financial losses, reputational damage, and legal penalties. Moreover, establishing trust through diligent data stewardship is increasingly recognized as vital for the sustainability of digital platforms and services.

In this digital milieu, companies amass vast quantities of data to drive advertising, market research, product development, and customer service. This data collection is motivated by a desire to decode consumer behaviors, preferences, and trends, enabling the creation of highly targeted marketing initiatives and customized user experiences. For example, the advertising sector leverages user data through sophisticated algorithms to deliver personalized ads, such as presenting sports apparel advertisements to a user frequently searching for running shoes. This tailored approach not only augments the efficacy of advertising campaigns but also boosts businesses' return on investment.

However, the shift toward cloud-based data storage introduces a new spectrum of security challenges, including vulnerabilities to unauthorized access and breaches. The cloud encompasses a vast network of remote servers globally interconnected to function as a cohesive ecosystem. These servers, designed to store, manage, and process data, offer users and organizations the capability to access and utilize software and databases over the internet. This eliminates the reliance on local servers or personal computers and provides advantages such as scalability, flexibility, cost-efficiency, and the convenience of accessing services and data from any location with an internet connection.

This transition toward cloud-based data storage necessitates that companies rigorously ensure their cloud storage solutions are equipped with vigorous security measures. To address the new spectrum of security challenges presented by the cloud, companies must implement stringent security protocols to identify and mitigate potential vulnerabilities before they can be exploited.

To safeguard data, companies implement various protective measures:

- **Encryption**: This makes data unreadable without the appropriate decryption key, providing a critical layer of security for intercepted or unauthorizedly accessed information.
- **Access Controls**: By limiting data access to authorized personnel, companies can significantly reduce the risk of data breaches.
- **Data Backup and Recovery**: Regular data backups and a solid disaster recovery strategy are essential for quick restoration in the event of data loss or corruption.
- **Compliance with Regulations**: Adherence to legal frameworks like the GDPR and CCPA is crucial for maintaining compliance and steering clear of financial penalties.

The imperative for companies to protect personal data from unauthorized threat actors transcends multiple facets of business operations, encompassing legal compliance, financial stability, customer trust, company reputation, intellectual property protection, and business continuity. Companies are mandated by data protection laws in the European Union and in California, among other regional and international regulations, to enforce mandated handling, processing, and protection of personal data, yet in many cases it is not enough.

Customer trust, which serves as a competitive advantage, is significantly bolstered by those companies who are fully committed to data privacy, as seen in Apple's emphasis on privacy as a core aspect of its products and services. This approach not only differentiates Apple in a saturated market but also cultivates consumer faith. Similarly, a company's reputation can suffer irreparable damage from data breaches, as evidenced by the Equifax incident, where the exposure of sensitive credit data of roughly 147 million individuals led to a sharp decline in stock value and public trust.

The economic fallout from data breaches extends beyond legal fines to include direct financial losses from legal fees, compensatory payments, and other breach-related expenses. The Target data breach from a few years ago exemplifies this, with costs surpassing $202 million, highlighting the substantial economic impact. Furthermore, breaches can result in the loss of intellectual property and sensitive business information, detrimental to a company's competitive edge, as demonstrated by the industrial espionage faced by Nortel Networks, which significantly affected its business operations.

Operational disruptions caused by data breaches, such as the WannaCry ransomware attack that impacted the UK's National Health Service and businesses globally, emphasize the importance of data protection for ensuring the continuity of services and products. Protecting personal data, therefore, is not merely a legal obligation but a critical component of safeguarding the company's reputation, protecting intellectual property, and ensuring the uninterrupted operation of business functions. The examples highlighted herein illustrate the broad and significant impact of data breaches and the indispensable nature of top-level data protection measures, yet for the customer whose private data have been compromised or stolen there are frequently few equitable remedies beyond receiving a year's worth of free credit checking.

Weighing the collection and utilization of data with ethical and legal considerations is paramount. Companies must balance the delicate act of obtaining explicit consent from individuals before collecting their data, ensuring transparency in their data collection practices, and offering mechanisms for data correction or deletion. This equilibrium between innovation and individual rights is fundamental to the ethical use of data in the digital age, ensuring that the relentless pursuit of personalized experiences does not come at the cost of privacy, trust, and security.

Data Protection Laws in the European Union

The evolution of data protection laws in the United States and Europe has been significantly shaped by technological advancements and growing concerns over privacy. In the United States, data protection is governed by a patchwork of sector-specific laws and state-level regulations rather than a single, comprehensive federal law. Key federal examples include the **Health Insurance Portability and Accountability Act (HIPAA)** for health information, the **Gramm-Leach-Bliley Act (GLBA)** for financial information, and the **Children's Online Privacy Protection Act (COPPA)** for children's online privacy. Additionally, state laws like the **California Consumer Privacy Act (CCPA)** have introduced broader protections similar to those found in European regulations, covering consumer rights such as access, deletion, and the option to opt out of the sale of personal information. Enforcement actions in the United States can result in substantial fines and settlements, exemplified by Facebook's $5 billion settlement with the Federal Trade Commission (FTC) over privacy violations.

In contrast, Europe has adopted a more unified and comprehensive approach with the **General Data Protection Regulation (GDPR)**, which came into effect in May 2018. The GDPR was introduced in response to the profound changes in our lives brought about by the internet and technological advancements, aiming to modernize data protection laws to keep pace with these changes. It establishes strict requirements for data handling and grants individuals significant control over their personal data, including rights to access, rectify, erase, and object to data processing. The GDPR's broad scope applies to all organizations processing the personal data of EU citizens, regardless of the organization's location, making it a global standard for data protection.

Specifically, these are the key compliance requirements of the GDPR:

1. **Lawfulness, Fairness, and Transparency (Article 5):** Organizations must process data lawfully, fairly, and in a transparent manner in relation to the data subject.
2. **Purpose Limitation (Article 5):** Data must be collected for specified, explicit, and legitimate purposes and not further processed in a manner that is incompatible with those purposes.
3. **Data Minimization (Article 5):** The collection of data must be adequate, relevant, and limited to what is necessary in relation to the purposes for which they are processed.
4. **Accuracy (Article 5):** Organizations must ensure that personal data are accurate and, where necessary, kept up to date.
5. **Storage Limitation (Article 5):** Data should be kept in a form that permits identification of data subjects for no longer than is necessary for the purposes for which the personal data are processed.

6. **Integrity and Confidentiality (Article 5):** Data must be processed in a manner that ensures appropriate security of the personal data, including protection against unauthorized or unlawful processing and against accidental loss, destruction, or damage.
7. **Rights of the Data Subject (Articles 12–23):** GDPR provides data subjects with various rights, including the right to access their data, the right to have incorrect data corrected, the right to have their data erased (the right to be forgotten), the right to restrict processing, the right to data portability, and the right to object to processing.
8. **Data Protection by Design and by Default (Article 25):** Organizations must implement appropriate technical and organizational measures designed to implement data protection principles in an effective way and to integrate the necessary safeguards into the processing.
9. **Data Protection Impact Assessments (Article 35):** For processing that is likely to result in a high risk to the rights and freedoms of individuals, organizations must carry out assessments of the impact of the envisaged processing operations on the protection of personal data.
10. **Notification of a Data Breach (Articles 33 and 34):** In the event of a data breach, organizations must notify the appropriate data protection authority within seventy-two hours, unless the breach is unlikely to result in a risk to the rights and freedoms of individuals. When the breach is likely to result in a high risk to the rights and freedoms of natural persons, the organization must also communicate the breach to the affected data subjects without undue delay.

Consequences of Noncompliance

Organizations that fail to comply with the GDPR can face significant penalties, including fines of up to €20 million or 4 percent of the annual global revenue of the preceding financial year, whichever is higher. The level of fines depends on the severity of the breach, the nature of the data involved, the duration of the infringement, and the intentional or negligent character of the infringement, among other factors.

Real-world examples of penalties include Google's €50 million fine by France's data regulatory body for lack of transparency, inadequate information, and absence of valid consent regarding tailoring advertisements to individual viewers based on their unique preferences, behaviors, and demographics; and British Airways' £183 million fine for inadequacies in security that led to a data breach affecting hundreds of thousands of customers. Compliance with the GDPR is not just about avoiding fines but also about protecting individuals' rights and fostering confidence in the digital economy.

Reach of GDPR to United States

The GDPR casts a wide net in its applicability, significantly impacting a variety of entities, including those well beyond the borders of the European Union. At its core, the GDPR mandates compliance from organizations established within the European Union irrespective of where the actual data processing occurs. This encompasses all organizations operating within the European Union that handle personal data as part of their operations.

Moreover, the laws extend to organizations outside the European Union that offer goods or services to EU residents or monitor their behavior, such as Amazon, Instagram, and YouTube. These companies, despite being headquartered in the United States, find themselves needing to comply with the GDPR because they process the personal data of individuals residing in the European Union. This compliance is necessary not just for direct transactions but also in instances where these platforms monitor the behavior of EU residents, which is often integral to their business models, particularly in advertising and personalized content delivery.

Public authorities and bodies within the European Union are also required to comply with GDPR, though certain exemptions exist to cater to governmental and public institutions, tailoring the regulation's application to the public sector's unique context. Interestingly, in 2024, the European Commission was found to have violated these very laws when in its contract with Microsoft, the Commission did not sufficiently specify what types of personal data are to be collected and for which explicit and specified purposes when using Microsoft 365.

The GDPR delineates responsibilities and obligations for both "data controllers" and "data processors." Data controllers, which could be any of these companies when they determine how and why personal data are processed, bear the brunt of GDPR compliance, ensuring the protection of data subjects' rights and the prompt reporting of data breaches. Data processors, on the other hand, handle personal data on controllers' behalf and, while their direct responsibilities under the GDPR are somewhat lesser, they are still crucial to the regulation's overall framework, especially in terms of data security and breach notification.

For US citizens, the GDPR's influence is indirect but significant. While the regulation is designed to protect EU residents' data, many international companies have opted to elevate their privacy practices globally rather than implementing region-specific standards. This means that US citizens often benefit from enhanced privacy protections because of the wide data protection swath of the GDPR.

Right to Erase Digital Past

The European Union's data protection law introduces a novel legal concept that addresses the digital age's profound challenges to privacy and autonomy: the right to erasure, or more commonly referred to as the "right to be forgotten." This right underscore a dramatic shift from the traditional dynamic where forgetting was natural and remembering required effort. In today's digital environment, the opposite is true; the internet's vast memory banks retain information indefinitely, challenging the very notion of privacy and the individual's control over their personal history making it difficult for individuals to escape their past.

Article 17 of the GDPR offers a legal remedy to these challenges, allowing individuals to request the deletion of personal data under certain conditions, such as when the information is no longer necessary for its original collection purpose because it is out of date, inaccurate or no longer relevant.

One of the most highly reported cases addressing the right to erasure is the Google Spain case adjudicated by the European Court of Justice (See: *Google Inc. v. Agencia Española de Protección de Datos (AEPD)* 62012CJ0131—EN—EUR-Lex—European Union). This ruling established that individuals have the right to request search engines like Google to remove links to web pages that contain personal information that is inaccurate, inadequate, irrelevant, or excessive for the purposes of processing. The case stemmed from a Spanish citizen's complaint about search results linking to an auction notice of his repossessed home, which he argued was no longer relevant. The court's decision underscored the balance between the public's right to know and individuals' right to privacy, setting a precedent for future requests for link removal from search engines.

Beyond search engine delisting, the right to erasure extends to social media and other online platforms, where individuals can request the deletion of their personal data. This includes posts, comments, images, and videos that users may no longer wish to be publicly accessible. For instance, a former college student might request the deletion of old school photos from a social media platform when they no longer reflect the person's current professional image. Similarly, individuals have successfully requested the removal of their contributions from online forums or comments from news articles, asserting their right to control personal data that might affect their privacy, job status, or reputation.

Moreover, the right to erasure has practical applications in e-commerce and online services. Nearly all digital customers can relate to receiving unsolicited messages frequently receiving an email from an online store highlighting a flash sale, a tactic often used to reengage customers who have made purchases in the past. Similarly, telecommunications companies might send text messages offering special deals on new smart phone plans, specifically targeting users whose contracts are about to expire, aiming to retain them as customers. Additionally, social media platforms leverage targeted advertising, where users encounter ads for services such as fitness subscription or weight-loss programs. These ads are meticulously tailored based on the user's past interactions with related content or searches on the platform thanks to cookies, illustrating how digital footprints are used to personalize marketing efforts. Consumers can ask for their data to be deleted from online retailers' databases, including past purchase history or subscription services, to prevent unwanted marketing communications or simply to exercise control over their data track.

The implementation of the right to erasure has not been without its challenges and controversies. Data controllers, from multinational corporations to small websites, have grappled with the technical and procedural complexities of completely erasing data. In some cases, data that have been widely disseminated or replicated across the internet can be particularly difficult to remove fully. Furthermore, debates continue over the right's implications for freedom of expression, the public interest in accessing information dealing with ethical breaches and criminal conduct, and the archival value of digital content. For example, journalists and historians have raised concerns about the potential for the right to erasure to be used to rewrite history or suppress freedom of speech.

Despite these challenges, the right to erasure under the GDPR marks a consequential step forward in acknowledging and addressing the complexities of privacy in the digital age. By enabling individuals to have a say in the management of their personal data online, it lays the groundwork for a more privacy-respecting digital environment, offering a model that could inspire similar protections globally, including potential future legislation in the United States that addresses the unique challenges of digital memory and identity in the twenty-first century.

Data Protection Laws in the United States

It is becoming more evident that regulatory bodies find it comparatively simple to oversee and control the movement of people, goods, and services across borders than to effectively regulate the complex and boundless flow of data on a global scale. The rapid proliferation of digital information, facilitated by the internet and other communication technologies, presents a formidable challenge to traditional regulatory frameworks. The task of managing technology, which has grown to a scale beyond our immediate grasp, remains a continuous and intricate endeavor. This situation underscores the need for innovative approaches and collaborative efforts to ensure that the governance of data keeps pace with its expansion and impact on society.

States across the United States are spearheading initiatives to fill the void left by the lack of a unified federal digital data protection framework. This movement led by California aims to empower American consumers with greater autonomy over the collection, usage, and sharing of their personal data by businesses.

The **California Consumer Privacy Act (CCPA),** in force since 2020, and an amendment to the original Act, the **California Privacy Rights Act (CPRA**), effective January 1, 2023, are key pieces of groundbreaking legislation emphasizing the importance of consumer data privacy. These laws play a vital role for well-known websites, such as Instagram, YouTube, Amazon, X, and Google that conduct online business with the personal information of Californian residents. These statutes grant California residents various rights regarding their personal information, including the right to know what personal data are collected about them, the right to delete personal information, the right to opt out of the sale or sharing of their personal information, and more recently, rights to correct inaccurate information and limit the use of sensitive personal information.

While the **CCPA** and **CPRA** are designed with California residents in mind, explicitly limiting their scope to individuals residing within the state, their impact is not strictly confined to California's borders. Despite the clear delineation by the CCPA that a California resident includes any natural person living in the state, regardless of temporary absences, these protections are not formally afforded to residents of other US states. However, the influence of the CCPA and CPRA can be felt by non-California residents in several indirect ways. For instance, businesses striving to comply with these laws may choose to apply the data privacy standards uniformly to all their customers, not only those in California, resulting in enhanced privacy protections for individuals elsewhere as a by-product of streamlined business operations.

Furthermore, the CCPA has served as a pioneering model for data privacy legislation in other states such as Virginia, Colorado, and Nevada among a growing number of other states. These states have either enacted or are in the process of considering privacy laws inspired by California's example, potentially extending similar rights and protections to their residents. Additionally, the logistic challenges associated with segmenting data practices for different states have led some national and global companies to adopt a more uniform approach. These organizations may offer the rights and protections stipulated by the CCPA to all Americans, regardless of their state of residence, in an effort to maintain consistency in their privacy policies and practices.

Here's how CCPA/CPRA and Europe's GDPR are alike and dissimilar:

Similarities

Privacy Rights: All three regulations grant individuals certain rights over their personal data, including the right to access their data, the right to have incorrect data corrected, the right to have their data deleted, and the right to know how their data are being used.

Data Security: Each framework requires that businesses implement reasonable security measures to protect personal data from unauthorized access, disclosure, or destruction.

Transparency: GDPR, CCPA, and CPRA emphasize the importance of transparency in data collection and processing activities. Businesses must inform consumers about the types of personal data they collect and the purposes for which they use the data.

Differences

Scope and Applicability: GDPR applies to all organizations operating within the European Union and those outside the European Union that offer goods or services to, or monitor the behavior of, EU data subjects, regardless of the company's location.

CCPA initially targeted for-profit entities doing business in California that met certain thresholds (e.g., annual gross revenues over $25 million, etc.). CPRA expands on CCPA's provisions and applies similar thresholds.

Opt-In vs. Opt-Out: GDPR generally requires an opt-in consent for data processing, especially for sensitive data, meaning businesses must obtain explicit consent from individuals before collecting or processing their data.

CCPA/CPRA primarily operate on an opt-out model, where consumers have the right to opt out of the sale or sharing of their personal information.

Enforcement and Penalties: GDPR has stringent penalties for noncompliance, which can reach up to 4 percent of the company's annual global turnover or €20 million (whichever is greater).

CCPA penalties can be up to $7,500 for each intentional violation and $2,500 for each unintentional violation. CPRA introduces the possibility of triple penalties for violations involving minors' information.

Data Protection Officer (DPO): GDPR requires certain organizations to appoint a Data Protection Officer (DPO) to oversee data protection strategies and compliance.

CCPA/CPRA do not have a similar explicit requirement for a DPO, though businesses must designate individuals responsible for data privacy compliance.

Data Minimization: GDPR explicitly mentions the principle of data minimization, which means collecting only the data that are directly relevant and necessary to accomplish a specified purpose.

CCPA/CPRA include provisions related to the purpose limitation and storage limitation but do not explicitly define a data minimization principle as GDPR does.

Both the CCPA/CPRA and GDPR represent critical steps forward in the protection of personal data and privacy rights. However, their differences in scope, enforcement, jurisdiction, and specific requirements necessitate careful consideration by businesses to ensure compliance with each applicable regulation.

California Delete Act 2023

In late 2023, California further amended its initial data privacy protection laws by enacting the **Delete Act**. This new law targets data brokers, which are businesses that collect and sell personal information from consumers with whom they do not directly interact. This significant piece of legislation requires data brokers to enable California residents to request the deletion of their personal information through a centralized platform, essentially a "one-stop-shop" for privacy requests.

Why is this significant? Well, because here's a breakdown of data brokers and how they operate:

Data Collection: Data brokers acquire information from various sources, often without your direct knowledge. These sources can include:

Public records (property ownership, marriage licenses).
Online activity (browsing history, social media profiles).
Loyalty programs and purchase history.
Data breaches and leaks from other companies.

Data Aggregation: Data brokers compile information from various sources to create detailed profiles on individuals. These profiles can include demographics, interests, purchasing habits, and even web-browsing behavior.

Data Analysis: Data brokers analyze the information they collect to identify patterns and trends. This allows them to categorize individuals into specific groups for targeted marketing purposes.

Data Selling: Data brokers sell the information they collect and analyze to other businesses. These businesses can include:

Advertisers: Target ads based on your interests and demographics.
Risk assessment companies: Evaluate your creditworthiness or insurance eligibility.
Political campaigns: Tailor messaging to specific voter groups.

California's Delete Act introduces significant benefits for California residents across all the activities conducted by data brokers that many consumers do not know are taking place. For instance, in California it impacts the work of credit bureaus Equifax and Experian and data technology and marketing firms Live Ramp and Epsilon. A key feature of this Act is the establishment of a single point of deletion, rather than swimming through the complex process of submitting individual deletion requests to each data broker. California residents can use a centralized mechanism to request the erasure of their personal information across all registered data brokers in the state. This streamlined approach not only simplifies the deletion process but also reduces the time and effort required from consumers to protect their privacy.

Additionally, the Delete Act empowers consumers with opt-out rights, allowing them to prevent the sale or sharing of their data by data brokers in the future, thereby offering a layer of ongoing data privacy protection. Moreover, the legislation imposes a continuous deletion obligation on data brokers, mandating them to periodically, at least every forty-five days, remove consumers' information to prevent the reaccumulating of data.

According to the State of California's Department of Justice website, a leading online food delivery already has run afoul of data privacy protection laws including the Delete Act. DoorDash Inc. agreed to a $375,000 settlement to address accusations that it violated the CCPA and COPP by selling its customers' personal information without proper notification or offering an opt-out option. This breach of privacy regulations occurred as part of DoorDash's engagement in marketing cooperatives, where the personal information of customers was exchanged among businesses to mutually enhance advertising opportunities. However, it was discovered that Door Dash's customer data were not only shared with cooperative participants but also with external entities, including a data broker who further sold the information multiple times.

In a separate privacy incident, Google settled for $93 million in a case alleging that the tech giant violated California's consumer protection laws through its location-privacy practices. Over several years, it was found that Google misleadingly collected, stored, and used users' location data for profiling and advertising without their consent. To rectify these practices, Google agreed to enhance transparency around location tracking, including providing users with additional information upon activating location-related settings, ensuring clear communication regarding its location-tracking practices, and subjecting any significant privacy-impacting changes to its location settings and ads personalization disclosures to an internal review by its Privacy Working Group.

Meanwhile, Kaiser Foundation Health Plan Inc. and Kaiser Foundation Hospitals, collectively known as Kaiser, agreed to a $49 million settlement to address accusations of improperly disposing of medical and hazardous waste along with protected health information across their statewide facilities. This conclusion came after undercover investigations revealed the mishandling of sensitive patient records, also a compliance issue for HIPAA, and waste materials. Kaiser's settlement includes over $42 million in civil penalties and costs. Agreed upon measures to prevent future violations include the appointment of an independent auditor for compliance monitoring concerning the proper disposal of regulated wastes and protected personal health information.

Finally, Sephora Inc., faced a $1.2 million penalty for breaching the CCPA by not adequately informing consumers about the sale of their personal information and failing to honor opt-out requests via user-enabled global privacy controls. The settlement mandates Sephora to revise its online disclosures and privacy policy to allow clearer opt-out options for consumers, align its service provider agreements with CCPA standards, and submit compliance reports to California's attorney general.

According to the latest polling data, more than 80 percent of all US citizens believe that there is a need for uniform federal data privacy legislation. Until then, more and more state legislatures are left with the responsibility of enacting data privacy protection laws for their residents. Here is a summary of the latest consumer protection data laws:

Virginia Consumer Data Protection Act (VCDPA)

The **VCDPA** focuses on fundamental consumer protections and clearly outlines business obligations. It grants consumers rights to access, correct, delete, and port their data and opt out of processing for targeted advertising or significant decisions. Applicable to businesses processing data of over 100,000 consumers or earning more than 50 percent of gross revenue from selling that data, it necessitates data protection assessments for targeted marketing. Importantly, it enforces consent for collecting and processing sensitive personal information and contractual obligations with service providers, aligning closely with the CCPA while forging its path toward consumer data protection.

Colorado Privacy Act (CPA)

Colorado became the third state to enact a comprehensive privacy law. It introduces obligations for businesses interacting with Colorado residents, including rights for consumers to access, correct, and delete their data, and opt out of personal data processing for targeted advertising. The CPA specifies seven controller obligations, such as transparency, data minimization, and safeguarding sensitive data, pushing businesses toward more accountable data handling practices.

Connecticut Data Privacy Act (CTDPA)

Mirroring aspects of Virginia's VCDPA and Colorado's CPA, the CTDPA emphasizes consumer-oriented privacy protections. It establishes a framework for data control and processing, empowering consumers with rights similar to those in Virginia and Colorado.

Utah Consumer Privacy Act (UCPA)

Taking effect on the last day of 2023, the UCPA adopts a more business-friendly approach compared to its counterparts. With higher compliance thresholds, it offers exemptions to small and medium-sized businesses. The act mirrors the VCDPA in many respects but differentiates itself by tailoring requirements to facilitate business operations while still providing essential consumer protections.

New York Privacy Act

The New York Privacy Act covers wide-ranging privacy protections, including a broad definition of personal information and comprehensive consumer rights such as the ability to request data deletion and corrections. A feature that was long awaited by data privacy experts is the introduction of a data fiduciary duty, requiring businesses to prioritize consumer data protection over profit motives. This positions businesses as guardians of consumer data, responsible for its safekeeping, and marks a significant shift toward prioritizing consumer interests lodged in more traditional negligence language.

Massachusetts Data Privacy Law

Massachusetts's approach to data privacy encompasses several key elements from the CCPA, adapting them to the specific needs of its residents. It grants consumers access to their personal information, the right to request deletion, and the ability to opt out of third-party information sharing. Furthermore, Massachusetts law empowers consumers with the ability to initiate class-action lawsuits against entities that breach data privacy, providing a stronger deterrent against negligent data practices.

Maryland Personal Information Protection Act (PIPA)

Maryland's PIPA enhances consumer protections by mandating timely notifications in the event of data breaches, thereby allowing individuals to take proactive measures to protect their information. The law also requires explicit disclosure about third-party data sharing, ensuring consumers are aware of who has access to their information.

Nevada Privacy Law

Nevada's pioneering privacy law mandates clear privacy policies outlining the types of collected information, the recipients of such data, and how consumers can modify their information or exercise their opt-out rights. This law reflects Nevada's commitment to empowering consumers with greater control over their personal data.

Maine Act to Protect the Privacy of Online Customer Information

Maine's law uniquely targets broadband internet service providers (ISPs), prohibiting them from selling or sharing customer personal information without explicit consent. This includes sensitive data such as browsing history and geolocation information similar to the requirements of the Delete Act.

Hawaii Data Privacy Law

Hawaii's legislation shares similarities with California's privacy regulation but extends its reach globally, potentially applying to any company worldwide that processes data related to Hawaii and its residents. This ambitious scope in expanding Hawaii's jurisdiction over data privacy is similar to that of the GDPR. While it underscores Hawaii's proactive stance on privacy, it signals potential legal and technological challenges for global businesses in ensuring compliance.

The overarching hope from these state data protection privacy laws is that by imposing strict data protection standards and significant penalties for noncompliance, businesses are incentivized to bolster their cybersecurity measures. This proactive approach to data security aims to reduce the frequency and severity of data breaches, offering consumers better protection against unauthorized access to their personal information. By establishing clear legal frameworks for data privacy protection, where in the past there were none, and outlining the responsibilities of businesses, these laws provide consumers with pathways to hold companies accountable through regulatory actions or, in some cases, even private tort or class-action-based litigation.

Ultimately, the collection of current and forthcoming state regulations highlights the fragmented strategy toward data privacy in the United States. In several aspects, digital technology corporations possess greater influence and resources than certain governments that are making data protection policy. However, with increasing demands for a consolidated federal privacy framework, these state-level legislations are crucial in steering the nationwide discourse on privacy. They lay the groundwork for subsequent legislative initiatives in data protection, potentially extending to the federal domain in collaboration with international regulatory bodies and the IT and digital media companies themselves.

National Security Concerns

A significant shift in how the United States approaches both national security and data privacy occurred as a result of the September 11, 2001, terrorist attacks on US soil leading to the enactment of several laws designed to prevent future attacks. Among these, the **USA PATRIOT Act** and the subsequent reforms to the **Foreign Intelligence Surveillance Act (FISA)**, including the **FISA Amendments Act,** stand out for their impact on surveillance practices and civil liberties. Both of these acts have crucially influenced the risk of loss of data privacy for both individuals and business entities in the United States.

Under the USA PATRIOT Act, one of the most dramatic expansions of surveillance capabilities is the collection of a vast range of personal data, including telephone records, email communications, and financial transactions. The aim is to preempt terrorism and reinforce national security. **Section 215** of the Act, often highlighted for its controversial nature, allows investigative agencies to secure secret court orders compelling third parties—such as telecommunication companies and financial institutions—to hand over records without demonstrating probable cause of criminal activity. This provision impacts both individuals and businesses, as it can lead to the collection of personal information without the subjects' knowledge or consent, potentially breaching the **Fourth Amendment's** safeguard against unreasonable searches and seizures. For businesses, this could mean the disclosure of customer or client information, raising concerns about confidentiality and trust.

Furthermore, the PATRIOT Act's broad surveillance permissions have stoked fears about infringing upon **First Amendment** rights, affecting individuals' free speech and privacy. The Act's nebulous criteria for surveillance orders might result in monitoring based on online activities, purchases, or writings, posing a chilling effect on free expression and privacy.

The FISA Amendments Act, particularly through **Section 702**, modernizes surveillance laws to cater to the evolving nature of communication technology and terrorism. It authorizes the targeted collection of foreign intelligence information from non-US persons reasonably believed to be located outside the United States. Despite its intention for targeted surveillance, there is the issue of incidental collection of US persons' communications, which affects both individuals and businesses. This incidental collection can lead to unwarranted privacy intrusions, as communications involving Americans can be gathered and analyzed without their knowledge, even when they are not the primary targets of surveillance.

The oversight mechanisms in place, including the role of the Foreign Intelligence Surveillance Court (FISC), are designed to provide a level of checks and balances. However, the secretive nature of the court's proceedings and the government's unilateral representation have been criticized for lacking transparency, raising further concerns about the effectiveness of oversight in protecting data privacy. One of the most pointed criticisms is the high rate at which FISC approves surveillance requests. It has been reported that the court grants nearly all requests made by the government, which raises questions about the rigor of its review process and whether it effectively acts as a rubber stamp for surveillance activities.

In a step toward greater collaboration between industry and government, the **Cybersecurity Information Sharing Act (CISA) of 2015** was enacted. It allows companies to share details about cybersecurity risks and defensive actions without fear of legal trouble, as long as they follow the law and remove any unrelated personal information before sharing. Since CISA was put in place, there have been mixed opinions. Some people think it's great for improving national cybersecurity by making it easier for the private sector and government to work together. Others worry it could lead to privacy issues or too much government surveillance if personal data are accidentally shared. Details on specific cases of information sharing under CISA are kept private to protect sensitive information.

While the USA PATRIOT Act and the FISA Amendments Act are deemed crucial for national security by government officials, they also present significant implications for the data privacy of individuals and business entities. The collection and handling of personal information under these laws continues to spark debate over the balance between security and privacy, highlighting the need for ongoing scrutiny and perhaps reform.

Significant Cases of Leaking, Hacking, and Surveillance: National Security

In 2013, Edward Snowden, a former contractor for the CIA and National Security Agency (NSA), made headlines worldwide by disclosing a vast trove of classified information to *The Washington Post* and the *The Guardian*.

This information laid bare the sweeping extent of surveillance activities carried out by the NSA, igniting a global conversation about data privacy, security, and government overreach. Snowden's revelations shed light on several critical aspects of the NSA's operations, notably transforming public awareness and sparking debates on surveillance ethics and legality.

One of the most startling disclosures was the mass surveillance of phone and internet communications by the NSA. Snowden revealed that the agency was amassing phone records of millions of Americans, in addition to tapping into the servers of major internet companies such as Facebook, Google, Microsoft, and Yahoo through a program known as PRISM. This program enabled the NSA to monitor online communications in real-time, raising dramatic privacy concerns. Moreover, Snowden's leaks uncovered the NSA's global surveillance operations, which included over 61,000 hacking operations worldwide, targeting not only potential threats but also government allies and private individuals. This capability to hack network backbones allowed the NSA unparalleled access to the communications of hundreds of thousands of computers globally without needing to compromise each one individually.

Another significant aspect of Snowden's disclosure was the compromising of encryption. He exposed that the NSA, alongside British intelligence, had succeeded in breaking or bypassing a substantial portion of the online encryption relied upon for data security. This was achieved not only through advanced code-cracking techniques but also via agreements with industry players to insert backdoors into commercial encryption software, thus undermining global data security.

The surveillance of allies, including the eavesdropping on European Union offices and the personal phone conversations of leaders such as German Chancellor Angela Merkel, was among the more diplomatically explosive revelations. These actions sparked considerable diplomatic tensions and raised questions about the depth and breadth of US surveillance on its allies.

Snowden's disclosures also brought to light serious concerns regarding the oversight and legality of the NSA's surveillance activities. The incident where Director of National Intelligence James Clapper apologized for providing "clearly erroneous" statements to Congress—denying the collection of data on millions of Americans—underscored issues of transparency, truthfulness, and accountability within the surveillance apparatus.

Legally, the NSA's actions, as revealed by Snowden, potentially conflicted with several laws and constitutional protections. The mass collection of phone records without probable cause could be seen as infringing upon the Fourth Amendment, which guards against unreasonable searches and seizures. While the NSA's surveillance activities were authorized under the FISA and the Amendments Act and expanded by the PATRIOT Act, the scale and nature of the surveillance led to debates about whether these laws were being overly broadly interpreted or even violated.

In response to Snowden's actions, the US government charged him under the Espionage Act of 1917 that makes it a crime to leak classified information to the public or foreign entities, a move that sparked further debate about the appropriateness of such a law for whistleblowers who expose governmental misdeeds. This charge highlights the complex interplay between national security, individual rights, and the public's right to know about government actions that may infringe upon their privacy and freedoms.

The aftermath of Snowden's revelations has seen some reforms to surveillance practices, yet the fundamental legal and policy frameworks enabling mass surveillance have remained largely unchanged.

The issue of leaking government secrets has ensnared several American citizens beyond Edward Snowden, leading to additional legal and ethical debates surrounding whistleblowing, government transparency, data privacy, and national security. Among these individuals is Chelsea Manning, a former US Army intelligence analyst, who faced charges under the **Espionage Act of 1917**. In 2010, Manning disclosed a vast array of classified documents to WikiLeaks, which included videos of airstrikes in Iraq and Afghanistan, diplomatic communications, and profiles of Guantanamo Bay detainees. These leaks offered a startling glimpse into the US military's operations and diplomatic communications, sparking global discussions on the ethics of whistleblowing, national security breaches by a military officer revealing real-time operations, and the public's right to know. Manning was initially sentenced to thirty-five years in prison for her actions. However, after serving seven years, her sentence was commuted by President Barack Obama.

WikiLeaks, the platform that published the materials provided by Manning, has itself been central to several controversies involving the leak of classified information. Julian Assange, the organization's founder, has faced legal battles, including charges under the Espionage Act of 1917 for his role in disseminating classified documents. Assange's legal troubles escalated when he was arrested in April 2019 in the United Kingdom after spending seven years in the Ecuadorian embassy in London to avoid extradition. His case has raised critical questions about press freedoms, the definition of journalism in the digital age, and the legal boundaries of publishing classified information.

The cases of Snowden, Manning, and WikiLeaks underscore the contentious intersection between the public's right to know and the government's duty to safeguard national security information. Critics contend that the Espionage Act lacks provisions for a public interest defense, effectively silencing whistleblowers and journalists who might expose government wrongdoing. These cases have ignited debates over the adequacy of current laws to address the complexities of digital-age whistleblowing and journalism, the protection of civil liberties, and the imperative of national security. The ongoing discussions reflect the evolving nature of transparency, ethics, and accountability in the context of modern governance and technology.

A broad spectrum of issues at the intersection of technology, data privacy, national security, and global politics are further encapsulated by two recent controversies surrounding Huawei's role in 5G infrastructure development and TikTok's operations in the United States. These cases address apprehension over the influence of Chinese technology companies and their potential implications for espionage, data security, and geopolitical dynamics.

Huawei, a leading global provider of telecommunications equipment and a major player in the development of 5G technology, has faced scrutiny and allegations from the United States and other Western nations. Concerns center on the potential for Huawei's equipment to be used for espionage activities by the Chinese government, attributed to Huawei's perceived close ties with China's leadership and laws that may compel Chinese companies to assist in intelligence operations. This scenario has elevated Huawei to a focal point of US–China geopolitical tensions, with significant implications for global trade, technological advancement, and the principles of free market competition.

The critical issue surrounding Huawei has broader repercussions, touching upon the future of international trade and the risk of technology-related protectionism. As countries grapple with balancing economic interests against national security concerns in an increasingly data-centric world, the Huawei case raises fundamental questions about the future direction of global trade policies, especially in sectors deemed vital to national security

Parallel to the Huawei controversy, TikTok, a popular social media platform owned by the Chinese company ByteDance, has come under intense scrutiny in the United States. Lawmakers express concern that TikTok could become a conduit for the Chinese government to access the data of American users or to exert influence and spread disinformation within the United States. These concerns are amplified by incidents where ByteDance employees allegedly misused their access to surveil Americans, raising fears about TikTok's potential as a tool for Chinese surveillance and influence operations.

The bipartisan momentum in Congress to address these issues, potentially through legislation that would ban TikTok or force its divestiture from Chinese ownership, underscores the gravity of these national security concerns. This legislative push enacted into law reflects a broader public policy consensus on the need to safeguard American data and prevent foreign influence through digital platforms.

Both the Huawei and TikTok cases illuminate the delicate balance between safeguarding national security and upholding the principles of free speech and open markets. The measures taken against these companies, while rooted in legitimate security concerns, also pose questions about the impact on First Amendment rights of TikTok users, especially younger digital media fans who use TikTok as their principal source of news and information, and the global internet ecosystem. The potential for these actions to set precedents for how governments manage or restrict access to technology and information raises critical considerations about the future of digital expression and international commerce.

Computer Fraud and Abuse Act

The Computer Fraud and Abuse Act (CFAA) was inspired by the 1983 movie *WarGames*. In the movie, a young hacker, played by Matthew Broderick, unwittingly accesses a US military supercomputer programmed to predict possible outcomes of nuclear war. Thinking he's playing a computer game, the protagonist almost starts World War III, highlighting potential vulnerabilities in computer systems and the need for stronger security measures. The film prompted Congress to enact legislation to safeguard sensitive information and prevent similar scenarios at a time when hacking was a relatively unknown phenomenon.

The Act criminalizes the intentional accessing of a computer without authorization or exceeding authorized access, thereby covering a spectrum of activities from traditional hacking to unauthorized data retrieval and the infliction of harm on digital systems. For instance, the NSA and Environmental Protection Agency accused hackers of acting in concert with Iran's Revolutionary Guards to disable a controller at a water facility in Pennsylvania, which "compromised information technology of multiple critical infrastructure systems, including drinking water, in the United States and its territories." The penalties for such violations range from monetary fines to imprisonment, contingent on the offense's gravity. This broad applicability has enabled the prosecution of diverse activities under the CFAA, highlighting its significance in the legal arsenal against cybercrime, yet stymied by lack of jurisdiction over foreign adversaries.

However, the CFAA has been the subject of extensive debate and criticism, primarily due to its broad language—especially the phrases "without authorization" and "exceeding authorized access"—which has led to varied interpretations and applications by courts. This legal ambiguity has raised concerns about the Act's clarity, due process, fairness, and its potential to criminalize benign online activities not intended as malicious. For instance, activities such as data scraping (the process of using software to automatically collect information like prices, email addresses, contract terms, etc., from websites) or infringing upon a website's terms and conditions of service have faced legal challenges under the CFAA, sparking debates on the balance between system protection and the inhibition of innovation or freedom of expression. Moreover, the stringent penalties and broad application associated with the CFAA may deter security research and innovation, as individuals fear legal repercussions for conducting vulnerability assessments or exploring system weaknesses—activities vital for advancing cybersecurity.

The call for legislative reform aims to refine the CFAA's scope, offering clearer definitions of prohibited actions and focusing on malicious intent to distinguish between criminal conduct and activities that, while technically in violation, do not pose a significant threat. The Supreme Court's decision in *Van Buren v. United States* (141 S. Ct. 1648 (2021)), which narrowed the interpretation of "exceeding authorized access," represents a judicial step toward addressing some of the criticisms and ambiguities associated with the CFAA.

The significance of the CFAA in combating cybercrime is undisputed by most experts, yet the discourse surrounding its scope and enforcement underscores the necessity of reform to ensure the law remains effective and equitable in the face of evolving digital realities. The Act's broad application has been illustrated in several notable legal cases:

1. *United States v. Nosal* (676 F.3d 854 (9th Cir. 2012)), where the former employee's act of enlisting colleagues to access and download information from a former employer's database raised questions about what constitutes "exceeding authorized access" under the CFAA.
2. *United States v. Auernheimer ("Weev")* (748 F.3d 525 (3d Cir. 2014)), which involved the exposure of a security flaw in AT&T's system, challenged the application of the CFAA in cases where the accessed information was not used for harm.
3. *United States v. Keys* (143 F.3d 479 (9th Cir. 1998)), where the indictment for providing hackers access to a media company's systems underscored the government's use of the CFAA to address facilitation of unauthorized access and system damage.

These cases highlight the CFAA's extensive reach and the ongoing debate over its interpretation, particularly concerning "authorized" versus "unauthorized" access and the suitable penalties for violations. The complexities surrounding the CFAA exemplify the broader challenge of ensuring that laws governing digital conduct and cybersecurity keep pace with technological advancements, adequately protect data privacy and security, and do not unduly impede innovation or digital freedoms.

Future Challenges and Developments

Artificial Intelligence (AI) is reshaping the cybersecurity landscape, offering both remarkable opportunities and formidable challenges for data protection and national security. The adoption of AI in cybersecurity strategies enhances capabilities in threat detection, predictive analytics, and incident response. AI's ability to process vast amounts of data swiftly allows for the detection of anomalies and patterns indicative of security threats, enabling organizations to respond more rapidly than traditional methods permit. Innovations such as AI-powered systems by cyber-technology companies like Darktrace demonstrate this advantage by identifying and neutralizing threats in real-time, showcasing a significant leap over conventional security tools. Moreover, predictive analytics powered by AI holds the potential to foresee the nature and timing of future attacks, setting the stage for preemptive defense measures developed by cybersecurity firms like Cylance and CrowdStrike.

Despite these advancements, the integration of AI into cybersecurity is not without its pitfalls. Cybercriminals are leveraging AI to develop advanced malware that can alter its code to evade detection, complicating the detection process. Furthermore, AI-enhanced social engineering attacks, including sophisticated phishing schemes, present a growing challenge for security measures. The risk extends to AI systems themselves, which can become direct targets of cyberattacks, as evidenced by incidents like the ChatGPT data breach. There's also the issue of feeding misleading data to machine-learning models, potentially skewing threat detection. Ethical and privacy concerns further complicate the use of AI in cybersecurity, demanding a delicate balance between enhancing security and respecting user privacy.

Looking forward, the role of AI in cybersecurity is poised for significant growth, with its market size projected to reach $102 billion by 2032. This development signifies AI's evolving role as both a defensive and offensive tool in cybersecurity. As such, organizations must remain vigilant, continuously updating their cybersecurity strategies to incorporate the latest AI advancements while adhering to responsible AI practices that have yet to be fully formed. For those interested in learning more about the benefits and concerns over living and working with AI, a recommended reading is Ethan Mollick's lucid and reasoned guidebook: *Co-Intelligence*.

On another front, the increasing necessity for international cooperation in cybersecurity underscores the global nature of cyber threats. International collaboration is crucial for sharing intelligence, coordinating responses to cyber incidents, and developing unified strategies to combat cyber threats. Despite challenges such as differing national laws and the complex issue of attributing cyberattacks, the future of international cybersecurity cooperation looks toward more coordinated frameworks, shared best practices, and dedicated task forces to tackle the evolving cyber threat landscape.

Summary

This chapter on national security, hacking and defending the digital frontier examines the multifaceted challenges encountered in safeguarding digital information, providing an extensive examination of data protection legislations and their effectiveness in today's technology-driven world. It looks into the various types of data breaches, such as unauthorized access, phishing attacks, malware infections, insider threats, and ransomware attacks, each illustrating the complexity and evolving nature of cyber threats. The material underscores the significant financial and reputational harm inflicted by data breaches, detailing the costs associated with breach remediation, legal fees, and compliance penalties, alongside the long-term reputational damage that can erode customer trust and diminish brand value.

The chapter discussion on data protection highlights the fragmented landscape in the United States, characterized by a lack of a uniform federal data protection law at a time when nearly every American experiences some form of data privacy breach on an annual basis. This has led to a piecemeal, state-by-state approach to data privacy, with California leading the charge through the California Consumer Privacy Act (CCPA), which, in many ways, mirrors the European Union's General Data Protection Regulation (GDPR). This segment of the chapter critiques the inefficiencies and complexities of social media companies and websites having multiple regulatory environments, stressing the need for a comprehensive federal data protection standard that aligns more closely with the GDPR to provide broad, enforceable protections for US citizens' privacy.

On national security, the narrative shifts to the post-September 11 era, marked by the United States enacting increased government surveillance laws, notably the PATRIOT Act and subsequent amendments to other legislation to protect against terrorist acts. These measures, aimed at strengthening national security, have not been without controversy. The chapter explores the criticism these actions have attracted, particularly highlighting Edward Snowden's revelations. Snowden's sharing of classified

National Security Agency documents with the media, allegedly in violation of the Espionage Act of 1917, exposed the extent of data privacy intrusions by government agencies marked by lack of constitutional protections, sparking a global debate on the balance between security and data privacy and asking where transparency and notice fits within the two competing concerns.

The role of artificial intelligence (AI) in predicting cybersecurity threats is acknowledged as a significant advancement to prevent data breaches. However, the curse of open AI systems is that bad actors can misuse AI, feeding machine-learning algorithms with malicious information to enhance the effectiveness of cyberattacks.

To effectively address the complexities of the digital age, a balanced strategy is crucial. This approach should utilize technological innovations, such as AI, for defense, while enforcing adequate measures to prevent misuse. Moreover, it necessitates collaboration with global partners to establish a clear data protection standard that both recognizes and safeguards data privacy. Additionally, it must ensure that wrongdoers are held accountable, all the while prioritizing the preservation of privacy and individual freedoms.

Discussion Questions

1. How do the principles of data protection and privacy differ between the United States and the European Union, and what impacts do these differences have on international businesses?
2. In the context of national security, where should the line be drawn between surveillance for protection and the invasion of privacy?
3. How has recent privacy legislation in the United States, such as the CCPA, influenced the approach to data breaches and consumer privacy, and how does it compare to the GDPR in the European Union?
4. What constitutional protections exist to safeguard individual privacy and how do they stand up against the government's digital surveillance tactics?
5. Discuss the implications of banning social media platforms like TikTok on the grounds of national security. Do the benefits outweigh the potential drawbacks regarding freedom of speech and access to information?

6. How is evolving case law adapting to the challenges of cyber security and privacy in the digital age? Provide examples of landmark cases that have shaped current policies.
7. What role do artificial intelligence and machine learning play in enhancing cybersecurity measures, and what ethical considerations arise from their use?
8. How effective are current cybersecurity strategies in predicting and mitigating future threats, and what improvements could be made?
9. Considering the balance between privacy and security, what reforms would you propose to current legislation to better protect individuals from future cyber threats?
10. Discuss the potential impacts of future cybersecurity threats on global economies and political landscapes. How should nations prepare to defend against these evolving threats while ensuring the privacy and freedoms of their citizens?

Works Referenced

Chen, Brian X. "The Battle for Digital Privacy Is Reshaping the Internet." *The New York Times*, September 16, 2021, updated June 23, 2023, accessed at https://www.nytimes.com/2021/09/16/technology/digital-privacy.html

Crocetti, Paul, Peterson, Stacey, and Hefner, Kim. "What Is Data Protection and Why Is It Important?" *Tech Target*, accessed at https://www.techtarget.com/searchdatabackup/definition/data-protection

Davis, Betsy, Houston, Patrick, and Besteman, Vivi. "Computer Fraud and Abuse Act: Supreme Court Ruling." Whiteford, August 10, 2021, accessed at https://www.whitefordlaw.com/news-events/computer-fraud-and-abuse-act-supreme-court-ruling

Evanko, Lizzie. "FISA and the USA PATRIOT Act: Reforms and Legal Implications." *Princeton Legal Journal*, Vol. 3, No. 2 (2023), accessed at https://legaljournal.princeton.edu/fisa-and-the-usa-patriot-act-reforms-and-legal-implications

Fomperosa Rivero, Álvaro. "Right to Be Forgotten in the European Court of Justice Google Spain Case: The Right Balance of Privacy Rights, Procedure, and Extraterritoriality." Stanford Law School Publications, February 2017, accessed at https://law.stanford.edu/publications/right-to-be-forgotten-in-the-european-court-of-justice-google-spain-case-the-right-balance-of-privacy-rights-procedure-and-extraterritoriality

Geveye, Michelle Ofir. "Top US State Data Privacy Laws to Watch Out for in 2024." Centraleyes, December 1, 2023, accessed at https://www.centraleyes.com/top-10-us-state-data-privacy-laws-to-watch-out-for-in-2022

Gibson, Derek W., and Camm, Jeffrey D. *Data Duped*. Rowman & Littlefield, Lanham, MD, 2023.

Hojjati, Avesta. "The Future Role of AI in Cybersecurity." digicert, September 28, 2023, accessed at https://www.digicert.com/blog/the-future-role-of-ai-in-cybersecurity

Kukava, Ketevan. "Right to Erasure (Right to Be Forgotten) under the GDPR—the Danger of 'Rewriting History' or the Individual's Chance to Leave the Past Behind." *EU Law Analysis* (blog), May 25, 2018, accessed at http://eulawanalysis.blogspot.com/2018/05/right-to-erasure-right-to-be-forgotten.html?m=1

Macaskill, Ewen, and Dance, Gabriel. "NSA Files: Decoded." *The Guardian*, November 1, 2013, accessed at https://www.theguardian.com/world/interactive/2013/nov/01/snowden-nsa-files-surveillance-revelations-decoded#section/1

Mollick, Ethan. *Co-Intelligence*. Penguin Books, New York, 2024.

Murray, Conor. "U.S. Data Privacy Protection Laws: A Comprehensive Guide." *Forbes*, April 25, 2023, accessed at https://www.forbes.com/sites/conormurray/2023/04/21/us-data-privacy-protection-laws-a-comprehensive-guide/?sh=39061b0e5f92

Petrosyan, Ani. "Number of Data Compromises and Impacted Individuals in U.S. 2005–2023." Statista, February 12, 2024, accessed at https://www.statista.com/statistics/273550/data-breaches-recorded-in-the-united-states-by-number-of-breaches-and-records-exposed

Porter, Ethan. "Mis-information and Dis-information." Labs, Institute for Data, Democracy and Politics, accessed at https://iddp.gwu.edu/misinformationdisinformation-lab

Ross, Jeremy. "What Is Data Protection and Privacy?" Cloudian, accessed at https://cloudian.com/guides/data-protection/data-protection-and-privacy-7-ways-to-protect-user-data/amp

Savage, Charles. "U.S. to Ask Court to Reauthorize Disputed Surveillance Program for a Year." *The New York Times*, February 28, 2024, accessed at https://www.nytimes.com/2024/02/28/us/politics/nsa-fbi-surveillance-program.html

Satter, Raphael. "US Warns that Hackers Are Carrying Out Disruptive Attacks on Water Systems." March 20, 2024, Reuters, accessed at https://finance.yahoo.com/news/us-warns-hackers-carrying-disruptive-153129211.html

8

Digital Media Contracts, Blockchain Technology, Cryptocurrencies, NFTs, and the Metaverse

A contract is a promise.

—Sir William Blackstone, jurist

As we have learned in previous chapters, the digital era has dramatically altered various aspects of personal and business life, including how agreements and contracts are conceived, executed, and preserved. The inception of digital media contracts, riding on the back of this digital wave, represents a decisive transformation in the realm of legal agreements, particularly in the creative and technology sectors. These contracts, existing entirely in an electronic milieu, have not only redefined the commercial environment of agreement management but also introduced a synergy with cutting-edge technologies like blockchain to enhance integrity, productivity, and trust.

Digital media contracts are essentially agreements that are created, signed, and maintained in a digital format, specifically tailored for the media industry. They govern the creation, distribution, and use of digital media content, including videos, music, articles, and photographs, among others. This evolution from paper-based to digital documents signifies a leap toward embracing a more sustainable, agile, and interconnected global digital economy.

Sir William Blackstone, a preeminent English jurist, eloquently encapsulated the essence of a contract as a promise. This foundational principle remains at the heart of all agreements, including digital media contracts. However, the digitalization of contracts amplifies their capability, making them not just a promise but a dynamic tool for ensuring that promises are kept, efficiently, securely, and transparently, but not without some critical limitations.

Blockchain Technology and Digital Media Contracts

This chapter also focuses on blockchain technology, a decentralized ledger that records transactions across many computers in a manner that ensures the security and integrity of the record, offering a natural complement to digital media contracts. By integrating blockchain technology, these contracts can achieve unprecedented levels of verifiability and enforceability. This is because blockchain's inherent characteristics—immutability, transparency, and security—align perfectly with the core needs of digital contracts. Every transaction or agreement recorded on a blockchain is virtually tamper proof, providing a framework against fraud and unauthorized alterations.

The application of blockchain extends to "smart contracts," which are self-executing contracts—that is, agreements where the terms and conditions are automatically enforced or carried out without the need for any additional action, with the terms of the agreement directly written into lines of code. In the context of digital media, smart contracts can automate the enforcement of agreements, such as releasing payments to content creators once their work achieves certain milestones or conditions (e.g., a specified number of downloads or views). This not only enhances the efficiency of transactions but also significantly reduces the potential for disputes, as the terms and their execution are transparent and immutable.

A practical demonstration of smart contracts within the digital media realm can be seen in how blockchain technology streamlines the payment process for content creators upon the fulfillment of certain predefined milestones. Consider a scenario where an advertiser collaborates with a social media influencer for a promotional campaign. The agreement stipulates that payment to the influencer hinges on the attainment of a specific number of legitimate purchases by followers, facilitated by a unique discount code provided by the advertiser. Here's the operational breakdown of such an arrangement.

First, the creation of the smart contract involves a mutual understanding between the advertiser and the influencer regarding the campaign's specifics, including the payment sum and the purchase targets linked to the discount code. Following this agreement, the terms are encoded within a smart contract on a blockchain platform. This contract is designed with an "if-then" logic; for instance, if the influencer's post generates 100 legitimate purchases, the smart contract is then programmed to release the payment to the influencer automatically.

The enforcement of the contract is overseen by an oracle—a system that relays external data to the blockchain. This oracle tracks the count of purchases attributed to the discount code. Upon verification that the agreed milestone has been achieved, the smart contract is activated.

Consequently, the contract executes the stipulated action autonomously, effecting the transfer of payment from the advertiser to the influencer's digital wallet.

This streamlined approach not only ensures timely compensation for the influencer upon the successful achievement of the campaign's objectives but also offers assurance to the advertiser of their investment's value, paying strictly for tangible results. By employing smart contracts, the process mitigates administrative overhead and curtails the likelihood of disputes, courtesy of its transparent terms and immutable, automated execution process.

In the scenario where social media influencers engage with digital smart contracts, the emergence of cryptocurrency introduces a novel method for executing payment transactions. Cryptocurrencies, such as Bitcoin, tether or Ethereum, which are viewed as digital assets by the US government and not actual currency, are integral parts of the digital environment and can be leveraged for transactions within these contracts instead of using more traditional forms of payments. As stated before, when the predefined conditions of a smart contract are met—such as achieving a certain number of views or likes—an oracle verifies the accomplishment and triggers the contract. The payment is then automatically processed using the chosen cryptocurrency, transferring the funds from the advertiser's digital currency account to the influencer's digital wallet.

A digital wallet is a software-based system that securely stores users' payment information and passwords for numerous payment methods and websites. By using a digital wallet, payments can be made quickly and securely online. Digital wallets are especially conducive to cryptocurrency transactions, as they can hold various types of digital currencies and allow for immediate, borderless transactions, which are recorded on the blockchain for added security and transparency. This system ensures that influencers receive their payments automatically, without the need for traditional banking procedures, while allowing both parties to benefit from the reduced transaction fees and the quick clearance times associated with cryptocurrency payments.

Notwithstanding the benefits of smart contracts, their deployment comes with challenges that need careful consideration. The creation and management of smart contracts demand substantial technical knowledge in blockchain and programming, which can be daunting and expensive for those new to blockchain and small businesses, in particular. Smart contracts, while designed to reduce human error, are not immune to flaws. They are only as good as the code they are written with, meaning any bugs or vulnerabilities in the code can lead to incorrect execution or exploitation. The reliance on external data sources, or oracles, to execute contracts introduces risks of inaccuracies, potentially leading to disputes or premature payments if the data are incorrect. Legal and regulatory uncertainties also pose significant hurdles, as the legal status of smart contracts and the resolution of disputes remain in flux, complicated further by jurisdictional issues across states and countries.

Once smart contracts are deployed, their immutable nature means they cannot be easily modified, making error correction or updates challenging. Privacy is another concern since contracts on public blockchains are visible to all, which might not be desirable in all commercial dealings. Blockchain networks may also face scalability and performance limitations, affecting transactions' speed and cost. Moreover, the success of smart contracts depends on widespread adoption and the ability to work across different blockchain platforms, with interoperability issues potentially hindering execution.

Finally, it needs to be disclosed that governments have several reservations about the use of cryptocurrencies in digital transactions. They are worried about ensuring that such transactions follow financial laws, particularly with regard to anti-money laundering efforts, and they are working on tax measures to prevent evasion through the anonymity that cryptocurrencies provide. Additionally, the volatility of cryptocurrencies poses a risk to financial stability, and their potential for use in illegal activities like money laundering and terrorism financing is a significant concern. There is also an increased risk of fraud and scams associated with digital currencies, which is troubling due to the lack of consumer protection in this decentralized space. The collapse of FTX, a cryptocurrency exchange, in 2022 where upward of $8 billion was lost highlights worries within the cryptocurrency market. FTX's founder, Sam Bankman-Fried, pled guilty to criminal charges, including wire fraud and securities fraud. He faces up to twenty-five years in jail. Market manipulation and cybersecurity are further issues, as the digital nature of these assets makes them vulnerable to hacking and other cyber threats, leading regulators to consider how to safeguard digital infrastructures effectively.

Blockchain Technology: Fundamentals and Operation, and NFTs

At the core of blockchain technology lies its revolutionary distributed ledger system, which marks a consequential departure from the centralized databases that have dominated data storage for decades. Unlike traditional systems where data are housed on a single server or location, blockchain disperses this information across an extensive network of computers. This decentralization not only enhances the overall security of the system but also imbues it with a resistance to unauthorized alterations and cyber threats, making it a formidable fortress against digital malfeasance. Immutability stands as another foundational pillar of blockchain technology. Once data are recorded on a blockchain, they become indelible, immune to alteration or deletion. This permanence ensures a transparent and incontrovertible record of all transactions, offering an invaluable asset in contexts that demand high levels of traceability and auditability.

Whether it's tracking financial exchanges, monitoring supply chain movements, or recording creative asset ownership, blockchain's ledger provides an unassailable record of events and transactions. Blockchain's defense mechanisms are fortified by sophisticated cryptographic techniques, which play a key role in validating transactions and safeguarding data from unauthorized breaches. These cryptographic measures encrypt each transaction and securely link it to the preceding one, thereby weaving a chain of trust that spans the entire ledger. This encryption not only protects the integrity of the data but also ensures that each transaction is authenticated and verifiable, bolstering the system's security and reliability.

To demystify blockchain's workings, imagine it as a sophisticated, shared spreadsheet replicated across a network of computers globally. In digital media, entertainment, and the arts, this spreadsheet doesn't just track numbers, but could include copyright information, digital art ownership, or streaming revenues. When a new piece of content is created, or ownership changes hands, this information is recorded and instantly updated on every copy of the spreadsheet. Such transparency means that artists, creators, and consumers all see the same unchangeable dataset.

The impact of blockchain in these creative industries is profound, promising a future where digital media transactions are transparent and every creator is in theory fairly compensated. Imagine a musician directly receiving royalties without delay, a digital artist maintaining indisputable proof of ownership, or a filmmaker managing the rights to their films with unassailable accuracy.

The ripple effect of blockchain extends beyond just transactional clarity. In the entertainment sector, it could dismantle monopolistic structures, enabling independent artists to retain more control and revenue. In arts and media, it guarantees the authenticity and originality of works, adding value to digital ownership in ways that were previously difficult or impossible, especially in the fine arts.

A real-life example of blockchain's ripple effect in the entertainment industry is the platform known as "Audius." This music streaming service utilizes blockchain technology to connect audio creators directly with listeners, bypassing traditional music industry intermediaries. Independent artists on Audius retain a much higher degree of control over their work, including setting their own monetization terms. They can receive payment directly from listeners through cryptocurrencies, ensuring immediate and transparent compensation for their streams and interactions, which is often higher compared to conventional streaming services.

Chapter 8: Digital Media Contracts, Blockchain Technology 241

The emergence of blockchain in the art world has been groundbreaking, particularly with the introduction of Non-Fungible Tokens (NFTs). NFTs are digital certificates of authenticity and ownership for unique items or content, and they have become particularly prominent in the realm of art. Each NFT is distinctive, with information and ownership details stored on the blockchain, making it impossible to replicate or forge. This technology has opened up new possibilities for digital artists, allowing them to monetize their work in ways that were not possible before.

Beeple, a digital artist whose real name is Mike Winkelmann, provides a compelling case study. In 2021, Beeple made headlines when he sold an NFT of his artwork titled "Everydays: The First 5000 Days" for a staggering $69 million at Christie's, a well-known auction house. The sale was a landmark event in both the art and blockchain communities, signifying one of the first times a major auction house sold a purely digital work of art with an NFT.

This event did more than just showcase the monetary value of digital art; it represented a seismic shift in how digital art is valued,

Figure 8.1 Beeple non-fungible token for sale by Christie's Auction House.

authenticated, and owned. With NFTs, digital artists can sell their work directly to collectors without the need for galleries or even auction houses, which traditionally take a significant portion or commission of the sales proceeds. Furthermore, NFTs can be programmed to provide artists with a percentage of sales whenever the art is resold, ensuring that creators can benefit from increases in the value of their work over time a concept foreign to the American art market.

Moreover, the proof of authenticity and ownership provided by NFTs via the blockchain stands to protect both artists and buyers. Collectors can be confident that the digital artwork they purchase is genuine and not a copy, while artists can safeguard their intellectual property rights. This level of security in verifying authenticity is unprecedented in the digital domain and is particularly valuable given the ease with which digital works can be copied and distributed.

Differences between a Physical Work of Art and an NFT

It's important to understand that owning an NFT is fundamentally different from possessing a physical piece of art in several respects. First, NFTs are digital assets that signify ownership or proof of authenticity for a digital item secured on a blockchain, whereas physical artworks are tangible items that can be physically displayed or stored. The ownership of an NFT is validated through the blockchain, providing a clear, immutable history of transactions, a stark contrast to physical art, where authenticity and ownership proof may depend on certificates, provenance history, or the reputation of the selling parties.

The process of transferring or selling an NFT is streamlined and secure, facilitated directly through blockchain technology without intermediaries, unlike the potentially complicated process involved with physical art, which may include authentication, valuation, and logistic challenges of storing, shipping, and insuring. Additionally, while digital files associated with NFTs can be viewed or copied by anyone, the NFT itself represents verified ownership of the original digital work, offering a unique claim that doesn't apply in the same way to physical art, where ownership is tied to the physical object itself, despite the existence of replicas.

Furthermore, NFTs can be programmed with specific features, such as artist royalties on resale or interactive elements, introducing a level of dynamism and interactivity not inherent in physical artworks. This utilization of blockchain technology with NFTs ushers in a novel paradigm for digital ownership, authenticity, and the transaction of art assets, distinguishing digital art ownership substantively from traditional physical art ownership.

It's fair to say that blockchain and NFTs are revolutionizing the art industry by enhancing the intrinsic value of digital creations, providing artists with more autonomy, and ensuring that ownership rights are clear and enforceable. This technological advancement is not only changing the way we think about digital artwork but is also setting a new standard for how art is bought, sold, and collected in the digital media age. Yet admiring a physical work of art, whether it's hanging on a wall or displayed on a mantel, often evokes a distinct emotional or intellectual response that may not be fully replicated when viewing digital art on devices like iPads or smartphones. The tangible presence and texture of physical art pieces, along with their scale in real space, contribute to this unique experience and value.

The ownership of NFTs brings with it a range of contradictions and potential drawbacks. Environmental concerns are at the forefront, with the substantial energy consumption of many blockchain networks, particularly those utilizing Proof of Work (PoW) mechanisms, raising alarms over their carbon footprint. Additionally, the NFT market is characterized by its high volatility, where the value of NFTs can experience rapid and significant fluctuations, posing a risk of considerable financial loss to investors and collectors. The relatively unregulated nature of the NFT space further complicates matters, leaving room for fraud, scams, and a lack of consumer protections that are typically available in more established markets.

Copyright, trademark and publicity rights issues also present infringement concerns, as there have been instances where artists' works were tokenized and sold without their consent, complicating the legal landscape around digital content ownership. There also have been cases of cybersquatting—that is, registering one NFT related domain name confusingly similar to an existing NFT registered domain name. Liquidity issues represent another matter; although some NFTs may sell for high amounts, finding a buyer at the desired price point like in any market can become knotty, particularly for less sought-after tokens by lesser known or established digital artists. The complexity of NFTs and blockchain technology, combined with the necessity for cryptocurrency and digital wallets, presents a barrier to entry for many, further complicated by the possibility for loss through human error or technological failures, such as misdirected transactions with no means of recovery.

Moreover, the hype surrounding NFTs has led to worries about overvaluation and the formation of market bubbles, with critics cautioning that the inflated prices of some NFTs may not be sustainable in the long term, as is true for nearly any visual art, potentially leading to significant market adjustments. NFTs' values can swing wildly based on market trends, collector interest, and even social media buzz. This volatility is underscored by two high-profile cases:

The Bored Ape Yacht Club (BAYC) has found itself embroiled in several legal battles, testing the boundaries of intellectual property in the burgeoning world of NFTs. Here's a look into these disputes:

The Rivalry with Ripps: Yuga Labs, the creators of BAYC, clashed with conceptional artists Ryder Ripps and Jeremy Cahen over trademark infringement. The BAYC is a collection of 10,000 unique *Bored Ape* NFTs—unique digital collectibles living on the Ethereum blockchain. Ripps launched a collection called "RR/BAYC" featuring altered versions of the BAYC apes, claiming it was protected fair use in the form of artistic commentary. Both the BAYC's NFTs and Ripp's "RR/BAYC" NFTs could be traded on OpenSea, one of the leading NFT marketplaces. However, Yuga Labs argued these NFTs too closely resembled their own, potentially confusing consumers. Yuga Labs also alleged that Ripps made a copycat version of the Bored Ape Yacht Club Twitter (now X) account, causing further confusion. The court sided with Yuga Labs finding Ripps liable for trademark infringement and cybersquatting (registering domain names mimicking BAYC's). This landmark decision awarded Yuga Labs nearly $1.6 million, but a key question remained unanswered. Ripps countersued, arguing the BAYC images lacked originality due to their computer-generated nature, raising doubts about copyright protection for algorithmic art in the NFT space. The court ultimately focused on the trademark violation, leaving the copyright question unresolved for now.

Cracking Down on Counterfeits: Yuga Labs took aim at NFT marketplace developers Thomas Lehman and Ryan Hickman. The accusation? Creating a fake marketplace selling counterfeit BAYC NFTs. These NFTs mimicked

Figure 8.2 On the left is the BAYC "Bored Apes" image, and on the right is the "RR/BAYC" image in dispute.

the BAYC apes visually but lacked the official branding and weren't part of the legitimate collection. While the lawsuit details are confidential, Yuga Labs reportedly reached a settlement with Lehman, suggesting they successfully defended their intellectual property.

Facing Investor Scrutiny: The tables turned when Yuga Labs found itself on the receiving end of a lawsuit. A class-action suit alleged Yuga Labs manipulated the BAYC NFT market through misleading marketing and celebrity endorsements. The lawsuit claims these tactics artificially inflated the value of BAYC NFTs, leading to financial losses for investors. This case highlights the potential for manipulation within the NFT market and the growing focus on responsible celebrity involvement under FTC rules.

CryptoPunks, launched in 2017, are considered pioneers in the NFT space. These algorithmically generated pixel-art characters, each with unique traits and variations, captured the imagination of early NFT enthusiasts. At a minting price of just around $38 each, they offered a relatively inexpensive entry point into the NFT world. Their popularity soared over the years, with some fetching millions at auction in 2021. This meteoric rise showcased the immense potential for value creation within NFTs.

However, CryptoPunks' journey also serves as a cautionary tale about the inherent volatility of the NFT market. The broader market correction in 2022 saw a significant dip in CryptoPunk prices. While they remain valuable collectibles, the dramatic price swings highlight the speculative nature of the NFT market. This rollercoaster ride underscores the importance of approaching NFT investment with caution and a clear understanding of the risks involved. Unlike traditional assets with established valuation metrics, the worth of NFTs can be heavily influenced by hype, trend cycles, and overall market sentiment.

Figure 8.3 CryptoPunks.

For many sports-minded fans there is the allure of owning a part of the game. For example, NBA Top Shot has become a game-changer for fan engagement, blurring the lines between watching and owning a piece of the action. This platform operates on the blockchain, a secure digital ledger, and uses NFTs to represent unique, officially licensed NBA eclectic moments. Imagine owning a LeBron James highlight reel from a historic playoff game, where his clutch 3-pointer secured victory. This digital collectible, minted as an NFT on NBA Top Shot, can be bought, sold, and traded among fans. Some of these coveted moments have fetched tens of thousands of dollars, showcasing the immense potential of NFTs to expand fan engagement beyond traditional jerseys and memorabilia.

The excitement extends beyond league-sanctioned platforms like NBA Top Shot. Individual athletes are also getting in on the action, launching their own NFT collections. Take NFL tight end legend Rob Gronkowski or Simone Biles, the record-breaking Olympic gymnast. These athletes have used NFTs to offer fans a unique way to connect with their careers. Their NFT collections feature iconic moments like Gronkowski's game-winning touchdown catches or Biles's gravity-defying gymnastic routines. These NFTs hold value not just as digital collectibles, but often come with additional perks. Owning an NFT from an athlete's collection could grant exclusive access to virtual meet-and-greets, signed memorabilia, or even behind-the-scenes content. This added utility layer makes athlete-driven NFTs potentially more stable investments in the long run, compared to purely speculative NFT art pieces.

Beyond the realm of sports, celebrities from various walks of fame are venturing into the NFT space, but this foray isn't without its complexities. Take Tom Hanks, the award-winning actor, who auctioned off an NFT collection. This collection wasn't your typical digital art; it featured unique digital representations of vintage typewriters owned by Hanks.

The intersection of sports, celebrities, digital art, and NFT technology underscores a broader trend: the expansion of NFTs into various sectors, providing new opportunities for fans, collectors, and creators alike. However, the speculative nature of the market, coupled with concerns about environmental impact, market manipulation, and intellectual property infringement issues, suggests that operating in the NFT space requires careful consideration and an understanding of its inherent risks and rewards.

Virtual Worlds: Beyond Screens and into the Metaverse

The evolution of the digital landscape has brought us to a new era where traditional boundaries, borders, and rules are increasingly blurred. The inception of the internet, known as Web 1, was marked by the dominance of desktop computers and the foundational elements of a digital society, including traditional advertising models, an information-based economy, and the necessity for usernames and passwords. This period was characterized by the reliance on physical contracts, credit cards for transactions, and an internet experience primarily navigated through websites, anchoring users in a predominantly physical reality.

Transitioning from Web 1, the advent of Web 2 introduced significant shifts toward a more interactive and user-driven internet. This era was defined by the ubiquity of mobile devices and the emergence of digital assets. Algorithms began to play a pivotal role in shaping user behavior as witnessed by the movie *Social Dilemma*, while videos, digital signatures, apps, and augmented reality started to merge the digital with the physical. The introduction of payment aggregators like PayPal and the rise of social media platforms further facilitated this integration, marking a departure from the static nature of its predecessor.

Currently, we are witnessing the dawn of what is referred to as Web 3, a term popularized by tech visionaries like Elon Musk. This latest iteration of the internet is characterized by a plethora of cutting-edge technologies, including wearable devices, open-source software, NFTs, blockchain technology, cryptocurrencies, artificial intelligence, deepfakes, gaming engines, mixed reality, and the concept of metaverses. In this new digital world, wearable technology from Fitbits to smart compression shirts not only track our physical activities, such as heartbeat and daily steps, but also act as a personal sleep coach, ensuring optimal rest. It's a world we are fast approaching, as nearly one in three Americans uses a wearable device, such as a smart watch or band, to track their health and fitness. Web 3 signifies a paradigm shift from merely consuming information and interacting through social media to a more immersive experience. It offers an integrated reality where the physical and virtual worlds blend seamlessly, allowing users to create and interact within their own chosen realities, thereby molding their own futures. This progression reflects a journey from surfing the internet for information to engaging in social media, and ultimately, to being transported into alternate realities where the distinction between the virtual and the physical becomes increasingly indistinct.

The concept of a virtual world or universe extends far beyond the limitations of our physical reality and even the familiar landscape of the internet. Imagine a space that transcends the confines of a screen, where you can not only see and interact with digital information but truly feel like you're inhabiting it. This is the essence of virtual reality (VR).

In contrast to the tangible nature of the real world, VR offers an entirely simulated environment, meticulously crafted with advanced headsets and sophisticated software like the Apple Vision Pro. This innovative technology allows individuals to traverse otherworldly terrains, engage in epic battles against legendary creatures, or partake in virtual concerts, all from the sanctuary of their own homes. While the internet serves as a gateway for connectivity and information retrieval, VR emphasizes total immersion, plunging users directly into the vibrant core of digital realms.

Among the vanguard of VR's widespread adoption are virtual games, which ingeniously blend elements of play with perceptual reality. Titles such as "Beat Saber," a rhythm game where players slash through beats with lightsabers, and "Half-Life: Alyx," a first-person shooter that has redefined immersive storytelling in VR, exemplify the potential of VR gaming. These experiences can simulate physical sensations, such as the gust of wind on your face while scaling a majestic mountain in a fantastical setting or the adrenaline rush of engaging in combat with a computer-generated adversary.

Blockchain technology and NFTs play pivotal roles in further enriching these virtual experiences. NFTs enable the unique ownership of digital items within these games, ranging from exclusive weapons to bespoke virtual real estate and distinctive avatars that signify your digital persona. These digital possessions are not merely cosmetic or trivial; they embody real-world value, fostering novel in-game economies and player opportunities. For instance, in games like "Decentraland" or "The Sandbox," players can buy, sell, or trade virtual plots of land and other assets using cryptocurrencies, which might soon become the universal currency of the metaverse. This integration of blockchain and NFTs into VR games not only enhances the immersion and ownership but also introduces a groundbreaking economic model where virtual assets offered by real-world brands transcend digital boundaries, possessing tangible economic impact.

Cryptocurrencies play an indispensable role in this burgeoning ecosystem, acting as the lifeblood for transactions within these virtual worlds. The purchase of NFTs and various digital assets through cryptocurrencies exemplifies a seamless integration of digital finance and virtual experiences. Cryptocurrencies, such as Ethereum, which is widely used for NFT transactions, provide a secure, transparent, and efficient means of acquiring digital goods. This digital currency facilitates the exchange of value in a way that mirrors real-world transactions but with the added benefits of blockchain technology, including immutability, decentralization, and reduced risk of fraud.

The use of cryptocurrencies in buying NFTs and other digital assets underscores a noteworthy shift toward a digital economy where virtual goods have tangible value. This economic model not only democratizes ownership by making it accessible to anyone with an internet connection and digital wallet but also fosters a direct relationship between creators and consumers. Artists, game developers, and content creators can monetize their digital creations directly, without the need for intermediaries, thus ensuring a fairer distribution of income.

Moreover, the reciprocal operability of assets across different games and virtual platforms, facilitated by blockchain technology, promises a future where digital possessions can be used and showcased across multiple metaverses, enhancing the user's digital identity and experience. This transition highlights the role of cryptocurrencies not just as a medium of exchange but as a foundational component of a new Web 3 digital economy.

Finally, the exploration into VR worlds, particularly through the lens of wearable technology for gaming and virtual experiences, unveils a complex array of potential drawbacks spanning health, mental well-being, financial stability, and losing the distinction between reality and virtuality. A research summary by *Common Sense Media* examines these concerns with a multifaceted approach.

Health Concerns are notably significant, with VR headsets implicated in vision problems due to the vergence-accommodation conflict, which misaligns the eye-brain coordination for focusing, potentially impairing vision development in children. Furthermore, the risk of motion sickness and the discomfort from prolonged headset use are noteworthy. Additionally, while VR has the potential to encourage physical activity, its propensity to substitute for real-world outdoor activities could inversely affect physical health by reducing engagement in essential physical exercises.

Mental Health and Development issues are critical, particularly for children who are at a developmental stage where distinguishing between reality and fiction is crucial. VR's immersive nature might exacerbate this difficulty, possibly affecting their understanding of real-world consequences and psychological development. The accessibility of age-inappropriate content within these virtual environments raises alarms about exposure to sexually explicit material, abusive language, and predatory behaviors, posing risks to psychological health. Moreover, the potential for social isolation is significant, as virtual interactions lack the complexity and depth of real-life human connections, which could hinder social and emotional development.

Financial Concerns emerge within the virtual economy, characterized by digital advertising, NFTs, and cryptocurrencies, introducing new dimensions of spending that may promote financial irresponsibility among users, especially young ones. The realms of virtual spending and the engagement in gambling-like behaviors through the integration of cryptocurrencies in gaming platforms highlight the risks of addiction and excessive financial expenditure in virtual pursuits.

Safety and Privacy considerations are paramount, with VR platforms capable of collecting sensitive information, including biometric data, such as fingerprints, voiceprints, iris scans, and facial recognition, which poses substantial privacy concerns. The anonymity provided by VR can also amplify vulnerabilities to online predators and cyberbullying, making personal safety a salient issue.

While VR technology presents groundbreaking opportunities for immersive experiences, the importance of cautious integration into our lives, especially concerning children, cannot be overstated.

The Metaverse: A Vision for the Future

The metaverse, as conceptualized by Meta (formerly Facebook) under the guidance of CEO Mark Zuckerberg, signifies a monumental shift in our engagement with digital realms. This ambitious vision transcends traditional gaming, offering a digital expanse where users can immerse themselves in virtually every aspect of life—from work and socialization to education and entertainment—within a network of interconnected virtual realities. This fusion of VR, augmented reality (AR)—a technology that superimposes computer-generated enhancements atop an existing reality, and conventional internet elements aims to forge a cohesive and immersive digital universe, heralding a new era of online interaction.

Table 8.1 Key Differences between Virtual Reality, Augmented Reality, and the Metaverse

Feature	VR	AR	Metaverse
Immersion Level	Completely immersive	Overlays digital on real world	Combines VR & AR, persistent world
Device	VR headset	AR glasses/devices	Both VR & AR
Focus	Transportation to virtual worlds	Enhancing real-world experiences	Network of interconnected spaces
Role in the Metaverse	Immersive component	Practical interaction component	Foundation for the entire concept

Table 8.1 summarizes the key differences between VR, AR, and the metaverse:

At the core of Meta's blueprint for the metaverse is the creation of unique digital identities through customizable avatars, to wit, a three-dimensional character that represents a real person in the virtual world. These avatars are envisioned to traverse a plethora of virtual settings, participating in a wide range of activities such as attending live concerts, exploring digital reconstructions of renowned museums, and engaging in social gatherings within VR environments. The integration of AI is crucial in enabling these natural interactions and maintaining safety across the metaverse. Among the most avant-garde aspects of Meta's plan is the M2Meta initiative, which seeks to explore the feasibility of uploading human consciousness to a decentralized network.

The scope of the metaverse's potential applications is broad, brave, and diverse. In the educational sector, it could transform learning by allowing students to virtually immerse themselves in historical events or navigate the complexities of the human anatomy, thereby converting education into an engaging, interactive experience. Health care could witness significant advancements, with physicians performing remote surgeries or consultations in virtual spaces, thus overcoming geographical limitations and improving patient care. The entertainment industry might evolve to host virtual movie premieres, enabling fans to interact with celebrities in a digital realm, or create virtual theme parks that provide thrilling experiences devoid of physical constraints.

For the business community, in particular, the metaverse heralds a new era for expansion and growth, transforming traditional sectors and introducing novel concepts within the digital landscape. In virtual commerce and retail, the metaverse allows for the creation of immersive shopping experiences where customers via avatars can move through virtual stores, try on outfits in a digital format, and make purchases with cryptocurrencies, all within a virtual environment. This revolutionizes the retail experience by boosting customer interaction and allowing them to share design concepts with fashion designers or shop alongside their preferred celebrity endorsers, thereby setting the stage for groundbreaking retail concepts.

In the realm of real estate and virtual land, the metaverse offers unprecedented options. Companies can acquire digital plots to establish virtual offices, lease spaces, buy and sell, or advertise spaces, essentially generating a new category of digital assets and investment possibilities.

Marketing and brand engagement are reimagined in the metaverse, offering creative avenues for brands to connect with their audience. Through virtual events, concerts, and interactive advertisements, brands can craft unique and engaging experiences that forge stronger consumer relationships and elevate brand loyalty.

The metaverse also redefines work and collaboration, providing an alternative to traditional remote work solutions like video online conferencing. Virtual workspaces potentially enable more dynamic meetings, team-building exercises, and international conferences, eliminating the logistic constraints of physical presence and travel.

In education and training, the metaverse and virtual reality technologies present transformative opportunities. Businesses can utilize realistic simulations for training, while educational institutions can deliver immersive learning experiences that exceed the limitations of conventional classroom settings, making education more engaging and effective.

However, the journey into the metaverse is not without its challenges. Ethical considerations are paramount, with a need to foster a metaverse that upholds positive values and safeguards against harmful content and behaviors. This includes protecting user privacy and ensuring safe, respectful virtual interactions.

The societal impact of the metaverse, particularly its potential to deepen social inequalities or contribute to digital media addiction, warrants careful attention as described earlier. Promoting equitable access and encouraging healthy digital practices are critical to ensuring that the metaverse benefits all segments of society. Finally, environmental concerns, such as the monumental energy demands and carbon footprint associated with running complex virtual worlds, cannot be overlooked. The development of sustainable technologies and practices will be crucial in minimizing the environmental impact of the metaverse.

Digital Media Advertising

Digital advertising's transformative impact on brand-consumer interaction is exemplified through interactive and personalized experiences, a shift from the passive reception of traditional advertising to active engagement. This evolution is vividly illustrated by real-world examples where brands like Nike leverage digital platforms to create customizable sneaker experiences, inviting consumers to design their shoes online. This level of customization and interaction fosters a deeper connection and loyalty, a feat traditional advertising mediums struggle to achieve.

The agility of digital advertising is demonstrated through platforms like Google AdWords, allowing businesses to adjust their campaigns in real time based on performance data. This capability is crucial in the digital age, where trends and consumer preferences evolve swiftly. For instance, during the 2020 pandemic, many retailers quickly shifted their advertising strategies to highlight online shopping options and contactless delivery, responding to changing consumer needs with unprecedented speed.

Targeting and efficiency also differ markedly between the two. Traditional advertising, while capable of reaching a wide audience, often lacks the precision of digital advertising, leading to potentially higher costs from reaching non-targeted audiences. The inability to precisely target can obscure the efficiency of the spending in relation to actual audience interest. Digital advertising, however, with its granular targeting capabilities based on demographics, interests, and behaviors enhanced by the application of AI, provides a more cost-efficient way to reach the intended audience segments. The real-time tracking and measurement of engagement allow for ongoing optimization of spending on ads to maximize return on investment (ROI).

The comparison between the costs of digital and traditional ad campaigns reveals significant variations influenced by factors such as the campaign's scale, the specificity of the targeted audience, and the choice of advertising platforms or mediums. Traditional advertising channels like TV, radio, and print typically demand a higher initial investment. The production of TV commercials, for instance, involves considerable costs for scriptwriting, hiring actors, filming, and postproduction. Similarly, billboards and print ads require expenditures for design, printing, and the rental of physical space. In contrast, digital advertising campaigns can be launched with relatively lower upfront costs. The creation of digital content can be more economical, with expenses varying with the ad design's complexity and flexibility with pricing models such as pay-per-click (PPC) for search ads or cost-per-impression (CPI) for social media and display ads. This flexibility enables advertisers to set budget limits and pay only for the actual engagement or exposure, offering better cost control. The direct online management of these campaigns further reduces initial setup costs.

The transition from traditional to digital advertising reflects a significant shift in how brands approach marketing communications. While traditional advertising has been dominated by broad-reach platforms like television and billboards, exemplified by memorable Super Bowl commercials that reach millions, these methods lack the direct interaction and personalization that digital channels offer. Digital advertising, in contrast, enables brands to deliver targeted messages to specific audiences, enhancing the relevance and effectiveness of their marketing efforts. Facebook's targeted ads, for instance, allow small businesses and large corporations alike to reach specific demographics, interests, and behaviors, optimizing their marketing spend with precision.

The digital landscape offers a diversity of channels for brand engagement, from search and display advertising to social media, video, and influencer marketing. Influencer partnerships, such as those by beauty brands like Glossier, demonstrate the power of leveraging social media personalities to reach niche audiences, blending authenticity with targeted reach. Meanwhile, AI-driven platforms like The Trade Desk empower advertisers to optimize their digital campaigns across multiple channels, adapting to real-time feedback and trends for maximum impact. The importance of adhering to regulations and ethical standards in digital advertising cannot be overstated, with bodies like the FTC ensuring that advertisements are both honest and substantiated by evidence.

As digital technology continues to evolve, the advertising landscape becomes increasingly complex and dynamic. Brands face the challenge of staying abreast of regulatory changes and technological advancements to remain competitive. The evolution to digital advertising underscores a fundamental change in marketing, emphasizing the importance of targeted engagement, personalized messaging, and measurable outcomes. In this vibrant and challenging arena, the brands that succeed are those that adapt to these changes with agility and strategic foresight, ensuring their marketing efforts resonate deeply with their intended audiences.

Regulatory and Compliance Issues in Blockchain and Smart Contracts

The regulatory and compliance environment for blockchain technology and smart contracts within the digital media realm is both intricate and rapidly evolving, presenting a host of challenges for entities involved in this space. These tests are not only technical but also legal, as blockchain technology transcends traditional sectoral boundaries, jurisdictions, and legal frameworks, leading to potential conflicts with existing laws and creating a regulatory environment that is often unclear or overlapping. One significant area of concern is intellectual property (IP) rights in the context of blockchain's decentralized nature, which complicates traditional IP protection mechanisms and raises questions about ownership and the unauthorized use of copyrighted and trademarked material.

Additionally, the marketing of blockchain-based assets, such as cryptocurrencies and crypto tokens, faces intense regulatory scrutiny. Various jurisdictions have expressed concerns over misleading claims and the potential for fraud, prompting entities like the US Securities and Exchange Commission (SEC) to issue guidance and take enforcement actions against misleading initial coin offerings (ICOs). This scrutiny extends to digital advertising platforms, which must carefully consider whether to accept ads for these blockchain-based products and services.

Complicating the regulatory environment further are anti-money laundering (AML) and know-your-customer (KYC) regulations, which are particularly onerous given the anonymity and cross-border nature of blockchain transactions. Platforms operating within the blockchain space might be required to implement AML and KYC procedures to prevent illicit activities, necessitating innovative solutions to comply with legal requirements without compromising the benefits of decentralization.

Moreover, there's the issue of ensuring that blockchain and smart contract deployments do not inadvertently facilitate unethical marketing practices. The transparency and immutability of blockchain, while generally seen as advantages, could paradoxically be used to lend a veneer of credibility to false or misleading advertising campaigns. This necessitates the development of new standards and best practices by regulators and industry bodies that do not currently exist to govern the ethical use of blockchain technology, aiming to enhance consumer trust rather than undermine it.

The integration of smart contracts into the legal system as legally binding agreements presents another layer of complexity. Traditional legal frameworks, designed around centralized parties and clear jurisdictional boundaries, are ill-equipped to handle the decentralized and autonomous nature of blockchain-based transactions. This raises numerous legal questions regarding the validity of smart contracts, the attribution of liability, especially in cases of coding errors leading to financial losses, and the enforcement of terms across different jurisdictions. The global and borderless nature of blockchain technology means that a single transaction can involve parties from multiple countries, each with its own legal system and regulatory standards, further complicating regulatory compliance.

Summary

This chapter explores the dynamic and rapidly changing ecosystem of digital media, examining the integration and implications of cutting-edge technologies such as blockchain, smart contracts, cryptocurrencies, non-fungible tokens (NFTs), augmented reality (AR), virtual reality (VR), and the metaverse. Blockchain technology and smart contracts are heralded for introducing unprecedented levels of security, transparency, and efficiency in digital transactions, enabling the creation and exchange of digital assets like NFTs with verifiable ownership and authenticity. NFTs have particularly revolutionized the digital art world and content creation, providing artists and creators with new avenues for monetization and copyright protection. Meanwhile, AR and VR technologies have altered user experiences, offering immersive and interactive digital environments that extend from entertainment to educational applications, fundamentally changing how content is consumed and interacted with. The concept of the metaverse, a collective virtual shared space, further integrates these technologies, promising a future where digital and physical realities converge to create fully immersive, persistent worlds where people can meet, work, and play.

However, this rapid technological advancement and integration presents significant challenges, especially in terms of regulation, privacy, health, and security. The decentralized nature of blockchain and the global scope of digital assets like NFTs raise complex legal and regulatory issues, from intellectual property rights to compliance with anti-money laundering directives. The introduction of cryptocurrencies in this technology-enabled environment allows direct, decentralized transactions, reducing the need for intermediaries and potentially lowering costs for digital media platforms and consumers. It also offers new monetization models for content creators allowing for more flexible and equitable compensation. Cryptocurrencies can enhance user privacy and security, providing anonymous transactions and secure payment methods. However, volatility and regulatory uncertainty of cryptocurrencies can pose financial risks to creators, advertisers, and platforms, complicating budgeting and financial planning. The anonymity afforded by cryptocurrencies, while beneficial for privacy, can facilitate illicit activities, including copyright infringement and the distribution of unauthorized content. Additionally, the environmental impact of cryptocurrency mining on the energy grid, particularly for those using proof-of-work mechanisms, has raised sustainability concerns.

The anonymity afforded by these technologies also poses risks of fraudulent activities and scams, necessitating security measures and ethical guidelines. Privacy concerns are particularly pronounced with AR and VR, as these technologies require the collection and processing of vast amounts of personal data to create personalized experiences. Additionally, the burgeoning development of the metaverse introduces questions about data governance, user safety, and the potential for creating monopolistic digital ecosystems controlled by a few large entities.

Overall, while the integration of blockchain, NFTs, AR, VR, and the metaverse within digital media offers evolutionary potential, it also requires careful understanding of the accompanying challenges. Stakeholders must engage in ongoing dialogue and collaboration to establish regulatory frameworks, ethical standards, and security protocols that ensure these technologies not only foster innovation and creativity but also safeguard user rights and promote a healthy digital ecosystem.

Discussion Questions

1. How do blockchain technology and smart contracts revolutionize transactions and ownership in the digital world, and what are the implications for creators and consumers?
2. In what ways do NFTs impact the economics of digital art and content creation, and how do they address issues of copyright and ownership?
3. What ethical considerations arise from the monetization of digital assets through NFTs, and how should the digital community address potential concerns of inequality and accessibility?
4. How do augmented reality (AR) and virtual reality (VR) technologies alter user experiences in digital media, and what industries stand to benefit the most from these changes?
5. As the metaverse begins to take shape, what are the potential social, economic, and psychological impacts of living and interacting in fully immersive digital environments?
6. Discuss the privacy and security challenges associated with AR and VR technologies, especially in relation to the collection and use of personal data from children. How should these concerns be mitigated?
7. What are the key regulatory challenges posed by the global and decentralized nature of blockchain technology, especially concerning NFTs, and how can they be addressed to ensure market integrity and consumer protection?
8. Consider the implications of the metaverse for digital identity. How can users' identities and personal information be protected in these virtual spaces, and what role should anonymity play?

9. Explore the potential risks and downsides of creating monopolistic digital ecosystems by a few large entities within the metaverse. How can diversity and competition be encouraged to foster a healthy digital economy?
10. What role should international cooperation play in the regulation of blockchain technology, smart contracts, NFTs, and the metaverse? How can countries work together to create standards that promote innovation while protecting users and maintaining market integrity?

Works Referenced

Buzu, Irina. "Blockchain, Smart Contracts and Copyright Management Disruption." SSRN, March 5, 2021, accessed at https://papers.ssrn.com/sol3/papers.cfm?abstract_id=3759260

Chynoweth, Victoria. "Exploring the Future of Crypto Gaming in 2024." *Forbes*, January 22, 2024, accessed at https://www.forbes.com/sites/digital-assets/2024/01/22/exploring-the-future-of-crypto-gaming-in-2024/?sh=664d3dc565f2

Ding, Yuanjun, Li Yang, Wenfeng Shi, and Xuliang Duan. "The Digital Copyright Management System Based on Blockchain." IEEE 2nd International Conference on Computer and Communication Engineering Technology (CCET), August 2019, accessed at https://www.researchgate.net/publication/339170641_The_Digital_Copyright_Management_System_Based_on_Blockchain

Ghaffary, Shirin. "Why You Should Care about Facebook's Big Push into the Metaverse." *Vox*, November 24, 2021, accessed at https://www.vox.com/recode/22799665/facebook-metaverse-meta-zuckerberg-oculus-vr-ar

Hulse, Spencer. "Smart Contracts and Intellectual Property: Protecting Creators." *BlockTelegraph*, August 31, 2023, accessed at https://blocktelegraph.io/smart-contracts-intellectual-property-creators

IBM. "What Are Smart Contracts on Blockchain?" IBM, accessed at https://www.ibm.com/topics/smart-contracts

Lennon, Hailey. "A Landmark NFT Lawsuit Seeks to Determine How Creators, Owners, and Investors Can Protect Their Intellectual Property and Monetize Assets Moving Forward." *Forbes*, July 5, 2022, accessed at https://www.forbes.com/sites/haileylennon/2022/07/05/a-landmark-nft-lawsuit-seeks-to-determine-how-creators-owners-and-investors-can-protect-their-intellectual-property-and-monetize-assets-moving-forward/?sh=5bfc795561ec

Liu, Yanhui, Jianbiao Zhang, Shupei Wu, and Pathan, Muhammad Salman. "Research on Digital Copyright Protection Based on the Hyperledger Fabric Blockchain Network Technology." National Library of Medicine, September 17, 2021, accessed at https://www.ncbi.nlm.nih.gov/pmc/articles/PMC8459789

Pacheco, Guilliean. "10 Examples of Smart Contracts on Blockchain." *TechTarget*, August 31, 2023, accessed at https://www.techtarget.com/searchcio/feature/Examples-of-smart-contracts-on-blockchain

Aiswarya, P.M. "How Non-Fungible Tokens Are Revolutionising Digital Ownership?" *Analytics Insight*, September 22, 2020, accessed at https://www.analyticsinsight.net/how-non-fungible-tokens-are-revolutionising-digital-ownership

Rejolut. "Blockchain in Media Advertising and Entertainment Market." Rejolut, accessed at https://rejolut.com/blog/blockchain-in-media-advertising-and-entertainment-market

Shah, Pritesh, Forester, Daniel, Berberich, Matthias, and Raspé, Carolin. "Blockchain Technology: Data Privacy Issues and Potential Mitigation Strategies." Practical Law, 2019, accessed at https://www.davispolk.com/sites/default/files/blockchain_technology_data_privacy_issues_and_potential_mitigation_strategies_w-021-8235.pdf

Silicon Valley Innovation Center. "Intellectual Property and Digital Rights Management with Blockchain: Safeguarding Creative Content in the Digital Age." Silicon Valley Innovation Center, August 9, 2023, accessed at https://siliconvalley.center/blog/intellectual-property-and-digital-rights-management-with-blockchain-safeguarding-creative-content-in-the-digital-age

Singh, Menga. "Traditional Advertising vs Digital Advertising—Key Differences." The Media Ant January 22, 2024, accessed at https://www.themediaant.com/blog/traditional-advertising-vs-digital-advertising

SMU. "Blockchain: The Future of Digital Art and Design." SMU, February 19, 2024, accessed at https://www.smu.edu/meadows/newsandevents/news/2024/blockchain-the-future-of-digital-art-and-design

Technology Innovators. "Regulatory Challenges in Blockchain: Navigating Compliance and Legal Frameworks." Technology Innovators, accessed at https://www.technology-innovators.com/regulatory-challenges-in-blockchain-navigating-compliance-and-legal-frameworks

The Compliance Digest. "Blockchain and Smart Contracts in Compliance." The Compliance Digest, February 13, 2024, accessed at https://thecompliancedigest.com/2024/02/13/blockchain-and-smart-contracts-in-compliance

Walker, Beth. "What Is Digital Advertising and How Does It Work?" SMA Marketing, April 28, 2022, SMA Marketing, accessed at https://www.smamarketing.net/blog/what-is-digital-advertising-and-how-does-it-work

9

Big Data Battles: Antitrust Law in an Age of Tech Giants and Market Dominance

> *The greatest concentration of economic and social power in a few hands since the rise of industrial monopolies in the Gilded Age. This is not capitalism. This is something new.*
>
> —Shoshana Zuboff, author of
> *The Age of Surveillance Capitalism*

In today's era, giants of digital information technology and communications like Amazon, Apple, Alphabet's Google, and Meta Platforms have emerged as pivotal elements of the US economy and societal framework. Their influence stretches far beyond their market footprint, intricately weaving into the socioeconomic fabric of the country. This significant prominence as pronounced by keen observers like *The Age of Surveillance Capitalism* author Shoshana Zuboff has drawn concentrated attention from US institutions such as the Congress, the White House, federal agencies and courts, all keenly observing the operational strategies of these behemoths. As primary channels of online interaction, these digital media corporations hold considerable sway over commercial and political landscapes, frequently spotlighting their CEOs and highlighting their critical role in the nation's economic and social realms.

Antitrust regulators, aware of the vast scope of these companies' activities and their impact on consumers, businesses, and the workforce, are increasingly scrutinizing their conduct. The challenge, however, lies in aligning the business maneuvers of these digital titans with the principles of US antitrust law, established in 1890 but based on even older common law traditions. The advent of modern technology markets presents unique hurdles for antitrust enforcement and judicial systems, necessitating focused analysis and innovative approaches to adapt age-old laws to contemporary technological realms. Despite the adaptable nature of antitrust legislation, designed to grow with evolving markets and technologies, applying these laws to the new dynamics of technology markets continues to provoke intricate questions and challenges that are the focus of this chapter.

For similar reasons, the European Union (EU) expresses concern over the concentration of power among major digital media firms reflecting its commitment to maintaining a fair, competitive, and innovative digital market that protects consumer rights: Both the United States with its market-driven regulatory model and the European Union with its rights-driven model face the challenge of balancing the need for robust antitrust enforcement with the desire to promote innovation and economic growth. As digital media firms continue to expand their influence, regulators must adapt their strategies to ensure that competition thrives and consumer interests are safeguarded in the rapidly evolving digital landscape.

Meanwhile, China in direct competition with the United States and European Union, is racing to win the global battle to regulate the dominant digital media powers. China's approach to regulating big tech and major media firms involves a comprehensive set of regulations and actions aimed at curbing monopolistic practices, ensuring data security, with a strong focus on maintaining state control over the rapidly growing digital economy.

History of Antitrust Law in the United States

The history of antitrust law in the United States is intricately tied to the nation's economic progression and the evolution of its market dynamics. Originating in the late nineteenth century, these laws emerged as a legislative response to the burgeoning power of monopolies and trusts, which, by controlling vast sectors of the economy, were stifling competition and adversely affecting consumers. This period of rapid industrial growth and consolidation gave rise to public and governmental concern over the unchecked power of these entities, leading to the development of a legal framework aimed at preserving market competition and protecting consumer interests.

Sherman Antitrust Act of 1890

The Sherman Antitrust Act of 1890 is a foundational statute in United States antitrust law that aims to maintain a competitive marketplace by prohibiting certain business behaviors that restrict competition. The Act's two main provisions, Sections 1 and 2, address different aspects of anticompetitive conduct. Section 1 targets agreements that restrain trade, such as cartels and collusive practices, while Section 2 focuses on unilateral conduct that monopolizes or attempts to monopolize a market. These are the key provision of the Sherman Act:

- **Section 1** prohibits "every contract, combination in the form of trust or otherwise, or conspiracy, in restraint of trade or commerce among the several States, or with foreign nations."
- **Section 2** makes it a felony to "monopolize, or attempt to monopolize, or combine or conspire with any other person or persons, to monopolize any part of the trade or commerce among the several States, or with foreign nations."

Under the Sherman Act, the remedies available to address anticompetitive practices include injunctions, allowing courts to issue orders halting these practices. Civil penalties can be levied on corporations and individuals found in violation, as determined in cases brought by the federal government. Furthermore, criminal penalties, including fines and/or imprisonment, can be imposed for violations of the Act. Individuals or businesses harmed by antitrust violations have the right to initiate private actions, suing for triple (treble) damages and attorney's fees. Additionally, courts have the authority to mandate divestiture, requiring a company to sell off certain assets or parts of its business to reinstate competitive market conditions.

The Sherman Act has been the subject of numerous landmark court cases that have shaped its interpretation and application. These cases have grappled with defining the boundaries of acceptable business practices and the government's role in fostering competition. Here are some of the most compelling cases that have illuminated the power and complexities of the Sherman Act.

United States v. E. C. Knight Co. (156 U.S. 1 (1895)): This case, also known as the "Sugar Trust Case," was one of the first antitrust cases in the United States. The Supreme Court ruled that manufacturing was not subject to federal regulation under the Sherman Act, as it was not considered interstate commerce. This decision limited the government's ability to apply antitrust laws to manufacturing monopolies within a state.

Northern Securities Co. v. United States (193 U.S. 197 (1904)): The Supreme Court ruled that the Northern Securities Company, a large railroad trust, violated the Sherman Act. The decision set a precedent for the government to break up monopolies and promote competition in the marketplace, which remains a guiding principle of US antitrust law today.

United States v. American Tobacco Co. (221 U.S. 106 (1911)): This was a decision by the Supreme Court, which held that the combination in this case is one in restraint of trade and an attempt to monopolize the business of tobacco in interstate commerce within the prohibitions of the Sherman Act. The American Tobacco Co. was ordered to dissolve into four separate entities to restore competition.

United States v. Alcoa (148 F.2d 416 (1945)): The Court of Appeals for the Second Circuit, in an opinion by Judge Learned Hand who heard the case by a special act of Congress because the Supreme Court could not hear the case due to disqualification of too many justices, found that the Aluminum Company of America (Alcoa) had illegally monopolized the aluminum market. This case is noteworthy for its discussion of the control of market share and the concept of "intent" in monopolization.

United States v. Paramount Pictures, Inc. (334 U.S. 131 (1948)): Known as the "Hollywood Antitrust Case of 1948," this landmark decision by the Supreme Court dealt with the control major film studios had over the movie industry. The Court found that the vertical integration of film production, distribution, and exhibition violated antitrust laws, leading to the mandatory divestiture of theater chains by the studios. This case dramatically altered how movies were distributed and shown in the United States.

Broadcast Music, Inc. v. CBS, Inc. (441 U.S. 1 (1979)): Authored by Justice Byron White, this Supreme Court ruling determined that Broadcast

Music Inc. (BMI)'s practice of issuing blanket licenses to copyrighted musical compositions did not inherently constitute price fixing under antitrust laws. Blanket licenses give the licensees the right to perform any and all of the compositions owned by the members or affiliates as often as the licensee's desire for a stated term. The Court recognized potential pro-competitive benefits of this practice, such as enhanced efficiency in music licensing, highlighting a case-by-case approach to antitrust evaluations.

United States v. AT&T (552 F. Supp. 131 (1982)): The case against AT&T led to the breakup of the Bell System into seven smaller companies, fundamentally changing the telecommunications industry in the United States. The government argued that AT&T had used its monopoly power to stifle competition and innovation in the market for telephone services and equipment. The settlement, known as the Modification of Final Judgment, resulted in AT&T divesting its local exchange service operating companies, facilitating the entry of new competitors into the market.

United States v. Visa U.S.A., Inc., and MasterCard International Inc. (163 F. Supp. 322 (2001)): This case addressed the issue of Visa and MasterCard's control over the credit card market. The US Department of Justice argued that the companies' practices restricted competition by enforcing rules that prevented banks from issuing cards from competing networks, such as American Express and Discover. The court's decision forced Visa and MasterCard to alter their policies, opening up the market to greater competition.

United States v. Microsoft Corp. (253 F.3d 34 (2001)): This groundbreaking case found that Microsoft had maintained its monopoly in the PC operating systems market through anticompetitive actions that violated Section 2 of the Sherman Act. Specifically, Microsoft was accused of illegally monopolizing the web browser market for Windows, primarily through the legal and technical restrictions it put on the abilities of PC manufacturers (OEMs) and users to uninstall Internet Explorer and use other programs such as Netscape and Java. The case was settled with Microsoft agreeing to a consent decree that imposed various restrictions on its business practices.

FTC v. Qualcomm Inc. (935 F.3d. 752 (9th Cir. 2019)): Though not a Sherman Act case initiated by the Department of Justice, this Federal Trade Commission (FTC) case against Qualcomm is significant in the context of antitrust discussions around technology and patents. The FTC alleged that Qualcomm engaged in anticompetitive patent licensing practices to maintain a monopoly in the cellular modem chip market. Initially, the district court ruled against Qualcomm, but the decision was overturned on appeal. The case highlights the complexities of applying antitrust laws to the tech industry's patent and licensing practices.

The Sherman Act has been subject to various interpretations over time, as illustrated by the above cases, with federal courts playing a crucial role in defining what constitutes illegal restraint of trade or monopolization. The Act's general terms have allowed it to be applied to a wide range of business practices and market conditions, from the era of horse and buggies to the digital age.

In what is perhaps the most important antitrust case brought by the Department of Justice (DOJ) against a digital media company, in 2023, the DOJ, along with thirty-eight state and territory attorneys general, brought a lawsuit against Google, alleging that the company has violated Section 2 of the Sherman Act.

The case focuses on several key issues, including whether Google's browser agreements are exclusive or de facto exclusive, thereby potentially stifling competition. These agreements, particularly with Apple and Mozilla, make Google the dominant default search engine on their browsers, which the DOJ argues biases users toward sticking with Google due to the effort and knowledge required to switch to a different search engine.

Another significant aspect of the case concerns Google's agreements regarding Android devices. Google has entered into Mobile Application Distribution Agreements (MADAs) and Revenue Share Agreements (RSAs) with device manufacturers and wireless carriers. While MADAs are nonexclusive, allowing the preinstallation of Google apps alongside non-Google search apps, RSAs require Google to be the exclusive preinstalled search app, creating a strong economic incentive for device makers and carriers. This arrangement is argued to effectively make MADAs exclusive contracts leading to the unlawful monopoly argument.

The DOJ has raised concerns that Google's dominance in the search engine market is less about the superiority of its product and more about its strategies, such as making its search engine the preloaded, default option on various devices. This situation, the DOJ argues, leads to Google amassing millions more search queries and much more data, potentially without enhancing its service as occurred when AT&T dominated the telecommunications industry. This, they suggest, could hurt consumers either through lower-quality search results or compromised privacy, without Google losing market share.

Yet, this perspective is challenged by the argument that, despite a so-called "default bias," changing search engines is a simple task requiring only a few clicks. Historical examples, such as Internet Explorer's decline despite its default status on PCs—a situation that previously brought Microsoft under antitrust scrutiny—demonstrate that consumer preferences can shift, leading to the rise of alternatives like Firefox, DuckDuckGo, and Chrome, and now newer search engine alternatives that contain machine-learning algorithm-driven capabilities like ChatGPT, OpenAI, Bing AI, Midjourney, and Perplexity AI.

The Sherman Act's enduring legacy is its role in shaping the competitive landscape of American business to prevent practices that significantly diminish competition or tend toward establishing a monopoly. By providing a legal framework to challenge anticompetitive practices the Act works to ensure that no single firm can unduly dominate a market to the detriment of consumers and competition. However, there's a crucial legal distinction between acquiring and preserving market share through fair competition and efficiency, which benefits consumers by delivering superior products, and engaging in practices that exclude potential competitors in a way that could disadvantage consumers. The Act continues to be a vital tool for antitrust enforcement depending in large part on which political party controls the White House.

The Clayton Act of 1914 and the Federal Trade Commission Act

The Clayton Act of 1914 and the Federal Trade Commission (FTC) Act are cornerstones of US antitrust legislation, complementing the Sherman Act of 1890 by addressing specific anticompetitive practices and establishing a regulatory body to enforce these laws. The Clayton Act focuses on particular behaviors that could lead to reduced competition, while the FTC Act created the FTC to prevent unfair trade practices and promote consumer protection.

The Clayton Act was designed to address and prevent specific anticompetitive practices not explicitly covered by the Sherman Act. Key provisions include:

- **Price Discrimination (Section 2):** Prohibits selling the same product to different buyers at different prices if it lessens competition.
- **Exclusive Dealings and Tying Arrangements (Sections 3 and 7):** Bans exclusive dealing contracts, tying agreements, and certain mergers and acquisitions if they may substantially lessen competition or tend to create a monopoly.
- **Interlocking Directorates (Section 8):** Forbids directors from serving on the boards of competing companies simultaneously if it would reduce competition.

Under the Clayton Act several remedies are available. It allows for preventive measures, enabling intervention before certain mergers and acquisitions are completed to avert potential harm to competition. The Act authorizes the use of injunctions to prohibit practices that may harm competitive market conditions. In terms of enforcement, civil penalties can be sought for violations of the Act, providing a deterrent against anticompetitive behavior. Individuals or entities injured by such practices have the right to initiate private actions, seeking damages for the harm incurred. The Act also allows for conditions on mergers to be imposed, ensuring that approved mergers do not negatively impact competition, which may include requirements for divestitures or operational restrictions. Divestiture can be ordered by courts, compelling a company to sell off parts of its business or assets, thereby maintaining or restoring competitive balance within the marketplace. This comprehensive suite of remedies under the Clayton Act serves to prevent anticompetitive practices before they cause harm and to maintain the integrity of competitive markets.

The **Federal Trade Commission Act of 1914 (FTC Act)** was signed into law by President Woodrow Wilson as part of the administration's trust-busting efforts. The FTC Act established the Federal Trade Commission (FTC) to protect consumers and promote competition. Addressing concerns over unfair business practices and monopolies not fully addressed by the Sherman Act, the FTC Act endowed the FTC with various tools to fulfill its mission.

Key Sections and Elements of the FTC Act

- **Section 5: Unfair or Deceptive Acts or Practices:** Prohibits "unfair methods of competition" and "unfair or deceptive acts or practices in or affecting commerce," serving as the primary foundation for the FTC's operations. The FTC is authorized to issue administrative cease-and-desist orders to stop unfair competition or deceptive practices. The FTC can seek civil penalties for violations of cease-and-desist orders and certain rule violations.
- **Section 6: Investigations and Reports:** Grants the FTC authority to investigate business practices and management of commerce entities. Empowers the FTC to require testimony and documentary evidence through subpoenas.
- **Section 7A: Premerger Notification:** This requires notification to the FTC and Department of Justice for certain large mergers or acquisitions, facilitating anticompetitive outcome reviews.
- **Section 12: Regulation of False Advertisements:** The FTC can act against false advertisements for various products and services.
- **Section 18: Rulemaking Authority:** Allows the FTC to define specific unfair or deceptive acts and establish preventive requirements.
- **Section 19: Redress and Penalties:** The FTC can seek monetary redress for consumers and impose penalties for rule violations.

The FTC's enforcement authority covers both antitrust laws and consumer protection, tackling issues from monopolistic practices to deceptive advertising. The FTC's proactive and reactive measures aim to prevent unfair business practices from becoming prevalent. Though not explicitly mentioned in the FTC Act's original text, the FTC includes consumer privacy protection in its mandate, vital in the digital age where personal data are highly valued, as discussed in a prior chapter.

In another significant case filed, but yet to be resolved, by the Federal Trade Commission and several states, this lawsuit against Facebook (now Meta Platforms Inc.) challenges the company's dominance in social networking. The complaint centers on acquisitions of Instagram and WhatsApp, critiquing them as means to maintain a monopoly. This ongoing case exemplifies the complexities of applying antitrust laws in the digital arena, with potential far-reaching effects on digital market competition.

Competition and Antitrust in the Digital Age in the United States

Over the years, antitrust laws in the United States have slowly progressed to address the complexities of a changing economy, particularly with the rise of digital media and technology firms. These historical statutes and landmark cases have laid the groundwork for contemporary antitrust scrutiny, demonstrating the government's commitment to preserving competition, fostering innovation, and protecting consumers from monopolistic practices. As the economy continues to evolve, particularly with the digital revolution, antitrust law faces new challenges and opportunities to effectively govern companies that rival some countries in their size and economic, cultural, and political influence.

To put the growth of digital media platforms in perspective, the entities behind these services—Amazon, Apple, Facebook (now Meta), Google, Twitter (now X), and Netflix—were largely nonexistent in 1995, with the exception of Apple, which was then just a minor player. These companies dominate the realms of online shopping, search engines, social media, and digital advertising, and their stocks now represent roughly 14 percent of the total value of the US stock market.

In the traditional sense, antitrust laws rely on the delineation of clear, distinct markets to evaluate competitive forces and identify instances of monopolistic tendencies. However, the advent of digital platforms challenges this premise, as these entities often blur conventional market boundaries by offering a host of integrated services across diverse sectors. For example, Google extends beyond its search engine roots to provide cloud services, operating systems, and digital advertising, complicating the assessment of its market domain for antitrust scrutiny. Similarly, Facebook's (Meta's) expansion into digital marketplaces and virtual reality further muddies the waters for regulatory oversight. These examples highlight the difficulty in applying traditional market definitions to multifaceted digital platforms, complicating efforts to gauge monopoly power effectively.

The digital economy is remarkably influenced by network effects, where the utility of a service increases as more individuals uses it. This phenomenon is particularly evident in social media platforms like X and online marketplaces like eBay, where the first movers gain a significant advantage, potentially leading to natural monopolies. Moreover, the concentration of extensive data troves by a select few entities raises alarms regarding market power abuse and consumer exploitation. Historic antitrust frameworks fall short in addressing these distinctions, as they predominantly focus on pricing and not the overarching implications of data control on competitive dynamics and consumer choice.

In the past, antitrust actions have homed in on consumer harm manifested through price surges. Yet this model hits a snag in the digital realm, where many services, including social networking (Instagram) and video streaming (YouTube), are offered for free, generating revenue through advertising and data monetization. This paradigm shift prompts a reevaluation of what constitutes consumer harm, pushing beyond the conventional price metrics to include considerations like privacy erosion, diminished service diversity, and the manipulation of consumer preferences fostered by algorithms. The near-zero marginal cost of digital products further complicates the appraisal of pricing tactics and their broader implications on market health and consumer welfare.

There's a growing consensus around the necessity for antitrust theories to evolve in tandem with the digital market's complexities. This entails acknowledging the strategic role of data, the far-reaching effects of network externalities, and the cumulative impact on innovation and consumer well-being. Many experts assert that an adaptive antitrust framework is crucial for addressing the multifaceted challenges posed by the digital economy.

It's important to keep in mind that regulatory predictions of market domination do not always come true. For instance, once upon a time Blockbuster was the leading video rental company. It attempted to eliminate Netflix, a new entrant in the market, through aggressive pricing strategies. This occurred despite the FTC intervention to prevent Blockbuster's acquisition of Hollywood Video due to concerns over market power. Nevertheless, Netflix weathered the price competition, diversified into video streaming and content production, and continued to grow, whereas Blockbuster faced bankruptcy.

In a more recent critique, the FTC has accused Amazon of engaging in predatory pricing, arguing that the company's strategy of maintaining low prices is designed to undercut competition, a patience for profits that does not immediately suggest an intention to monopolize the market through price gouging. Amazon has maintained a policy of "everyday low prices" for over two decades, suggesting that the period during which it could recoup any losses from such a strategy by later raising prices may have already passed. The possibility remains that new competitors could enter the market or existing ones could scale up, challenging Amazon and preventing any attempt to significantly raise prices in the future.

The FTC's position, which de-emphasizes the need for demonstrating how a company might later recoup losses incurred from low pricing, shifts the focus of antitrust law from consumer welfare to the protection of existing competitors. While this perspective might safeguard certain competitors from being ousted from the market, it also risks stifling beneficial price competition that serves consumers, potentially inhibiting not just predatory practices but also legitimate competitive strategies that lead to lower prices and innovation. This approach highlights the complex balance regulators must strike between preserving competitive markets and preventing anticompetitive practices that harm both consumers and the overall health of the market.

Efforts to reform antitrust laws are underway in jurisdictions such as the United States and the European Union, aiming to more aptly address the unique challenges presented by digital giants. Initiatives include contemplating the regulation of significant platforms as utilities, designing legislation that targets digital monopolies explicitly, and refining enforcement strategies to better match the rapid pace of technological progress.

It is increasingly recognized that antitrust regulations alone may not suffice in mitigating the complexities introduced by digital media entities. Complementary measures, like robust data protection and privacy statutes, an approach the European Union is leading, are deemed essential for reining in the dominance of tech behemoths and safeguarding consumers against a spectrum of harms beyond just price effects. This holistic approach signifies a shift toward a more integrated regulatory framework, capable of addressing the unique challenges of the digital age.

The European Union's Approach to Regulating Tech and Digital Media Platforms

The European Union (EU) stands at the vanguard of regulatory efforts targeting technology and digital media platforms, with its overarching goal being to cultivate a competitive, consumer-friendly, and innovative digital marketplace. The enactment of the **Digital Markets Act (DMA)** alongside the **Digital Services Act (DSA)** epitomizes the EU's commitment to curbing the dominance of large online platforms, often referred to as "gatekeepers," and setting a global benchmark for digital economy regulation.

Introduced in July 2022, the DMA seeks to ensure fair play, competition, and innovation across Europe's digital landscape. It specifically addresses platforms providing critical services—such as social networking sites, search engines, messaging apps, and online retail services—that command a significant user base (over 45 million monthly active users in the EU). The DMA aims to thwart these gatekeepers from exploiting their market power to the detriment of smaller entities and to foster a more equitable competitive environment. These are the key DMA provisions:

- **Data Privacy and Consent**: Under the DMA, gatekeepers must secure explicit consent from users to process their data, emphasizing user privacy and data protection rights.
- **Interoperability Requirements**: The act mandates that messaging and social media platforms ensure interoperability, enabling users across different platforms to communicate seamlessly.
- **Freedom from Pre installed Software**: It empowers users with the choice to uninstall any preloaded applications, addressing concerns over forced software bundling and promoting software diversity.
- **Equitable Online Presence**: Prohibiting gatekeepers from preferentially promoting their products or services in search results, the DMA enforces equitable visibility for all market participants.

The DMA introduces severe penalties for breaches, including fines up to 10 percent (or 20 percent for repeat offenses) of a company's global turnover or revenue, and, in severe cases, may compel divestitures or bar future acquisitions.

The European Commission has initiated formal investigations into major digital media-tech entities—Apple, Alphabet's Google, and Meta—citing potential "noncompliance" with the newly enacted DMA. These proceedings represent the inaugural enforcement actions under this landmark digital regulation. The investigations primarily scrutinize whether these tech behemoths are adhering to the DMA's stipulations, which include provisions for enabling app downloads beyond their proprietary app stores and eliminating undue restrictions and limitations that could stifle market competition.

Specific areas of inquiry include examining Google's practices around its Play Store, Apple's App Store policies, and Meta's operations that may unfairly limit user choices or elevate their services unfairly over competitors. Additionally, the Commission is looking into how these companies handle user data, ensure interoperability of their messaging services, and comply with the DMA's requirements on self-preferencing to prevent these platforms from leveraging their dominance to disadvantage competitors.

The outcomes of these high-profile investigations are anticipated with keen interest by industry observers, regulatory bodies, and other digital market participants globally. They are expected to establish critical precedents regarding the enforcement of the DMA, shedding light on the legislation's practical impact on curtailing the market power of Big Tech firms. Moreover, these cases will likely offer insights into the adaptability of such companies to comply with stringent regulatory frameworks aimed at ensuring fair competition, transparency, and innovation in the digital marketplace.

As these investigations progress, they will not only test the DMA's operational efficacy in regulating some of the largest and most influential companies in the digital sphere but also signal the EU's resolve in pioneering comprehensive digital market regulation. The eventual rulings and potential penalties imposed could serve as a benchmark for future actions and influence similar regulatory efforts in jurisdictions outside the European Union, underscoring the global significance of these precedential cases.

Despite its groundbreaking nature, the DMA's implementation faces logistic hurdles, notably the EU's prior inconsistent tech sector regulation experiences discussed in an earlier chapter, like those with the **General Data Protection Regulation (GDPR)**. Anticipating these challenges, the DMA stipulates more substantial fines and establishes a dedicated enforcement body, albeit concerns linger over its adequacy given its modest staffing against the vast tech landscape. The DMA's influence extends globally, with nations from Japan to Brazil to India considering similar rights-driven regulatory frameworks as the de facto standard for digital media regulation in the democratic world.

In any event, it is clear that the digital economy is difficult to regulate given the sheer volume of regulatory activity oversight would require. For instance, according to the latest data, Facebook (Meta) has over

1.93 billion daily users and every minute these users upload more than 147,000 photos and share upward of 150,000 messages. During that same minute, YouTubers uploaded 500 hours of videos and Instagram posters shared nearly 350,000 stories. This overwhelming volume of content and interaction underscores the monumental task EU and US regulators face in creating and enforcing rules that effectively address the complexities and scale of the digital world.

Understanding the expansive digital influence of even relatively lesser-known media entities offers a prime example of the challenges faced by antitrust regulators when it comes to defining concepts such as market scope, monopoly power, and anticompetitive behaviors. Liberty Media, a company traditionally anchored in the cable and entertainment sectors, has initiated a wide-ranging strategy aimed at digital innovation. This shift has propelled the company beyond the confines of traditional media, showcasing the complexity of maneuvering through and regulating such dynamic digital landscapes.

The conglomerate's acquisition of Formula One in 2017 underscored this shift, demonstrating a keen focus on harnessing digital platforms to rejuvenate and broaden the appeal of its sporting properties. This approach is poised to further evolve with the recent announcement of Liberty Media's proposed $4.5 billion acquisition of MotoGP, the world's premier two-wheel motorcycle racing competition, pending approval from antitrust regulators. This move not only signifies a substantial investment in the realm of motorsports but also highlights Liberty Media's commitment to integrating these sports into the digital era.

Liberty Media has three separate divisions: Liberty SiriusXM Group that includes SiriusXM and Pandora, Formula One Group, and Liberty Live Group that includes the largest entertainment company in the world—Live Nation. Liberty Media's digital strategy, already in motion with Formula One through initiatives like the F1 TV streaming service, aims to enhance fan engagement and accessibility. F1 TV caters to a digitally savvy audience, offering live races, extensive on-demand content, and exclusive insights that appeal to a global audience. In parallel, Liberty Media has ramped up social media efforts to significantly bolster Formula One's online presence, creating a dynamic and interactive platform for fans worldwide. This data-driven approach, leveraging analytics to understand and anticipate fan preferences, exemplifies how Liberty Media plans to transform MotoGP's digital footprint.

The acquisition of MotoGP is expected to unfold a similar blueprint for digital engagement, suggesting a future where MotoGP enjoys increased accessibility through dedicated streaming services. Such platforms would not only democratize access to live races and enrich the viewing experience with on-demand content but also potentially introduce innovative features tailored to enhance fan interaction and immersion in the sport.

Moreover, Liberty Media is likely to invest in the creation of compelling digital content surrounding MotoGP, mirroring its successful content strategies with Formula One. This could range from immersive documentaries and behind-the-scenes footage to bite-sized, social media-optimized content designed to captivate and grow MotoGP's digital audience.

Another intriguing dimension of Liberty Media's digital strategy could involve the integration of esports with MotoGP. Recognizing the explosive growth and the passionate, engaged community within esports, Liberty Media might explore synergies between MotoGP and virtual racing competitions. This could involve setting up online leagues or tournaments that leverage the brand and fan base of MotoGP, thus tapping into the burgeoning market of competitive gaming and offering new ways for fans to engage with their favorite motorsport.

Liberty Media's adaptation to the digital media evolution and its aim to innovate in sports entertainment pose fascinating challenges for antitrust regulators, as they struggle to apply traditional market definitions and assess competitive impacts in a terrain characterized by rapid technological change and global reach. The dynamic nature of digital competition, alongside the need to weigh immediate consumer benefits against potential long-term market power abuses, complicates efforts to discern whether Liberty Media's strategies could lead to anticompetitive outcomes.

China's Regulatory Approach to Digital Media

China's regulatory framework for the digital media and technology sectors underscores a state-driven model that aims to utilize technology not just for economic growth and development but also as a means to enhance governmental oversight and control. This approach prioritizes the use of technology to bolster the Chinese Communist Party's influence across the domestic digital economy and media landscape. Through amending laws and introducing new regulations, the government seeks to mitigate monopolistic tendencies and promote competitive practices, albeit within a tightly controlled environment. Such regulatory efforts are accompanied by direct interventions in tech companies' operations, emphasizing the preservation of social harmony and control over citizens' communications. Moreover, this strategy involves leveraging technology for surveillance, control, and propaganda, thereby embedding a form of digital authoritarianism within Chinese society. This comprehensive regulatory stance not only targets economic objectives but also aligns the burgeoning digital domain with broader state interests, including national security and the centralization of power.

China's approach to managing competition in the digital media sector showcases a strategic blend of economic growth ambitions with stringent regulatory control. This intricate balance is achieved through the implementation of two pivotal laws: the **Anti-Monopoly Law (AML)** and the **Anti-Unfair Competition Law (AUCL)**, each addressing different facets of market behavior and fairness.

The AML specifically targets actions by dominant market players that could stifle competition, such as collusion between competitors (horizontal agreements), restrictive agreements in the supply chain (vertical agreements), and the abuse of market power to exclude or disadvantage competitors.

A prime example of the AML in action is the case against Alibaba, where the e-commerce giant faced a fine for allegedly exploiting its market dominance to hinder competition. Jack Ma, the cofounder and former CEO of Alibaba, played a significant role in the Chinese government's regulatory crackdown on Alibaba and the broader tech industry in China. The clampdown's timing was closely linked to public comments Ma made, where he criticized China's regulatory system for stifling innovation and compared Chinese banks to "pawnshops" for their reliance on collateral and guarantees. These comments were perceived as a direct challenge to the regulatory authorities and the financial regulatory framework in China.

Shortly after Ma's outspoken remarks, the Chinese regulators intervened in a dramatic fashion. One of the most immediate and visible impacts was the abrupt suspension of the highly anticipated Initial Public Offering (IPO) of Ant Group, Alibaba's fintech arm, which was set to be the largest IPO in history. The suspension occurred just days before the listing was scheduled, indicating a direct response to Ma's comments.

Following the halted IPO, Alibaba and Ant Group came under intense regulatory scrutiny. Alibaba was subjected to an antitrust investigation, which culminated with a record fine of approximately $2.8 billion for violating antitrust laws. The regulators accused Alibaba of engaging in monopolistic behavior, such as enforcing an "exclusivity" requirement on merchants, preventing them from selling on rival platforms. In addition to financial penalties, Alibaba and Ant Group were required to undergo significant restructuring of their operations, particularly around Ant Group's credit, insurance, and wealth management services.

Jack Ma's situation underscores the delicate balance between innovation and regulation in China's rapidly evolving tech landscape. His reduced public appearances following the crackdown reflect the broader implications for China's tech entrepreneurs, signaling a more constrained environment for outspoken business leaders and increased government oversight in the tech sector.

The blocking of Tencent's proposed merger with Huya and DouYu further illustrates another example of the Chinese government's dedication to preserving market diversity within its digital economy. This intervention against Tencent, a colossal entity in China's tech landscape, especially in the gaming and social media sectors, highlighted the regulatory body's vigilance against the consolidation of too much market power in the hands of a single corporation. By preventing the merger of these leading video game streaming platforms, the government aimed to avoid a scenario where Tencent could potentially monopolize the gaming content distribution market, thereby stifling competition and innovation. This action not only reinforced the government's resolve to enforce antitrust laws but also signaled to other market players the importance of maintaining a competitive environment that encourages a multitude of voices and services, ensuring that the market remains dynamic and accessible to new entrants.

Complementing the AML, the AUCL addresses broader unfair business practices including misleading marketing, commercial bribery, and the infringement of intellectual property rights. Recent enforcement includes crackdowns on fake reviews and misleading influencer marketing, as seen with fines levied against platforms like Weibo and Xiaohongshu. Additionally, the AUCL has been applied to combat price discrimination practices by e-commerce platforms, ensuring a fairer pricing strategy for consumers.

Together, these laws form an all-inclusive regulatory framework that allows the Chinese government to maintain a tight rein over the rapidly evolving digital media landscape. This includes interventions to prevent excessive consolidation of power among dominant digital media companies and ensuring consumer protection from deceptive business practices. Furthermore, this regulatory framework seeks to cultivate an environment conducive to innovation, deterring established players from using their market position to suppress emerging competitors.

However, the implementation of these laws does pose challenges, particularly in balancing the dual objectives of fostering a competitive market while ensuring state control. Concerns have been raised regarding the transparency and consistency of law enforcement, especially given the AML's allowance for substantial government discretion. Additionally, the evolving nature of China's regulatory landscape introduces elements of uncertainty for foreign companies looking to enter the market, reflecting the complex interplay between regulation, innovation, and international business dynamics.

China's data protection landscape is undergoing significant transformation, marked by the introduction of the **Data Security Law (DSL)** and the **Personal Information Protection Law (PIPL)**. These legislative moves signify China's attempt to balance the dual objectives of safeguarding national security and individual data privacy while maintaining its stronghold on data control and content regulation. The DSL and PIPL draw parallels with global data protection standards like the EU's General Data Protection Regulation (GDPR), emphasizing user consent, data minimization, and the protection of personal information. However, they also reflect unique aspects of China's approach to data security, including stringent requirements for data classification, restrictions on international data transfers, and the deletion of content that contradicts national interests. These regulations underscore China's commitment to collecting data for national development and security, raising questions about the implications for freedom of expression and global internet governance.

The challenges posed by these regulations are particularly pronounced for international companies operating in the Chinese market. One notable example is TikTok, a social media platform owned by the Chinese company ByteDance, which has found itself at the center of international disputes over data security concerns. Allegations that the Chinese government could access user data collected by TikTok have sparked debates in the United States and other countries, leading to calls for stringent measures to protect user data from potential foreign surveillance.

In response to these concerns, TikTok initiated "Project Texas," a strategic effort to segregate US user data and ensure their storage on servers located within the United States. This initiative includes partnerships with companies like Oracle to conduct independent security audits of TikTok's data practices and algorithmic operations. Despite these efforts, the challenges of weaving through China's regulatory environment, coupled with international scrutiny, highlight the complex interplay between data security, privacy, and geopolitical tensions.

Following its US IPO, Didi Chuxing, a prominent Chinese ride-hailing service, became the focus of a critical cybersecurity review by the Cyberspace Administration of China (CAC). This review, initiated shortly after Didi's IPO, which raised over $4 billion, was a defining demonstration of the regulatory hurdles companies face within China's digital economy. Conducted under the "Cybersecurity Review Measures," the scrutiny aimed to assess potential national security risks, including the risk of data theft or damage and compliance with Chinese laws. This led to the immediate suspension of new user registrations on Didi's platform, showcasing the direct operational consequences of failing to meet regulatory standards.

The implications of Didi's review extend beyond cybersecurity to encompass privacy concerns, reflecting the broader challenges of traversing regulatory compliance in China. Penalties imposed on Didi under China's Personal Information Protection Law (PIPL), signified a sizable financial impact, setting a precedent for the intersection of cybersecurity, privacy, and regulatory compliance. The investigation's outcome, characterized by a substantial fine and a lack of transparency in the regulatory process, underscored the formidable authority Beijing exercises over digital companies and highlighted the unpredictable nature of China's regulatory framework.

Finally, China is actively regulating the use of artificial intelligence (AI) in the digital media space with a focus on maintaining state control, promoting ethical use, and safeguarding national security and public interests. The Chinese government has implemented a series of measures and guidelines to oversee the development and deployment of AI technologies. These include strict data protection laws directly affecting AI applications in digital media.

Additionally, China has introduced specific regulations targeting the ethical development of AI, aiming to prevent the creation and spread of fake news and deepfake technology. Regulations now require that any AI-created content be clearly labeled to prevent misinformation and protect intellectual property rights. The Cyberspace Administration of China (CAC) plays a pivotal role in this regulatory framework, overseeing AI activities to ensure that they align with national interests and do not undermine social stability or security.

Traversing the evolving data protection framework in China poses both major risks and opportunities for foreign investors and companies operating within the digital media and technology sectors. The landscape is marked by regulatory uncertainty and the potential for increased costs related to compliance, presenting serious challenges. Compounding these difficulties is the use of exit bans by Chinese authorities, a practice that restricts the movement of foreign nationals embroiled in business disputes with Chinese companies, effectively confining them within China's borders without formal arrest. This tactic adds another layer of complexity to the already challenging operational environment for international digital media businesses.

Moreover, China's regulatory initiatives are closely aligned with its strategic goals, particularly in reinforcing industries critical to national security, such as semiconductor manufacturing and telecommunications. This focus underscores China's intent to attain technological self-sufficiency and lessen its reliance on foreign technologies amid rising global tensions. The intensified regulatory oversight, alongside more stringent investment guidelines from abroad, especially from the United States, injects further uncertainty into the investment climate. While some investors see this as a chance to enter the market at reduced valuations, others remain wary, apprehensive about the potential surge in operational expenses and the unpredictable outcomes of regulatory measures driven by wider political and economic agendas.

Summary

The relationship between antitrust laws and digital media spans various jurisdictions, each adopting distinct approaches tailored to their economic philosophies, regulatory environments, and strategic objectives. This multifaceted landscape is particularly evident in the case law system of the United States, the bureaucratic, rights-driven regulatory framework of the European Union (EU), and China's state-centric antitrust regulatory scheme.

In the United States, the antitrust regulatory approach is inherently market-driven, grounded in a case law system that prioritizes economic efficiency and consumer welfare. US antitrust laws, primarily the Sherman Act, the Clayton Act, and the Federal Trade Commission Act, aim to prevent monopolistic behaviors and promote fair competition without unduly interfering in the market dynamics. This approach has led to landmark cases against tech giants, scrutinizing their market practices to ensure they do not stifle competition or harm consumers. The US legal system's reliance on judicial precedents allows for a flexible, evolving interpretation of antitrust laws, adapting to the complexities of the digital age. However, critics argue this model sometimes falls short in addressing the rapid innovations and the dominance of tech giants in the digital media landscape.

Conversely, the European Union adopts a more bureaucratic, rights-driven approach to antitrust regulation, emphasizing market fairness, consumer rights, and data protection. The EU's regulatory framework, including the General Data Protection Regulation (GDPR) and the Digital Markets Act (DMA), reflects a comprehensive strategy to limit the power of digital media conglomerates and ensure they do not abuse their market positions. The EU's approach is characterized by stringent regulations, fines for noncompliance, and proactive measures to safeguard consumer privacy and data sovereignty. This model aims to create a level playing field, encouraging competition and innovation while protecting individual rights. The EU's regulatory actions against major tech companies underscore its commitment to enforcing these principles, though such measures sometimes face criticism for their complexity and potential to stifle market dynamics.

In contrast, China's antitrust regulatory framework is centered on state control, integrating economic goals with broader political and social objectives. Unlike the market-driven approach of the United States and the rights-driven focus of the European Union, China's model emphasizes the primacy of state interests, using antitrust laws as tools to regulate the digital economy, support state-owned enterprises, and foster domestic innovation. The Chinese government employs antitrust laws not only to prevent monopolistic practices but also to advance national security and development priorities. This approach includes rigorous scrutiny of tech firms, data security laws, and measures to ensure digital platforms align with state policies. While this model has enabled rapid growth and innovation in China's digital media sector, it also raises concerns about the implications for competition, free expression, and the global digital marketplace.

Each of these approaches—market-driven in the United States, rights-driven in the European Union, and state-controlled in China—reflects the broader legal, economic, and cultural contexts within which they operate. The differences highlight the challenges and opportunities in regulating the digital media landscape, emphasizing the need for astute understanding of antitrust laws as they intersect with global digital media practices. As digital media continues to transform to meet market demands, the effectiveness and adaptability of these regulatory frameworks will play a critical role in shaping the future of global digital markets, competition, and innovation.

Discussion Questions

1. How do US antitrust laws address the unique challenges posed by digital media conglomerates, and are these measures sufficient to ensure fair competition and consumer protection in the digital age?
2. In what ways does the EU's rights-driven regulatory approach to digital media and antitrust law differ from the US market-driven model, and what are the implications of these differences for global tech companies?
3. How does China's state-centric antitrust regulatory scheme reflect its broader economic and political goals, and what impact does this approach have on domestic and foreign digital media companies operating within its borders?

4. What are the potential benefits and drawbacks of the EU's General Data Protection Regulation (GDPR) and Digital Markets Act (DMA) in regulating digital media markets and protecting consumer rights?
5. Can the case law system in the United States adapt quickly enough to address the rapidly evolving nature of digital media and technology, or is there a need for more proactive legislative measures?
6. How do antitrust laws and regulations in these jurisdictions impact innovation within the digital media sector, and is there a risk of stifling technological advancement with overly stringent regulations?
7. Discuss the role of data protection and privacy in antitrust considerations within the digital media landscape. How do these concerns intersect with efforts to promote competition and curb monopolistic practices?
8. What are the ethical considerations for antitrust regulators when imposing fines and penalties on digital media companies, especially considering the global reach and influence of these entities?
9. How might emerging technologies, such as artificial intelligence and blockchain, challenge existing antitrust laws and regulatory frameworks in the context of digital media?
10. Considering the global nature of digital media, what steps can be taken to foster international cooperation and harmonization of antitrust laws and regulations to effectively address the dominance of digital media and tech giants?

Works Referenced

Bradford, Anu. *Digital Empires*. Oxford University Press, New York, 2023.

Crandall, Robert W., and Hazlett, Thomas W. "Antitrust Reform in the Digital Era: A Skeptical Perspective." *University of Chicago Business Law Review*, Vol. 2, No. 2, accessed at https://businesslawreview.uchicago.edu/print-archive/antitrust-reform-digital-era-skeptical-perspective

Douglas, Erika M., First, Harry, Lao, Marina, and Melamed, A. Douglas. "Insights on Applying U.S. Antitrust Laws to Digital Markets." Washington Center for Equitable Growth, December 2022, accessed at https://equitablegrowth.org/wp-content/uploads/2022/12/Judging-Big-Tech-Insights-on-applying-U.S.-antitrust-laws-to-digital-markets.pdf

Hayes, Adam. "Federal Trade Commission (FTC): What It Is and What It Does." *Investopedia*, April 21, 2022, accessed at https://www.investopedia.com/terms/f/ftc.asp

Hood, Bryan. "F1's Owner just Struck a $4.5 Billion Deal to Take Over MotoGP." *Robb Report*, April 2, 2024, accessed at https://uk.movies.yahoo.com/movies/f1-owner-just-struck-4-203000369.html

Jain, Vinod. "Competition and Antitrust in the Digital Age." *Forbes*, October 5, 2023, accessed at https://www.forbes.com/sites/forbesbusinesscouncil/2023/10/05/competition-and-antitrust-in-the-digital-age/?sh=4e42e18461b6

Liu, Qianer. "China to Lay Down AI Rules with Emphasis on Content Control." *Financial Times*, July 10, 2023, accessed at https://www.ft.com/content/1938b7b6-baf9-46bb-9eb7-70e9d32f4af0

Marar, Satya. "Antitrust Supreme Court Cases." *Justicia*, September 9, 2023, accessed at https://supreme.justia.com/cases-by-topic/antitrust

Ng, Wendy. "The Role of Competition Law in Regulating Data in China's Digital Economy." *Antitrust Law Journal*, Vol. 84, No. 3 (2022), accessed at https://www.americanbar.org/content/dam/aba/publications/antitrust/journal/84/3/role-of-competition-law-regulating-data-china-digital-economy.pdf

Phillips Sawyer, Laura. "US Antitrust Law and Policy in Historical Perspective." Harvard Business School Working Paper 19-110, 2019, accessed at https://www.hbs.edu/ris/Publication%20Files/19-110_e21447ad-d98a-451f-8ef0-ba42209018e6.pdf

Stokel-Walker, Chris. "China Is Tightening Its Grip on Big Tech." *Wired*, June 29, 2022, accessed at https://www.wired.com/story/china-big-tech-regulation

Stolton, Samuel, and Deutsch, Jillian. "Europe's Two-Track Approach to Policing Big Tech." *Bloomberg*, March 6, 2023, accessed at https://www.bloomberg.com/news/articles/2023-08-29/all-about-the-eu-s-dsa-and-dma-laws-to-rein-in-big-tech-platforms

"The Antitrust War against Google Fails Consumers." *The Hill*, accessed at https://thehill.com/opinion/technology/4199800-the-antitrust-war-against-google-fails-consumers

Zhang, Zoey. "China's Regulatory Plans for Technology Companies and the Platform Economy in 2022." *China Briefing*, February 9, 2022, accessed at https://www.china-briefing.com/news/new-government-document-indicates-chinas-regulatory-plans-for-technology-companies-platform-economy-in-2022

10

The Future of Digital Media Law: Navigating Ethics, AI, and Beyond

Nothing huge enters the lives of mortals without a curse.
—Sophocles

In an era where the boundaries of technology continually blur and expand, the prognostications of Elon Musk and Jamie Dimon represent not just speculative visions but potentially transformative realities. As we stand on the precipice of a new age, their bold predictions about artificial intelligence (AI) have ignited a global conversation on its implications. Musk, the thought leader behind Tesla and SpaceX, and Dimon, the astute chief executive and financial fortune teller of JPMorgan Chase, have both forecasted that AI will outstrip human intelligence and usher in societal transformations unparalleled in history. Their remarks reflect a growing sentiment among business leaders in digital media and technology about AI's potential to redefine the contours of daily life, economy, and human capability.

Elon Musk's assertion—that AI will surpass the collective intelligence of humans within a mere half-decade—resonates with the swift pace at which this technology evolves. Similarly, Dimon's analogy of AI's impact to groundbreaking inventions like the printing press and electricity underscores the magnitude of change anticipated. These statements are not isolated musings but are echoed by tech luminaries and innovators worldwide.

Yet, amid this chorus of optimism and alarm, critical voices emerge, questioning the immediacy and extent of AI's transformative power on business and digital media. Cognitive scientists like Gary Marcus caution against overestimating AI's current capabilities and underestimating the challenges that lie ahead. Skeptics like Damion Hankejh considered the inventor of e-Commerce and social engineer Angel Vossough remind us of the fundamental differences between digital computation and the sophisticated intelligence including emotional IQ of the human mind. These divergent views invite a broader discussion on AI's trajectory, its potential benefits, and the ethical considerations it entails within the world of digital media.

Justifiably, concerns about AI data centers' energy consumption highlight the tangible challenges of integrating AI into the fabric of business and society, including the digital media landscape. As digital media platforms increasingly rely on AI for content curation, personalized recommendations, and user engagement analytics, the energy demands of these AI systems grow exponentially. This not only impacts the environmental footprint of digital media companies but also raises questions about the sustainability of current practices in the face of rapid technological advancements. Addressing these concerns is crucial for ensuring that the assimilation of AI into digital media does not compromise environmental sustainability or exacerbate existing resource constraints.

The rapid evolution of artificial intelligence (AI) and its integration into digital media unfolds a panorama of unprecedented opportunities alongside compelling legal and ethical challenges. As AI becomes increasingly refined, digital media platforms are harnessing their capabilities to revolutionize content creation, distribution, and consumption. This transformation extends to personalized user experiences, where AI algorithms predict and deliver content aligned with individual preferences, enhancing engagement and satisfaction. Moreover, AI-driven analytics offer deep insights into user behavior, enabling media companies to tailor their strategies in real time for optimal impact. These advancements promise to redefine the media landscape, making it more dynamic, interactive, and responsive to user needs.

However, this technological leap forward brings with it a complex web of legal and ethical considerations. One of the most pressing issues is privacy. The data used to feed AI algorithms often include sensitive personal information, raising concerns about user consent, data protection, and the potential for surveillance. This intersects with legal frameworks such as the **General Data Protection Regulation (GDPR)** in the European Union, which mandates strict guidelines on data usage and user rights.

Compliance becomes a significant challenge as companies navigate the global patchwork of privacy laws, each with its own requirements and penalties.

Intellectual property (IP) rights present another legal quagmire. AI's ability to generate content autonomously—ranging from written articles to artwork and music—challenges traditional notions of authorship and copyright. Determining the ownership of AI-created works and the application of copyright laws in such scenarios is an evolving debate. It raises questions about the rights of creators versus the rights of those who own or develop AI technologies.

Ethical concerns also loom large, particularly around the potential for bias and misinformation. AI algorithms, shaped by the data they are trained on, can perpetuate and amplify biases, leading to unequal or unfair outcomes. Furthermore, the use of AI in creating and spreading deepfakes—highly realistic and manipulated content—poses a threat to trust and integrity in the digital media ecosystem. It can undermine public discourse, manipulate elections, and violate individual rights, prompting calls for ethical guidelines and regulatory measures to govern AI's application in media.

Also, the societal implications of AI in digital media extend to the workforce. Automation through AI could disrupt media jobs, from journalism to entertainment, necessitating a rethinking of skills, roles, and economic models in the digital age.

Looking toward the future, it becomes clear that a comprehensive understanding of digital media law and ethics in the context of AI is essential, given the myriad emerging concepts, cases, and concerns. This chapter seeks to study and question the diverse aspects of this debate by scrutinizing the technological advancements propelling AI's rapid development, the societal transformations it might prompt, and the profound philosophical inquiries it instigates regarding intelligence, consciousness, and the future trajectory of human civilization. Additionally, we will explore potential legal reforms, assess the societal repercussions of technological progress, and contemplate the crucial equilibrium between fostering innovation and safeguarding individual rights. This exploration is an endeavor to comprehend not merely the future potentials of AI on digital media, but also to unearth what these developments signify about our collective ambitions, apprehensions, and the core of human advancement. Serving as an introductory discourse, this chapter lays the groundwork for a more in-depth analysis of the intricate relationship between digital media law, ethics, and the revolutionary impact of artificial intelligence, marking the beginning of a new and profound examination of these vital topics.

The Future of Digital Media and AI

The integration of AI into digital media and the broader media and entertainment (M&E) industries heralds a period of revolutionary change, influencing technological progress, legal frameworks, and societal norms. As AI's capabilities expand, its impact is felt across various facets of digital media, from content creation to consumption, setting the stage for significant legal reforms and driving technological advancements with far-reaching societal implications.

Generative AI: The realm of media content creation is undergoing a seismic shift with the advent of generative AI technologies. These algorithms are becoming increasingly capable of producing complex and refined works, transcending traditional boundaries of creativity. AIVA (Artificial Intelligence Virtual Artist), an AI that composes original soundtrack music, exemplifies the potential of AI to partake in creative processes traditionally reserved for humans. Similarly, platforms like OpenAI's GPT series and Midjourney's AI apps have shown the capability to generate written content that mimics human writing styles, from poetry to news articles, demonstrating generative AI's potential to transform content production in journalism, literature, and beyond.

Beyond these examples, generative AI is making strides in video game development, where it can create dynamic, evolving landscapes and storylines that respond to player inputs in real time. AI-generated characters with complex behaviors and personalities enhance the gaming experience, making each playthrough unique and engaging. This popular online gaming platform leans heavily on generative AI. Roblox Studio, the development toolkit within Roblox, allows users to create game environments and objects. A key feature is its use of generative AI to procedurally generate textures and terrain, freeing up creators to focus on more design-oriented aspects. Imagine being able to design a world with rolling hills and lush forests, and the AI fills in the details with realistic

Chapter 10: The Future of Digital Media Law: Navigating Ethics, AI, and Beyond

Table 10.1 Key Differences between Generative AI and Traditional AI

Feature	Traditional AI	Generative AI
Main function	Analyze data and solve problems	Generate new data (text, code, images, etc.)
Data usage	Relies on predefined rules and data	Learns patterns from data to create new outputs
Strengths	Transparency, reliability in well-defined tasks	Creativity, adaptability, potential for new applications

textures and variations, further expanding the possibilities for creativity and innovation in game design. This integration of generative AI into Roblox exemplifies how technology is pushing the boundaries of what is possible in digital and interactive media, offering creators new tools to bring their visions to life in more vivid and complex ways than ever before.

Table 10.1 to summarizes the key differences between generative AI and more traditional AI:

They aren't mutually exclusive and can even be used together. For instance, a traditional AI could analyze user data, and a generative AI could use that analysis to create personalized advertising content.

Deepfakes and Synthetic Media: The evolution of deepfake technology and synthetic media, powered by advancements in AI, has indeed altered the landscape of digital content creation. From a technical perspective deepfakes and synthetic media are powered by a type of AI called Generative Adversarial Networks, or GANs. GANs work like a two-part team in constant competition. One part, the generator, creates the deepfake or synthetic media content. The other part, the discriminator, acts like a critic, trying to spot the forgery. This ongoing battle helps the generator produce increasingly realistic fakes.

Synthetic media encompasses a broad range of content created or altered through AI or machine-learning techniques. This category includes a wide variety of outputs, from AI-composed music and text generated by programs like Stable Diffusion to computer-generated imagery (CGI), virtual reality (VR), augmented reality (AR), and voice synthesis. The purpose of synthetic media spans from creative expression to practical applications, aiming to enhance or innovate within digital and interactive environments without inherently seeking to deceive.

Deepfakes, on the other hand, represent a narrower segment within synthetic media, with a focus primarily on the alteration or manipulation of visual and auditory information to produce highly realistic and often deceptive content. This includes videos where an individual's face is swapped with another, creating scenarios that can be indistinguishable from real-life recordings. Deepfakes are especially known for their potential use in misleading viewers, thanks to their ability to mimic real human appearances and sounds with a high degree of accuracy.

The creation of deepfakes usually employs sophisticated techniques in three main areas: face reenactment, which involves manipulating a real person's facial expressions and movements; face generation, the process of synthesizing entirely new facial images from a composite of many real faces, resulting in a likeness that doesn't correspond to any actual person; and speech synthesis, where software models a person's voice to produce audio that sounds like them speaking words they never actually said.

The fundamental distinction between synthetic media and deepfakes lies in their intent and application. While synthetic media broadly refers to AI-generated content designed for a variety of creative, educational, or practical purposes, deepfakes specifically aim to create content that is so convincingly real that it can easily be mistaken for genuine material, often with the intention of deception. This difference highlights the ethical considerations and potential impacts each has on society, although sometimes the terms are used interchangeably as they are within this chapter, with deepfakes raising significant concerns over misinformation and the erosion of trust in digital communications.

Entertainment: Synthetic media technology has significantly impacted the entertainment industry, offering innovative ways to create content, enhance storytelling, and even resurrect performances from actors who have passed away, while acknowledging publicity rights are at stake. This technology, which utilizes artificial intelligence to create hyper-realistic videos, audio, and images, has been employed in various notable instances across films, television, and other media platforms. Below are expanded examples and additional instances where deepfake technology has been used in the entertainment industry:

- **"The Irishman" by Martin Scorsese**: This film used de-aging technology to make actors like Robert De Niro, Al Pacino, and Joe Pesci appear younger in certain scenes. While not a synthetic media or deepfake in the strictest sense, the technology shares similarities with it involving sophisticated computer-generated imagery (special visual effects created using computer software) (CGI) to alter appearances.

- **"Rogue One: A Star Wars Story"**: The film famously used CGI and synthetic media-like technology to resurrect Peter Cushing as Grand Moff Tarkin and to create a younger version of Carrie Fisher as Princess Leia. This allowed the filmmakers to maintain continuity with the original Star Wars films.
- **"The Mandalorian"**: In the Star Wars TV series, a young Luke Skywalker makes an appearance, achieved through the use of synthetic media/deepfake technology. This allowed the character, originally played by Mark Hamill, to be featured in the series looking as he did in the original trilogy.
- **Elvis Presley on "America's Got Talent"**: A synthetic media/deepfake video of Elvis Presley was showcased, demonstrating the technology's ability to recreate performances from iconic musicians who are no longer alive.
- **Robert Kardashian Hologram**: Kim Kardashian presented a hologram of her late father, Robert Kardashian, who gained fame as one of O.J. Simpson's criminal defense lawyers, created using synthetic media technology. This instance highlighted the personal and emotional applications of deepfakes, allowing individuals to "reconnect" with loved ones.
- **David Beckham's Malaria Campaign**: Synthetic media technology enabled soccer star David Beckham to deliver a public service announcement on malaria in nine different languages, showcasing the technology's potential to break down language barriers and personalize messages for a global audience.
- **Randy Travis**: In the realm of digital media, country music legend Randy Travis serves as a compelling case study in the use of AI to synthesize music. After suffering a debilitating stroke in 2013 that left him unable to speak or sing properly, Travis released a new song titled "Where That Came From," marking his first track since the stroke. The vocals for the song were created using AI software and a surrogate singer, under the supervision of Travis and his longtime producer Kyle Lehning. Country singer James DuPre provided the initial vocals, which were then transformed into Travis's distinctive voice using AI, trained on forty-two isolated vocal recordings from

his previous work. The song is available on platforms like YouTube, Apple Music, and Spotify.
- **Salvador Dalí at The Dalí Museum**: An art installation used synthetic media technology to bring the surrealist artist Salvador Dalí back to life. Visitors could interact with a life-sized Dalí, who moved, spoke, and even took selfies with them, demonstrating deepfake's potential in creating immersive and interactive art experiences.

While the use of synthetic media and deepfake technology in resurrecting performances and enhancing storytelling offers exciting

Figure 10.1 A synthetic media interactive display of a deceased Salvadore Dalí at the Dalí Museum, St. Petersburg, Florida.

possibilities, it also raises ethical questions regarding consent, copyright, publicity rights, and the potential for misuse.

The entertainment industry continues to address these challenges, balancing concerns over job loss, compensation, and innovation with respect for the rights and legacies of the individuals portrayed. From resurrecting iconic characters and celebrities to enabling cross-language communication and creating immersive art installations, the potential applications are vast.

For example, the latest collective bargaining agreement between the Screen Actors Guild–American Federation of Television and Radio Artists (SAG-AFTRA) and the Alliance of Motion Picture and Television Producers (AMPTP), ratified in December 2023, represents a first of its kind effort in tackling the challenges presented by synthetic media and artificial intelligence within the entertainment industry. It lays out important distinctions and regulations concerning digital replicas of performers and the use of synthetic performers. For digital replicas created with a performer's involvement during their employment, the agreement mandates compensation equivalent to what the performer would have received for a physical presence. Conversely, for independently created digital replicas used for postproduction modifications, such as cosmetic changes or visual effects, the agreement does not require the performer's consent. A particularly innovative aspect of this agreement is its focus on "synthetic performers," which are entirely digitally created entities not based on real actors but developed through AI models. The production companies are obligated to inform SAG-AFTRA upon the creation of synthetic performers and to enter into negotiations regarding actor compensation and other relevant terms. This approach sets a precedent for addressing the proprietary and financial concerns over protecting performers' personality or publicity rights and job security in the age of AI and digital replication.

Advertising: Synthetic media technology has rapidly transformed the advertising and marketing sectors, introducing a range of innovative applications that significantly enhance consumer engagement and experience. By employing artificial intelligence and machine learning, deepfakes produce highly realistic videos or images, allowing individuals to appear as though they are saying or doing something they have not actually done. This capability has been creatively adopted in several ways across marketing strategies.

One of the standout uses of synthetic media technology is in virtual try-ons within the fashion industry. Retail giants like Zalando utilize deepfake technology to enable customers to visualize how clothes would look on them virtually, bypassing the need for physical fittings—an essential feature for enhancing the online shopping experience. Furthermore, Japanese AI company DataGrid expands this application by generating complete body models that customers can dress in various outfits, tailored to their body type and style preferences.

This same AI technology also allows for personalized advertisements, a strategy that has been embraced by major brands to create highly tailored marketing content. For example, Cadbury's innovative campaign, "Not Just a Cadbury Ad," featured deepfake-generated visuals of Bollywood superstar Shah Rukh Khan endorsing small businesses, providing a personalized touch. Similarly, Zomato leveraged deepfakes to depict Bollywood actor Hrithik Roshan enjoying meals from local eateries, with advertisements customized to the viewer's location via GPS technology.

Nostalgic marketing is another area where synthetic media have made a significant impact. Brands resurrect historical figures or late celebrities to forge an emotional connection with audiences. For instance, the Queen Sofía Foundation used synthetic media to bring artist Salvador Dalí back to life, creating a poignant marketing moment. Additionally, State Farm tapped into nostalgia by integrating deepfake technology in an advertisement that featured recreated 1998 Sportscenter footage for the documentary series "The Last Dance."

Beyond these creative uses, synthetic media technology is enhancing customer experiences through augmented reality (AR) features. Amazon's AR View app allows users to visualize how various products, like furniture and home decor, would fit and appear in their actual living spaces, merging virtual items with real-world environments.

While the applications of this AI technology in marketing are extensive and exciting, they come with significant ethical concerns and legal implications. The potential for misuse, such as creating unauthorized endorsements or manipulating consumer behavior, is substantial. Digital marketers must therefore navigate these challenges carefully, ensuring adherence to legal standards and maintaining transparency to preserve consumer trust. Overall, while synthetic media technology offers remarkable opportunities for hyper-personalization and immersive experiences in marketing, its use must be balanced with stringent ethical practices and legal compliance to protect both consumers and brands from potential abuses.

Education and Health: The advent of synthetic media has revolutionized various sectors, notably education and health care, by introducing innovative applications that enhance interaction, learning, and training experiences. In the educational sphere, synthetic media has transformed language learning by creating dynamic, adaptive lessons that cater to individual pacing and learning styles. This technology enables the creation of virtual characters with whom learners can engage in simulated conversations, offering a safe environment to practice language skills such as speaking and listening. This method not only makes learning more accessible and enjoyable for learners of all ages but also improves retention rates, significantly outperforming traditional language learning techniques.

Expanding further into education, synthetic media facilitates the customization of educational content to include diverse accents, dialects, and cultural contexts, making language learning more comprehensive and globally oriented. Moreover, it can recreate historical events or literary scenes, allowing students to explore and interact with the past in a virtual setup, thereby deepening their understanding and engagement with the subject matter.

In the health care sector, synthetic media is notably enhancing medical training by providing realistic simulations where professionals can practice procedures on virtual patients. This use of synthetic media is particularly beneficial for training in high-stakes areas such as surgery, emergency care, and anesthesiology, where the risk to real patients can be significant. For instance, surgeons can practice intricate surgical techniques in a controlled virtual environment that mimics real-life conditions, complete with immediate feedback on their techniques and decisions. This practice not only hones their skills but also prepares them to handle a variety of clinical scenarios they may encounter.

Businesses like NVIDIA, a publicly traded company that designs and manufactures graphic processing units (GPUs) for gaming, cryptocurrency mining, and professional applications as well as chip systems for use in vehicles, robotics, and other tools, have pushed the boundaries further by using synthetic media to generate medical images for training diagnostic algorithms. This approach helps overcome the limitations posed by data scarcity and privacy issues related to using real patient images. By creating extensive datasets of synthetic images that accurately replicate various pathological conditions, researchers can train algorithms with high precision, enhancing the capabilities of medical diagnostics. This advancement is crucial for early and accurate disease detection, potentially revolutionizing how health issues are identified and treated.

The potential of synthetic media stretches beyond just education and health care. For instance, in professional training, synthetic scenarios can simulate real-world challenges in fields like engineering and architecture, allowing professionals to test and refine their skills in a risk-free environment. Similarly, in customer service, synthetic media can be used to train agents through interactive role-playing scenarios that mimic complex customer interactions, thus improving service quality and problem-solving skills.

Documentary Films: Not surprisingly, artificial intelligence is rapidly transforming the landscape of news and documentary filmmaking, providing an array of tools that enhance narrative capabilities and offer educational insights in captivating ways. AI technologies facilitate the creation of realistic simulations and visualizations of both historical events and potential future scenarios, engaging audiences and provoking thoughtful discourse.

In the realm of historical event simulations, AI has demonstrated its potential to vividly recreate significant moments. A notable example is the project "In Event of Moon Disaster," where AI was used to fabricate a speech by President Richard Nixon, intended for a scenario where the Apollo 11 mission failed. This synthetic media installation vividly demonstrated how AI could recreate critical historical events that never occurred. Another compelling application was in the documentary "Finding Jack Charlton," where AI technology restored the voice of the late soccer manager Jack Charlton, enabling him to narrate his story posthumously, thereby adding a profound and personal touch to the documentary, while raising publicity rights and integrity in the storyline issues.

AI's capability extends to visualizing future scenarios that have not yet occurred, which is considered the next major technological leap for generative AI. For instance, documentaries addressing climate change have employed AI to project the consequences of global warming, such as rising sea levels and extreme weather conditions. These visualizations help audiences understand and internalize the potential impacts of environmental changes on familiar landscapes.

Moreover, AI combined with Virtual Reality (VR) technology is revolutionizing educational content by offering immersive experiences that are not possible through traditional media. Viewers can virtually walk through ancient cities, participate in significant historical events, or explore distant planets, gaining a firsthand understanding of these environments and their historical or scientific significance.

Enhanced storytelling is another significant benefit of AI in documentary filmmaking. AI enables the creation of interactive documentaries where the narrative can shift based on viewer choices or queries. This interactivity, facilitated by AI-driven characters who can respond in real-time, transforms the viewing experience into an engaging, personalized journey through the content.

While the integration of AI into filmmaking opens new frontiers for creators, it also introduces major ethical challenges, particularly concerning the authenticity of information and the potential for misinformation. The use of AI-generated content, especially in news and documentary contexts, necessitates a high level of transparency. Filmmakers must clearly disclose the use of AI to their audiences and ensure that such technology enhances the truthfulness of the narrative rather than distorting it. The ethical use of AI is paramount to maintaining the credibility and integrity of films that aim to educate, inform, and inspire public discourse.

Virtual Games and Interactive Media: Synthetic media technology is also revolutionizing virtual games and interactive media, creating immersive experiences that blur the lines between reality and fiction. Game developers are utilizing deepfakes to generate lifelike characters and environments, enabling players to interact with game worlds that feel real. This technology can also adapt game narratives in real-time based on player choices, creating a personalized gaming experience.

For example, a company named Modulate has pioneered the development of "voice skins" tailored for use in online games and social platforms. These voices are available for gaming companies to purchase and integrate into their platforms, thereby enriching the user experience by offering customizable voice options. The vision of Modulate is to provide the opportunity to remain authentically human and emotionally expressive while having the ability to change their vocal identity. This allows users to adopt voices that perfectly align with their online avatars, such as matching their voice to the gruff timbre of a dwarf or the ethereal tone of an elf, enhancing the immersive experience when interacting with other players.

Moreover, the application of voice skins addresses concerns beyond mere personalization. It serves as a powerful tool for individuals prone to online harassment, including women and children, enabling them to conceal their gender or age to foster a safer online environment. Furthermore, it offers members of the transgender community the opportunity to use voice skins that more closely mirror their true identity, thereby providing a means of expression that aligns with their sense of self in online spaces.

Social Media: The advent of synthetic media technology on social media platforms has ushered in a new era of digital interaction, blending the lines between reality and virtuality with its vast potential for both innovation and deception. Leveraging advanced artificial intelligence, deepfake technology produces highly realistic manipulated content that thrives on platforms such as Facebook, Instagram, and TikTok. These platforms' vast reach and rapid dissemination capabilities allow deepfakes to serve not only as tools for creative entertainment and personalization but also as conduits for significant risks beyond the traditional concerns about fabricating news and spreading fictious statements by politicians to sway public opinion.

Social media platforms have embraced this evolving technology to offer users a range of personalized entertainment options, enhancing digital interactions with a touch of creativity. Platforms like Snapchat and Instagram have introduced filters that allow users to transform their features to resemble celebrities or historical figures, adding an element of fun to user experiences. Additionally, emerging applications are now offering voice cloning features, enabling users to send personalized messages or greetings in the voices of well-known figures, further enriching digital communication. Another popular use of this technology is the age and gender swap features, which let users alter their appearance in images and videos for humorous or educational purposes, demonstrating the lighter, more playful capabilities of synthetic media.

Despite the entertaining possibilities, deepfakes carry a substantial risk for harm, particularly through the spread of misinformation. Politically charged deepfakes, such as fabricated videos of politicians like the one featuring former President Barack Obama, have demonstrated their potential to influence public opinion and disrupt the democratic process by spreading false information. The realm of fabricated news also presents significant challenges; for instance, the use of Clint Eastwood's image in a *National Enquirer* publication could lead to viral hoaxes that mislead the

Figure 10.2 False reporting article using an image of Clint Eastwood.

public and damage reputations. Furthermore, there have been instances of financial fraud perpetrated through deepfake audio that mimics the voices of corporate leaders, resulting in substantial financial losses.

In response to these specific challenges posed by deepfakes, social media platforms and technological institutions are actively developing strategies to mitigate their misuse. This includes the advancement of AI detection tools designed to automatically identify and flag deepfake content, though perfecting these tools remains a daunting challenge, and experts like Ethan Mollick maintain that there is no effective deepfake detection technology. Additionally, collaborations with fact-checking organizations are crucial, helping to verify the authenticity of widely circulated content and quickly label deepfake materials. The European Union's **AI Act** has assumed a leadership role in this realm by requiring their creators to inform the public about the artificial nature of their work. Public awareness campaigns also play a vital role in educating the public about the nature of deepfakes, promoting critical engagement with online content, and empowering users to distinguish between authentic and manipulated media, thereby fostering a safer and more informed digital environment.

However, the impact of deepfakes extends into even more insidious areas on social media sites, particularly affecting younger audiences in educational environments. It was not long ago that schools across the United States were caught off guard by the sudden rise in popularity of AI-powered chatbots like ChatGPT, prompting them to take measures to prevent potential cheating by restricting access to these text-generating bots.

A new and more concerning AI phenomenon is now causing alarm within educational institutions. Boys in several states have been found using readily accessible "nudification" apps to manipulate real photos of their female classmates, taken at events such as school proms, into graphic and realistic images that depict the girls nude, with AI-generated breasts and genitalia. These manipulated images are often shared in school lunchrooms, on buses, or through group chats on platforms like Snapchat and Instagram. Known as "deepfakes" or "deepnudes," these digitally altered images can lead to severe consequences for the victims. Experts in child sexual exploitation highlight the dramatic harm these nonconsensual, AI-generated images can inflict on young women's mental health, reputations, and physical safety, potentially jeopardizing their future college and career opportunities. In response to this growing issue, the Federal Bureau of Investigation issued warnings stating that distributing computer-generated child sexual abuse material, including realistic AI-generated images of identifiable minors in sexually explicit conduct, is illegal.

Addressing the potential for serious mental health and well-being harm presented by these deepfakes, especially those young adults and children who are constantly engaged with the digital world via smartphones and social media, requires a well-rounded approach that encompasses both educational and legal strategies. First, incorporating media literacy into educational curricula is essential. This would equip students with the necessary skills to evaluate the truthfulness of digital content they come across. Educational initiatives should focus on teaching students to critically analyze the authenticity of online images and videos and to comprehend the ramifications of creating and sharing manipulated media. Programs provided by organizations like the Social Institute, which offer resources to schools on navigating social media and technology responsibly, exemplify the kind of efforts needed to boost media literacy.

On the legal front, there's an urgent need for comprehensive legal frameworks to tackle the unauthorized creation and dissemination of deepfakes. Legislation should be updated or newly introduced to make the production and sharing of such content illegal, with a particular emphasis on protecting minors. Moreover, many experts assert that this approach should hold social media platforms and content creators accountable despite protections afforded to social media sites and AI platforms by **Section 230 of the Communications Decency Act**, ensuring the swift removal of deepfake content. Notable legislative initiatives include a bill proposed in Alabama aimed at making the creation of deepfakes targeting children a felony, punishable by significant prison time, and model legislation from the American Legislative Exchange Council designed to encourage states to outlaw the possession and distribution of deepfakes depicting minors in explicit acts. By merging efforts in media literacy education with rigorous legal actions, society can offer better protection to young people from the detrimental effects of deepfake technology, thereby creating a more secure digital landscape for all.

Digital Media Employment: The intersection of technology and the labor market is a complex and dynamic area, characterized by both opportunities and challenges. Many observers view technological evolution as an inevitable force that follows its own intrinsic logic. However, as noted in the book *Power and Progress: Our 1,000-Year Struggle over Technology and Prosperity* by Daron Acemoglu and Simon Johnson, technology's trajectory is shaped by the decisions and visions of those in power. When technological control is concentrated among a select few, it often results in benefits accruing primarily to that elite, while the broader workforce may bear the costs, potentially for extended periods.

In the dynamic realm of digital media, artificial intelligence (AI) has transcended its role as just a technological enhancer to become a core element of strategic digital media innovation. With its superior capabilities in decision-making, language processing, and pattern recognition, AI is not only optimizing operations but is also redefining competitive landscapes. Industry leaders are increasingly integrating AI into their strategic plans, not merely for its operational benefits but as a pivotal driver of innovation and a key differentiator in the market. This growing reliance on AI is fueling a surge in demand for AI-focused careers, positioning AI expertise as essential for companies looking to maintain a competitive edge in today's digital economy.

The rapid advancement of artificial intelligence and technology presents a dual-edged sword significantly impacting job growth and loss. On one hand, AI introduces the potential for unprecedented efficiency and innovation, leading to the creation of new job opportunities and roles within the digital media space. In a first of its kind research study conducted by MIT, generative AI can improve a highly skilled worker's performance by as much as 40 percent compared with workers who don't use it. On the other hand, the automation capabilities of AI pose a threat to traditional jobs, particularly those involving routine tasks, potentially leading to significant job displacement.

AI and technology are catalysts for job growth in several ways. First, they drive the demand for new skill sets and specializations, such as AI development, data analysis, and digital marketing strategies that leverage AI-generated insights. For instance, the emergence of AI-powered analytics tools necessitates roles for professionals who can interpret and apply these insights to tailor content and marketing strategies. As firms invest more in artificial intelligence, there's a notable shift toward a more educated workforce, with a greater emphasis on STEM degrees and IT skills to fill critical AI jobs for the tech-heavy firms in the digital media space. AI can augment human capabilities, leading to the creation of jobs that focus on the symbiosis between human creativity and AI efficiency. In the digital media industry, this could manifest as roles for content creators who use AI to enhance storytelling, video editors who leverage AI for postproduction enhancements, and social media managers who utilize AI tools for personalized audience engagement.

Conversely, the automation capabilities of AI raise concerns about job displacement. Routine tasks, such as data entry, content curation, and even certain aspects of content creation, are increasingly being automated. This trend threatens to reduce the number of available positions for individuals whose jobs are centered on these tasks. The digital media space, with its reliance on content production and distribution, is particularly vulnerable to this shift. The automation of content generation and the use of AI to perform tasks traditionally done by humans, such as writing articles or creating visual content, could lead to a decrease in demand for human labor in these areas.

To address the future of employment in the digital media space amid these technological advancements, a multifaceted approach is required. This includes fostering a culture of continuous learning and adaptation among the workforces. Workers need to be encouraged and supported in acquiring new skills that complement AI technologies, ensuring they remain valuable in an evolving job market. Additionally, there is a need for a concerted effort among stakeholders, including businesses, educational institutions, and policymakers, to prioritize human-complementary technology development. This approach focuses on leveraging AI to enhance human work rather than replace it, creating opportunities for job growth in new and existing roles. Furthermore, the tech industry and corporate leaders in digital media must recognize the importance of human labor as a critical component of productivity and innovation.

Shifting the commerce mindset from viewing labor as a cost to be minimized to seeing it as a valuable resource to be developed can lead to more sustainable business practices and job growth in the digital media space. As the impact of artificial intelligence reshapes the digital media job market, leading to both job creation and job losses in uneven patterns, it becomes essential to support workers who are displaced by AI. Enhancing the social safety net and promoting retraining programs for these individuals are critical steps to ensure that all workers have the opportunity to adapt and thrive in this changing landscape. The key to unlocking these opportunities lies in strategic adaptation, continuous learning, and a value-based commitment to developing technologies that complement rather than replace human labor, which is no small task.

Lawyers in Digital Media: The impact of AI on legal professionals in the digital media representation field reflects a broader narrative about AI's role in transforming traditional professions.

AI technology offers substantial benefits to law firms by automating routine tasks that consume much of a lawyer's time. AI-driven tools can handle document review, conduct thorough legal research, and assist in drafting and analyzing contracts with speed and accuracy. This automation allows lawyers to dedicate more time to intricate legal issues and strategy development, thereby enhancing the quality of legal services and client advice. As AI takes over more of the time-consuming, administrative work, lawyers can focus on higher-level, value-added activities in their practice.

The integration of AI into digital media also opens up new avenues for legal specialization. Lawyers have the opportunity to become leading experts in fields like AI-related intellectual property, privacy laws, and compliance regarding digital content and AI technology usage. This expertise is crucial as businesses increasingly rely on AI for content creation and data analysis, raising complex legal questions that need informed and specialized responses.

While AI can streamline workflows, it also poses risks of job displacement within law practices. AI's capability to perform tasks traditionally handled by junior lawyers or paralegals—such as preliminary research or document management—might diminish the need for such roles. This technological shift could disrupt the conventional career trajectory in law, affecting job opportunities for newly graduated lawyers and those in early career stages.

The rapid advancement of AI technologies brings with it a plethora of ethical dilemmas and regulatory gaps. Lawyers specializing in digital media must navigate these emerging challenges, which include issues surrounding AI-generated content, data privacy, and the ethical implications of AI decisions. The fluid landscape of AI regulation requires lawyers to adopt innovative legal approaches and develop strategies that anticipate future legal trends.

To remain competent and effective, lawyers must engage in continuous professional development to keep pace with fast-evolving technologies like AI. This necessity spans understanding new legal precedents, technological capabilities, and potential legal risks associated with AI. Maintaining this level of expertise demands significant investment in learning and adaptation, posing challenges in terms of time and resource allocation but also offering opportunities for career advancement and specialization.

To successfully grasp the evolving landscape, lawyers should focus on cultivating skills that AI cannot replicate. These include complex problem-solving, ethical judgment, and nuanced understanding of human

Chapter 10: The Future of Digital Media Law: Navigating Ethics, AI, and Beyond

behavior, all of which are essential in legal reasoning and client relations. Lawyers should also emphasize soft skills such as empathy, negotiation, and advocacy, ensuring they remain indispensable in aspects of legal practice that require a human touch.

Engagement in the ongoing dialogue about AI's ethical use and the development of comprehensive legal frameworks to govern AI technology is crucial. By participating in these discussions, lawyers can help shape policies that ensure a balanced approach to AI integration that protects public interest and promotes fairness.

The impact of AI on lawyers in the digital media space is profoundly dualistic, offering opportunities for innovation and specialization while also demanding adaptability to new challenges. By leveraging AI to enhance their practices and focusing on uniquely human capabilities, lawyers can steer through these changes, ensuring their roles not only endure but also evolve in this new era.

Energy Concerns: The development and utilization of artificial intelligence, particularly in the realm of generative AI systems, has been a driving force in the tech and digital media industries, marking a new era of technological advancement with significant environmental implications. Companies like Google, Microsoft, OpenAI, and Facebook's parent company Meta are at the forefront, pushing the boundaries of AI capabilities from natural language processing to image generation. These innovations, however, demand substantial environmental resources, particularly in the chip design and manufacturing stages.

The design and production of AI chips, undertaken by giants like NVIDIA and Intel, are highly energy intensive. These chips are essential for AI's functionality and require precision engineering in cleanroom environments that consume large amounts of electricity. Additionally, the mining of rare earth elements, crucial for these chips, poses serious environmental risks. As AI technologies evolve rapidly, the increased obsolescence of devices contributes to a growing volume of electronic waste, which presents significant disposal and recycling challenges.

Training generative AI models also has a profound environmental impact. These models necessitate immense computational power, utilizing high-performance computers housed in data centers operated by services like Amazon Web Services (AWS) and Google Cloud. These facilities require vast amounts of electricity for operation and cooling, substantially contributing to greenhouse gas emissions and exacerbating climate change. The significant water uses for data center cooling further strains water resources, especially in arid regions.

To mitigate these environmental issues, the industry is exploring a variety of solutions. There is ongoing innovation in more energy-efficient chip architectures by companies like ARM and TSMC (Taiwan Semiconductor Company), aimed at reducing power consumption. Additionally, adopting renewable energy sources, such as solar panels and wind turbines, is gaining traction among firms like Google and Apple to power their operations more sustainably. Efforts are also being made to develop more efficient AI algorithms and training methods that require less power, showcasing initiatives like Google's AI for Social Good, which harnesses AI to tackle environmental challenges.

However, the industry faces the significant challenge of lacking standardized methods to measure the energy and environmental impact of AI systems accurately. For example, the business software company Salesforce is pushing for regulators to require digital media tech companies to disclose their AI emissions as well as to create standardized metrics for measuring and reporting environmental impacts associated with AI development and operations. This gap hinders the ability to fully assess AI's ecological footprint and monitor improvements effectively. Looking ahead, it is crucial for the tech industry to take decisive actions to address the environmental consequences of AI. This will involve collaborative efforts among companies, researchers, and policymakers to foster sustainable practices. By emphasizing energy efficiency, renewable energy, and optimization of AI technologies, the industry can aim for a future where AI advancement aligns with ecological sustainability, ensuring that technological growth does not come at the cost of our planet's health.

Summary

The digital media landscape is undergoing a profound transformation, shaped by the rapid evolution of technology and its pervasive integration into every aspect of our lives. This chapter explores the intricate interplay between law, ethics, and emerging technologies across various industries, including entertainment, social media, education, and the burgeoning fields of virtual (VR) and augmented reality (AR). As digital media continues to expand, it presents a multitude of challenges and opportunities that require careful and thoughtful consideration.

One of the most pressing challenges is the rise of deepfakes and synthetic media, which threaten to undermine public trust and manipulate political and social narratives. For instance, deepfake technology has been used to create convincingly fake videos of politicians, potentially swaying public opinion during critical times such as elections. Similarly, synthetic voice cloning can lead to fraudulent audio recordings that impersonate public figures, further complicating the information landscape.

The digital media environment poses significant risks to young people, impacting their privacy, mental health, and exposure to inappropriate content. A troubling example includes AI-generated explicit images of minors that have circulated on social media platforms, highlighting urgent concerns regarding the safeguarding of vulnerable groups.

AI's role in digital media is ambivalent. While it facilitates streamlined content creation and personalized user experiences, it also raises substantial ethical concerns. AI-driven recommendation algorithms on platforms like YouTube and TikTok can enhance engagement but may also funnel users, including impressionable teens, toward extremist content or perpetuate echo chambers.

Sector-Specific Challenges

- **Entertainment:** In this industry, the authenticity of content and the protection of intellectual property rights are paramount. The advent of AI in creating music, literature, and visual arts poses new challenges for copyright laws, which traditionally rely on human authorship.
- **Social Media:** Platforms face ongoing struggles with misinformation and the ethical implications of massive data collection. These platforms must balance algorithmic transparency with user privacy and the prevention of harmful content.
- **Education:** The integration of technology like AI and AR in educational settings must be managed carefully to ensure equitable access and uphold data security, preventing breaches that could expose sensitive information.

- **Virtual and Augmented Reality:** These technologies offer revolutionary user experiences but also raise significant safety concerns. The psychological effects of prolonged exposure to highly immersive environments are still not fully understood, necessitating guidelines to ensure user well-being.

The rapid advancement of digital media technologies has outpaced existing legal frameworks, creating a gap that must be addressed through updated regulations. This is particularly evident in the struggle to establish copyright norms for AI-generated content and the ethical management of biometric data used in VR and AR applications. The legal system must evolve to protect personal identity and ensure fair use of AI creations without stifling innovation. The IBM Policy Center recommends the following AI regulatory guidelines.

The role of various stakeholders—policymakers, industry leaders, legal experts, educators, and the public—is critical in shaping the responsible development of digital media. Collaborative efforts are necessary to address ethical dilemmas and to ensure that advancements in digital media technology are aligned with societal values and benefits.

The digital transformation promises new job opportunities in tech-driven sectors but also poses risks of displacement in traditional media roles. Strategic education and training initiatives are essential to equip the current and future workforce with the necessary skills to navigate the digital economy effectively.

Finally, this chapter advocates for a multidisciplinary approach to understanding and managing the future of digital media. By fostering robust legal and ethical frameworks and engaging a diverse array of stakeholders in meaningful dialogue, we can guide the development of new technologies to ensure they enhance societal welfare and reflect our collective ethical standards. The goal is to harness the potential of digital media as a force for good while mitigating its risks through informed and deliberate actions.

Discussion Questions

1. **Ethical Boundaries**: How should the legal system address the ethical concerns associated with AI-generated content, such as deepfakes, in a way that balances innovation with personal and societal safety?

2. **Regulatory Frameworks**: What specific changes or additions to current copyright laws and publicity rights are necessary to accommodate AI-generated works in the entertainment industry?
3. **Impact on Youth**: Given the risks associated with digital media's impact on young people, what policies should be implemented to protect minors from inappropriate content and privacy violations?
4. **Data Privacy**: How can social media platforms improve their handling of user data to protect privacy while still leveraging AI for personalized experiences?
5. **AI Accountability**: In cases where AI systems make decisions that have legal or ethical consequences, who should be held accountable—the developers, the users, or the AI itself?
6. **Public Trust:** What steps can be taken to restore or maintain public trust in digital media in the age of misinformation and AI manipulation?
7. **Deepfakes:** Do you view AI-generated deepfakes as a source for good or a curse, as Sophocles warned us?
8. **Energy Concerns:** Considering the significant environmental and climate impacts associated with manufacturing AI chips and training generative AI models, how important is addressing these issues to you?
9. **Stakeholder Roles:** How can collaboration among different stakeholders—policymakers, tech companies, legal experts, and the public—be effectively facilitated to guide the ethical development of digital media?
10. **Future Workforce:** What strategies should digital media industries and educational systems implement to prepare the workforce for the evolving job market created by advancements in AI and digital media?

Works Referenced

Acemoglu, Daron, and Johnson, Simon. "Choosing AI's Impact on the Future of Work." *Stanford Social Innovation Review*, October 25, 2023, accessed at https://ssir.org/articles/entry/ai-impact-on-jobs-and-work#

Askari, Javahir. "Deepfakes and Synthetic Media: What Are They and How Are techUK Members Taking Steps to Tackle Misinformation and

Fraud?" techUK, August 18, 2023, accessed at https://www.techuk.org/resource/synthetic-media-what-are-they-and-how-are-techuk-members-taking-steps-to-tackle-misinformation-and-fraud.html

Barney, Nick. "What Is Singularity?" TechTarget, accessed at https://www.techtarget.com/searchenterpriseai/definition/Singularity-the

Chu, S. C., Yim, M. Y. C., and Mundel, J. "Artificial Intelligence, Virtual and Augmented Reality, Social Media, Online Reviews, and Influencers: A Review of How Service Businesses Use Promotional Devices and Future Research Directions." *International Journal of Advertising* (2024), 1–31, accessed at https://doi.org/10.1080/02650487.2024.2325835

De Avila, Joseph. "Elon Musk and Jamie Dimon's AI Predictions and What They Mean for the Future of Humanity." *The Wall Street Journal*, April 10, 2024, accessed at https://www.wsj.com/tech/ai/elon-musk-and-jamie-dimons-ai-predictions-and-what-they-mean-for-the-future-of-humanity-d100b0c8

Khan, Yusuf. "Salesforce Calls for AI Emissions Regulations as Concerns Grow over Tech Sector's Carbon Footprint." *The Wall Street Journal*, April 22, 2024.

King of Digital Marketing. "The Impact of AI on Digital Marketing Jobs in Upcoming Years." King of Digital Marketing, March 21, 2024, accessed at https://www.kingofdigitalmarketing.com/blog/the-impact-of-ai-on-digital-marketing-jobs-in-upcoming-years.aspx

Mollick, Ethan. *Co-Intelligence*. Penguin Books, New York, 2024.

Morfoot, Addie. "Doc Filmmakers Debate Growing Use of AI in Non-Fiction Projects: 'We Are Supposed to Be the Truth.'" *Variety*, August 1, 2023, accessed at https://variety.com/2023/biz/news/documentary-filmmakers-debate-use-of-ai-1235681905

Panyatham, Paengsuda. "Deepfake Technology in the Entertainment industry: Potential Limitations and Protections." Arts Management and Technology Lab, March 10, 2020, accessed at https://amt-lab.org/blog/2020/3/deepfake-technology-in-the-entertainment-industry-potential-limitations-and-protections

Pulliam-Moore, Charles. "SAG-AFTRA's New Contract Hinges on Studios Acting Responsibly with AI." *The Verge*, November 18, 2023, accessed at https://www.theverge.com/2023/11/18/23962349/sag-aftra-tentative-agreement-generative-artificial-intelligence-vote

Singer, Natasha. "Teen Girls Confront an Epidemic of Deepfake Nudes in Schools." *The New York Times*, April 8, 2024, accessed at https://www.nytimes.com/2024/04/08/technology/deepfake-ai-nudes-westfield-high-school.html?searchResultPosition=1

Somers, Meredith. "Deepfakes, Explained." MIT Sloan School, July 21, 2020, accessed at https://mitsloan.mit.edu/ideas-made-to-matter/deepfakes-explained

Somers, Meredith. "*How* Generative *AI* Can Boost Highly Skilled Workers' Productivity." MIT Management, October 19, 2023, accessed at https://mitsloan.mit.edu/ideas-made-to-matter/how-generative-ai-can-boost-highly

Index

Aadhaar 77
access controls 205
accountability, anonymity and lack of 182
Acemoglu, Daron 305
ACPA. *See* Anticybersquatting Consumer Protection Act
actual malice, standard of 181
ADL. *See* Anti-Defamation League
Adobe Analytics 62
Age of Surveillance Capitalism, The (Zuboff) 263
Agreement on Trade-Related Aspects of Intellectual Property Rights (TRIPS) 93
AI. *See* artificial intelligence
AI Act 303–4
AI-generated content 5, 11, 78, 95–6, 183, 194–5, 294, 301, 308, 312
AIME. *See* Association for Information Media and Equipment
AIME v. Regents of the University of California 118–19
AIVA. *See* Artificial Intelligence Virtual Artist
Ai Weiwei 191
Albrecht, Jan Philipp 51
algorithmic bias 3
Alibaba 279–80
Alliance of Motion Picture and Television Producers (AMPTP) 297
Amazon 10, 37, 72, 141, 144, 263, 272, 298
 and COPPA violation 61–2

data breach 76
and data protection laws 212
FTC accusations 273–4
reach of GDPR to United States 209–10
revolutionizing retail industry 22
Amazon Web Services (AWS) 309
American Tobacco Co. *See United States v. American Tobacco Co.*
America's Got Talent 295
AML. *See* anti-money laundering; Anti-Monopoly Law
AMPTP. *See* Alliance of Motion Picture and Television Producers
Anadol, Refik 103–4
analytics, big data and
 Cambridge Analytica example 63–4
 COPPA violation example 61–2
 Google example 62–3
 sale of real-time location data 65–6
 Salesforce lawsuit 64–5
Andy Warhol Foundation for the Visual Arts, Inc. v. Goldsmith 119–21
Ant Group 280
Anticybersquatting Consumer Protection Act (ACPA) 140
Anti-Defamation League (ADL) 32
anti-money laundering (AML) 256–7
Anti-Monopoly Law (AML) 279–81
anti-Semitism 32, 41
Anti-SLAPP statutes 176–7
Anti-Terrorism Act 30
antitrust laws
 Chinese approach to digital media 278–83

Index

competition and 272–4
EU approach to regulating tech and digital media platforms 274–8
overview 263–5
summary of 284–5
in United States 264–74
Anti-Unfair Competition Law (AUCL) 279–81
API. *See* application programming interface
Apple 8–9, 144, 149, 205, 248, 263, 268, 272, 275–6, 296, 310
Apple Inc. 8–9
application programming interface (API) 77
Aqua (band) 155
AR. *See* augmented reality
Arab Spring 16
arbitrary marks 144
artificial intelligence (AI)
  advertising and 297–9
  big data and 68–72
  China regulating use of 283
  and copyright 96–8
  and copyright laws 88
  cyberscams 77–9
  and data protection 228–30
  and deceptive realm of deepfakes 6–8
  deepfakes 77–9
  deepfakes and synthetic media 293–4
  and defamation law 194–5
  digital media employment 305–7
  documentary films 300–1
  education and health 299–300
  energy concerns 309–10
  entertainment 294–9
  evolving role of 5–7
  and freedom of expression 20
  and future of digital media law 290–2
  generative AI 292–3
  lawyers and 307–9
  and social media 302–5

in Venezuela 183–4
virtual games and interactive media 301–2
Artificial Intelligence Virtual Artist (AIVA) 292
Aspirin, term 145
Assange, Julian 224–5
associational privacy 58
Association for Information Media and Equipment (AIME) 118–9
AT&T. *See* United States v. AT&T
Attribution (BY) 110
AUCL. *See* Anti-Unfair Competition Law
Audius, platform 240
augmented reality (AR) 72–4, 251–4, 257, 293, 298
Author's Guild v. HathiTrust, The 116–17
autonomy 58
A.V.E.L.A. Inc. 152
AWS. *See* Amazon Web Services
Axie Infinity 72

Bangladesh, defamation law in 189–90
"Barbie Girl" (song) 155
Barrett v. Rosenthal 177, 196
Battle Infinity 72
BAYC. *See* Bored Ape Yacht Club
Bayer 145
Beckham, David, campaign of 295
Beef Product's Inc. (BPI) 184
Berne Convention for the Protection of Literary and Artistic Works 98, 101
  brief history of 91–3
  and Copyright Directive 123–6
Betamax VCRs 115–16
Betty Boop, character 152
B.F. Goodrich Company 146
bias, moderation of 6
Biden, Joe 78, 181
big data
  and analytics 61–8

and artificial intelligence 68–72
role of companies of 67
Big Tech 72–4
binary signals 1, 12
Bing AI 269
Bitcoin 237
Black Lives Matter 16
Blockchain 20
blockchain technology
   and digital media contracts 235–9
   fundamentals and operation 239–42
   regulatory and compliance issues in 256–7
   ripple effect of 240
BMG Music v. Gonzalez 117–18
BMI. *See* Broadcast Music Inc.
bodily privacy 57
body image, negative impact on 33
Bored Ape Yacht Club (BAYC) 244–5
BPI. *See* Beef Product's Inc.
Brandeis, Louis 51–5
brand identity, foundation of 144–6
Braneis, Louis 51
Braque, Georges 112
Bridgeman Art Library, Ltd. v. Corel Corp 96–8
Broadcast Music, Inc. v. CBS, Inc. 266–7
Broadcast Music Inc. (BMI) 266–7
Brunetti 154
Burrow-Giles Lithographic Co. v. Sarony 98
business trade libel 180–4
Butts, Wally 171
BY. *See* Attribution
ByteDance 23, 282. *See also* TikTok

CAC. *See* Cyberspace Administration of China
CADA. *See* Colorado's Anti-Discrimination Act
Cahen, Jeremy 244
California, defamation law in 169

California Consumer Privacy Act (CCPA) 3, 60, 203, 207, 212–3, 230
California Delete Act 2023 215–7
California Law Review 52
California Privacy Rights Act (CPRA) 60, 212–3
Cambridge Analytica 63–4
Cambridge University Press 115
Cambridge University Press v. Patton 115
Cardi B 173
Carl Jóhann LILLIENDAHL v. Iceland 44
Carlson, Tucker 181
CC. *See* Creative Commons
CC0. *See* Creative Commons Zero
CCPA. *See* California Consumer Privacy Act
CDA. *See* Communications Decency Act
CD-ROMs 98
CFAA. *See* Computer Fraud and Abuse Act
CFPA. *See* Consumer Financial Protection Act
CFPB. *See* Consumer Financial Protection Bureau
ChatGPT 21, 194–5, 229, 269
children, Digital Services Act protections for 44–6
Children's Online Privacy Protection Act (COPPA) 61–2, 207
child sexual exploitation 33, 304
China 264
   AI regulations 283
   defamation law in 190–2
   regulatory approach to digital media 278–83
   trademark law in 133
Christie's Auction House 241–2
Chrome 269
Ciao Italia 103
CISA. *See* Cybersecurity Information Sharing Act

Civil Code (Japan) 189
Civil Rights Law 169
Clapper, James 223
Clayton Act of 1914 269–71
CNN 173
Code of Conduct, EU 41–6
Co-Intelligence (Mollick) 229
collaboration, promoting 109
Colorado Privacy Act (CPA) 218
Colorado's Anti-Discrimination Act (CADA) 28
Comcast 10
Comey, James 201
Commerce Clause, US Constitution 137
commercial applications. *See* deepfakes, deceptive realm of
Common Sense Media 250–1
communicational privacy 58
Communications Decency Act (CDA) 26, 30, 153, 176–9, 196, 305
comparison 34–5, 39, 169, 255
competition, antitrust and 272–4
compliance with regulations 205
Computer Fraud and Abuse Act (CFAA) 226–8
computer-generated imagery (CGI) 293
confirmation bias 182
Connecticut Data Privacy Act (CTDPA) 218
Consumer Financial Protection Act (CFPA) 186
Consumer Financial Protection Bureau (CFPB) 186–7
consumer privacy 58
consumer protection 184–8
Consumer Review Fairness Act (CRFA) 141
content
  AI-generated 5, 11, 78, 95–6, 183, 194–5, 294, 301, 308, 312
  amplifying 34
  creating 24, 72
  curating 17
  deepfake 303, 305
  distributing 89
  educational 299, 301
  moderating 196
  moderation of 6
  presenting 34
  sharing 88
  transmission of 12
  user-generated 4, 16, 20, 26, 30, 88, 102, 113, 122, 126, 153, 163, 178
content. *See also* various entries
Cookie Law. *See* ePrivacy Directive
cookies 59–61
COPPA. *See* Children's Online Privacy Protection Act
copyright 5
  benefits of 93–8
  brief history of copyright law 89–93
  creation of 93–8
  Creative Commons 108–10
  criteria to qualify for 94
  digital copyright 100–2
  Digital Millennium Copyright Act 121–3
  exceptions to ownership 104
  exclusive reproduction and derivative rights 105–6
  exclusive rights 99–100
  expression *vs.* idea dichotomy 102–4
  fair use 110–4
  infringement 107–8
  international dimensions of 123–6
  leading fair use cases 114–21
  overview of 87–9
  scope of 93–8
  summary of 126–7
Copyright, Designs and Patents Act 1988 125
Copyright Act of 1976 91, 94
  critical changes to 121–3
  and exceptions to ownership 104

and exclusive reproduction and
derivative rights 105-6
and fair use 111-4
Copyright Act of the United States 98, 100
Copyright Clause, Federal Constitution 90
Copyright Law of 1790 90
Corel Corporation 96-8
corporate privacy 58
cost-per-impression (CPI) 255
Counterman, Billy Raymond 28-9
Counterman v. Colorado 29, 41
countries, breaching 36
court cases. *See* Supreme Court
Covid-19 24
CPA. *See* Colorado Privacy Act
CPI. *See* cost-per-impression
CPRA. *See* California Privacy Rights Act
Creative Commons (CC) 108-10
Creative Commons Zero (CC0) 110
303 Creative LLC v. Elenis 4, 28
creative realism. *See* deepfakes, deceptive realm of
CRFA. *See* Consumer Review Fairness Act
Criminal Code, Article 230-1 of 188-9
CrowdStrike 229
cryptocurrencies 237, 249-51, 257
CryptoPunks 245
CTDPA. *See* Connecticut Data Privacy Act
Cubby v. CompuServe 178
Curtis Publishing Co. v. Butts 171, 172
cyberattack 74-7
cyberscams 77-9
Cybersecurity Information Sharing Act (CISA) 203, 222
Cyberspace Administration of China (CAC) 282-3
Cylance 229

DABUS 96
Dalí, Salvador 296
DALL-E 106
data, term 203-6
data backup and recovery 205
databases 102
data breaches 74-7, 202
data privacy 57
data protection
  Computer Fraud and Abuse Act 226-8
  differences 214-20
  EU data protection laws 206-12
  future challenges and developments 228-30
  importance of 203-6
  meaning of term *data* 203-6
  national security concerns 220-2
  overview 201-3
  significant cases involving 222-6
  similarities 213-4
  summary of 230-1
  transition toward cloud-based data storage 204-5
  US data protection laws 212-3
Data Protection Officer (DPO) 70, 214
Data Security Law (DSL) 281
DC Comics 149
DDoS. *See* Distributed Denial of Service
Decentraland 72
decentralized finance (DeFi) 146
deceptive realism. *See* deepfakes, deceptive realm of
decisional privacy 58
deepfakes 77-9, 293-4, 304
deepfakes, deceptive realm of 6-8
defamation claims, defenses to 175-7
defamation law
  artificial intelligence and 194-5
  brief history of 168-9
  business trade libel 180-4

Index

consumer protection in digital media 184–8
defenses to defamation claims 175–7
global perspectives 188–94
Infowars lawsuit 179–80
interests protected by 173
legal framework and challenges 177–9
overview 167–8
state *vs.* federal law 169–72
summary of 196–7
understanding in digital age 172–7
Defamation Mitigation Act 169–70
default bias 269
DeFi. *See* decentralized finance
Department of Justice (DOJ) 61, 268
derivative rights 105–6
derivative works, exclusive rights 99
descriptive marks 145
Devumi, LLC 185–6
DGMA. *See* Digital Millennium Copyright Act
digital age, understanding defamation law in 172–5
digital challenges, addressing 100–1
digital content 10, 88, 100–1, 123, 126–7, 157, 211, 243, 255, 293, 304
digital copyright 100–2
digital discourse, defining 24–30
digital expressions, digital copyright and 101–2
Digital Markets Act (DMA) 275–6
digital media. *See also* digital media law
advertising 254–6
contracts, blockchain technology and 235–9
defining digital discourse 24–30
driving 19
evolution of 18–24
rapidly changing ecosystem of 257–9
digital media law ix–x
antitrust laws 263–87

and artificial intelligence 5–6
blockchain technology 235–42
charting landscape of 1–13
copyrights 87–129
data protection 201–33
defamation law 167–99
digital media advertising 254–6
early evolution of 2–3
emerging complexities of 2–3
future of 289–315
legal conundrum 4–5
major digital media companies 8–10
metaverse 247–54
NFTs 239–47
safeguarding privacy 51–85
significance of studying 10–11
social media sphere 15–50
trademark management 131–65
Digital Millennium Copyright Act (DMCA) 4, 91, 121–3, 154
digital music 101–2
digital past, right to erase 210–2
digital replicas. *See* right of publicity
digital rights management systems (DRMs) 121
Digital Services Act (DSA) 44–6, 275
digital wallet 238–9
digital works, protection of 100
Dilution Act of 1996 140
Dimon 289
Dimon, Jamie 289
direct infringement 107
Discord 187
discussion questions
antitrust laws 285–6
charting digital media law landscape 11–12
copyright 127–8
data protection 231–2
defamation law 197–8
digital media 259–60
future of digital media law 312–3

privacy 83–4
social media sphere 47–50
trademarks 163–4
disinformation campaign 3
Disney+ 10
"Distracted Boyfriend," meme 113
Distributed Denial of Service (DDoS) 75, 203
distribution, exclusive rights 99
DMA. *See* Digital Markets Act
DMCA. *See* Digital Millennium Copyright Act
Dobbs v. Jackson Women's Health Organization 66
documentary films 300–1
Dominion v. Fox 196
Dominion v. Fox News 182–3
Dominion Voting Systems 181
Dong Cunrui 191
Douglas, William O. 56
DouYu 280
DPO. *See* Data Protection Officer
DRMs. *See* digital rights management systems
DSA. *See* Digital Services Act
DSL. *See* Data Security Law
DuckDuckGo 269
Duncan Toys Company 146

eBay 141
ebooks 102
echo chambers 182
ECHR. *See* European Court of Human Rights
ECJ. *See* European Court of Justice
e-commerce sales worldwide 22
economic incentives 182
economic interests, defamation law and 173
education and health 299–300
elaboration, Code of Conduct 41–2
ElevenLabs 21

Eleventh Circuit Court of Appeals 115
Elonis, Anthony 27
Elonis v. United States 27
email and correspondence privacy 58
emerging technologies 101
employment, digital media and 305–7
encryption 205
energy concerns, AI and 309–10
English common law, trademark system and 135–6
entertainment, AI and 294–9
ePrivacy Directive 59–61
Equifax 76
Escalator, term 146
Espionage Act of 1917 25, 224–5
Esposito, Mary Ann 103
ethical considerations. *See* deepfakes, deceptive realm of
ethical standards 182–3
EU. *See* European Union
EU Directive on Copyright in the Digital Single Market 123–6
EUIPO. *See* European Union Intellectual Property Office
European Commission 275–76
European Court of Human Rights (ECHR) 44, 194
European Court of Justice (ECJ) 159
European Human Rights Convention 38, 44
European Luxury Goods vs. Asian Manufacturer 161
European Union (EU) 136, 265
AI Act 303–4
consequences of noncompliance 208–9
cookie laws in 59–61
Copyright Directive of 123–6
copyright mandate of 96
data privacy laws in 69–70
data protection laws in 206–12
2008 Framework Decision 43–4

Index

General Data Protection Regulation (GDPR) in 60
  hate speech in 38
  legal standards 40–1
  reach of GDPR to United States 209–10
  regulating tech and digital media platforms 274–8
  right to erase digital past 210–2
  trademark laws in 157–9
  voluntary Code of Conduct 41–6
European Union Intellectual Property Office (EUIPO) 158
"Everydays: The First 5000 Days" 241–2
exclusive rights
  copyright and 99–100
  and reproduction derivative rights 105–6
  violation of 17
expansion, EU Code of Conduct 42–3
expression vs. idea dichotomy 102–4

Facebook 2, 196, 223, 251, 271–2, 276, 309
  Big Data and analytics 61–4
  controversies of 63–4
  data breach 76
  defining digital discourse 24–30
  and EU voluntary Coe of Conduct 43
  and evolution of digital media 18
  Fraley v. Facebook 80–1
  and importance of freedom of expression 16
  legal framework and challenges 177–9
  policies on regulating free speech 32–4
  rebranding of 147
  and right of publicity 81
  state lawmakers and 30–2
facial recognition privacy 58
Facial Recognition Technology (FRT) 70–1

fair use
  boundaries of 154–6
  as critical doctrine 110–14
  leading cases involving 114–21
false advertising 151–4
family privacy 58
fanciful marks 144
FasterCapital 65
FDA. *See* Food and Drug Administration
Federal Communications Commission 26, 39
Federal Trade Commission Act 185
Federal Trade Commission Act of 194, 269–71
Federal Trade Commission (FTC) 141, 207
  Amazon accusations 273–4
  consumer protection 184–7
  and false advertising 152–3
  and FTC Act 269–71
  and Sherman Antitrust Act of 1890 267–9
Federal Trade Commission v. Devumi LLC 152
Feist Publications, Inc. v. Rural Telephone Service Co., Inc. 95
Fight Online Sex Trafficking Act (FOSTA) 142
financial privacy 57
Finding Jack Charlton (film) 300
Firefox 269
First Amendment (US Constitution) 54–5, 56, 221
  as bedrock of American democracy 15–16
  boundaries of fair trademark use 154
  and copyright laws 89
  defining digital discourse 24–30
  and fair use cases 114–21
  and history of trademark law 138–9

international perspectives on online free speech 37–41
and regulating social media content 34–7
and right of publicity 80
FISA. *See* Foreign Intelligence Surveillance Act
FISA Amendments Act 221–2
FISC. *See* Foreign Intelligence Surveillance Court
Fleischer Studios, Inc. v. A.V.E.L.A., Inc. 152
Fleischer Studios Inc. 152
Food and Drug Administration (FDA) 24, 154
Foreign Intelligence Surveillance Act (FISA) 221–2
Foreign Intelligence Surveillance Court (FISC) 221–2
Formula One, acquisition of 277
FOSTA. *See* Fight Online Sex Trafficking Act
Fourteenth Amendment, US Constitution 114
Fourth Amendment (US Constitution) 221
Fox News 10, 181–2
Fraley v. Facebook 80–1
France, trademark law 134–5
Frank, Jerome 79
freedom of expression
　defamation law and 173
　impact of digital media on 18–24
　importance of 16–8
free speech
　cases of 24–30
　international perspectives on online free speech 37–41
　policies on regulating online speech 32–4
FRT. *See* Facial Recognition Technology
FTC. *See* Federal Trade Commission
FTC v. Devumi 185

FTC v. Qualcomm Inc. 267–8
FTX, cryptocurrency exchange 239
future of digital media law
　advertising 297–9
　deepfakes and synthetic media 293–4
　digital media and AI 292–310
　digital media employment 305–7
　documentary films 300–1
　education and health 299–300
　energy concerns 309–10
　entertainment 294–9
　generative AI 292–3
　lawyers 307–9
　overview 289–92
　social media 302–5
　summary of 310–11
　virtual games and interactive media 301–2

GameStop 106
GANs. *See* Generative Adversarial Networks
GDPR. *See* General Data Protection Regulation
General Data Protection Regulation (GDPR) 3, 60, 69–70, 202, 207–8, 230, 276, 281, 290–1
Generative Adversarial Network (GANs) 293
genericization 145–6
generic terms 145–6
Georgia State University (GSU) 115
Gertz, Elmer 171–2
Gertz v. Robert Welch, Inc. 171–2
Getty Images 106
GLBA. *See* Gramm-Leach-Bliley Act
global perspectives, defamation law
　Australia 188
　Bangladesh 190
　China 190–2
　Japan 188–9
　New Zealand 188

Index

Nigeria 192
Pakistan 189
Russia 192–3
Southeast Asia 189–90
United Kingdom 188
Glossier 255
Goldsmith, Lynn 119–21
Gonzalez, Cecilia 117
Gonzalez v. Google 29–30, 36
Google 9, 18, 46, 62, 72, 254, 263, 275, 309–10
  AdWords 254
  agreements regarding Android devices 268–9
  Arts & Culture initiative 122
  California Delete Act 2023 215–6
  Cloud 309
  competition and antitrust 272
  and data protection laws 212
  as dominant default search engine 268–9
  employ targeting advertising 63
  exclusive reproduction and derivative rights 106
  "Images" feature of 122
  leaking case 222–3
  right to erase digital past 210
  Supreme Court case involving 29–30, 36–7
  targeted advertising of 63
  and trademark law 144
  and trademark infringement 147
Google Inc. v. Agencia Española de Protección de Datos 210–1
Google LLC v. American Blind & Wallpaper Factory, Inc. 147
Gorsuch, Neil 28
GPUs. *See* graphic processing units
Gramm-Leach-Bliley Act (GLBA) 207
graphic processing units (GPUs) 299
"Gravity's Rainbow" 103–4
Grindr 65

Griswold v. Connecticut 54, 55–6
Gronkowski, Rob 246–7
GSU. *See* Georgia State University
Guardian 222
Guggenheim Museum 91
guilds, trademark and 133–4
Gutenberg, Johannes 89–90

hacking, significant cases of 222–6
Haelan Laboratories, Inc. v. Topps Chewing Gum, Inc. 79
Halleck, DeeDee 27–8
Hand, Learned 266
Hankejh, Damion 290
Haring, Keith 103
Harry Potter, name 156–7
Harvard Law Review 51
hate speech 3
hate speech, instances of 17–18
HathiTrust 116
Haute Diggity Dog 155
Haute Diggity Dog, LLC v. Hartman 155
Hawaii Data Privacy Law 219
Health Insurance Portability and Accountability Act (HIPAA) 67–8, 154, 207
Hermès 142–3
Hickman, Ryan 244–5
HIPAA. *See* Health Insurance Portability and Accountability Act
Hollywood Antitrust Case of 1948. *See United States v. Paramount Pictures, Inc.*
Holmes, Oliver Wendell, Jr. 24, 26
Huawei 225–6
Hulu 10
Hustler Magazine, Inc. v. Falwell 114
Huya 280

Iancu v. Brunetti 138
ICCPR. *See* International Covenant on Civil and Political Rights

ICOs. *See* initial coin offerings
idea *vs.* expression dichotomy 102–4
"if-then" logic 237
Indeed 187
indirect infringement 107
informational privacy 57
Information Technology (IT) 190
information wars 3
Infowars 179–80
infringement
  copyright 107–8
  trademarks and 146–9
initial coin offerings (ICOs) 256
Initial Public Offering (IPO) 280, 282
innovation, promoting 109
insider threats 75
Instagram 5, 9, 20, 22, 24, 31, 187, 196, 209, 212, 271, 273, 277
  deepfakes on 304
  and fair use 112
  filters on 302
  online speech regulation 33–4
  policies on regulating free speech 33
Intel 309
intellectual property rights. *See* copyrights
intellectual property (IP) 131, 256, 291
interactive media 301–2
International Covenant on Civil and Political Rights (ICCPR) 193–4
international harmonization 101
international trademark law 156–61
Internet Research Agency (IRA) 31, 183
Internet Service Provider (ISP) 91, 121, 177
intimacy privacy 58
IP. *See* intellectual property
IPO. *See* Initial Public Offering
IRA. *See* Internet Research Agency
Irishman, The 294–5
ISP. *See* Internet Service Provider
IT. *See* Information Technology

Jack Daniel's Properties, Inc. v. VIP Products LLC 154–6
Japan, defamation law in 188–9
Jobs, Steve 8, 112–13
Johnson, Simon 305
Jones, Alex 179–80
Jordan, Michael 80
jurisdiction, defining 93

Kagan, Elena 29
Kaplan, Lewis 98
Kardashian, Kim 187
Kardashian, Robert, hologram of 295
Katz v. United States 56–7
Kee, Latasha 174
Khan, Shah Rukh 298
Kickstarter 17
Kimura, Hana 188–9
Kimzey v. Yelp! Inc. 153
knowledge and culture, increasing access to 109
know-your-customer (KYC) 256–7
Kogan, Aleksandr 63–4
Korea Air 102–3
Kozinski, Alex 167
KYC. *See* know-your-customer

labor market, digital media 305–7
Labs, Yuga 244–5
Lanham Act 137–8, 147, 151, 154
Last Dance, The (documentary) 298
laws, data protection
  consequences of noncompliance 208–9
  in European Union 206–8
  reach of GDPR to United States 209–10
  right to erase digital past 210–12
  in United States 212–3
lawyers, AI and 307–9
leaking, significant cases of 222–6
legal and legislative responses. *See* deepfakes, deceptive realm of

legal clarity and certainty, providing 109
legal conundrums 4–5
legal landscape, navigating 1–2
legal sharing and reuse, facilitating 109
legal standards 182–3
Lehman, Thomas 244–5
liar's dividend 183–4
Liberty Media 277–8
licensing and distribution models 101
Lilly, Eli 24–5
LinkedIn 152
Louboutin 159
Luo Changping 191

Ma, Jack 279–80
MADAs. *See* Mobile Application Distribution Agreements
Madrid System 160
Maine Act to Protect the Privacy of Online Customer Information 219
Mair, Liz 177
malicious applications. *See* deepfakes, deceptive realm of
malware attacks 75
Mandalorian, The 295
Manhattan Community Access Corp. (MCAC) 27–8
Manhattan Community Access Corp. v. Halleck 27–8
manipulation 183
Manning, Chelsea 224
Marcus, Gary 289–90
marital privacy 58
market domination 3
Marriott International 76
Marvel 149
Maryland Personal Information Protection Act (PIPA) 219
Massachusetts Data Privacy Law 219
MasterCard. *See United States v. Visa U.S.A., Inc., and MasterCard International Inc.*

Masterpiece Cakeshop v. Colorado Civil Rights Commission 28
Matal v. Tam 138
Mattel, Inc. v. MCA Records, Inc. 155
MCAC. *See* Manhattan Community Access Corp.
M&E. *See* media and entertainment
media and entertainment (M&E) 292
medical privacy 58
Melendez, Jesus Papoleto 27–8
"meme stock" phenomenon 186–7, 196
mental health issues 33
Merchandise Marks Act of 1862 135
Merkel, Angela 223
Mesopotamia, trademark law in 133
Meta 5, 9, 37, 62, 72, 263, 271–2, 275, 309
  Big Data and analytics 63
  controversies of 63–4
  and importance of freedom of expression 16
  and metaverse 251
  pivoting approach 31
  rebranding 147–8
MetaBirkins 142–3
Metacapital 147
Meta Platforms Inc. 9
metaverse
  and freedom of expression 20–1
  key differences 251–4
  overview of 72–4, 257
  virtual worlds and 247–51
  and vision for future 251–4
MeToo 16
Microsoft Teams 23
Microsoft 21, 23, 25, 37, 76, 148, 209, 223, 267, 269
Midjourney 269
Minecraft 72
Mirage Editions, Inc. v. Albuquerque A.R.T. Co. 105–6
Mobile Application Distribution Agreements (MADAs) 268

Modulate 302
Mollick, Ethan 229, 303
Morol, Abdul Latif 190
MotoGP 277–8
Mugler v. Kansas 53
Musk, Elon 5, 147, 173–4, 289
My Neighbor Alice 72

National Conference of State Legislatures 31
National Enquirer 302
national security, data protection and 222–6
National Security Agency (NSA) 222–4
NBA Top Shot 246–7
NC. *See* Noncommercial Use
ND. *See* No Derivatives
Netflix 10, 272
Nevada Privacy Law 219
"never-off" nature of mobile connectivity 20
New York Privacy Act 218
New York Times 76, 170–1
New York Times Co. v. Sullivan 170–1, 181
NFTs. *See* Non-Fungible Tokens
Nigeria, defamation law in 192
Nike 141, 254
Ninth Amendment, US Constitution 56
Ninth Circuit Court of Appeals 153
No Artificial Intelligence Fake Replicas and Unauthorized Duplications Act 8
No Derivatives (ND) 110
Noncommercial Use (NC) 110
Non-Fungible Tokens (NFTs) 142, 257
  differences between physical art and 242–7
  introduction of 241–2
  legal battles involving 244–7
  overview 88–9
  ownership concerns of 243–4
  process of transferring and selling 242
  programming 243
North American Software Developer vs. Computer Hardware Manufacturer 161
Northern Securities Co. v. United States 266
Northern Securities Company 266
NSA. *See* National Security Agency
Nunes, Devin 177
NVIDIA 39, 299, 309
Nyquil chicken, recipe 24

Obama, Barack 78, 224, 302
Occupy Wall Street 16
OEMs 267
Ofcom 39
Olmstead, Roy 54–5
Olmstead v. United States 54–5
online articles 102
Online Safety Act 35, 38–9
  criticisms of 39–40
OpenAI 173, 194–5, 269, 309
Otis Elevator Company 146
ownership, AI 5
ownership, exception to 104

Packingham, Lester 27
Packingham v. North Carolina 4, 27
Pakistan, defamation law in 189–90
Panavision International, L.P. v. Toeppen 140
Pandora 277
parody, trademark law and 154–6
password guessing 75
PATA. *See* Platform Accountability and Transparency Act
partial privacy 57
Patreon 17
PATRIOT Act 230
PayPal 173

pay-per-click (PPC) 255
peer-to-peer (P2P) 117–18, 146
performance, exclusive rights 99
Perplexity AI 269
Personal Information Protection Law (PIPL) 281, 282
personal relationships, privacy of 58
Phillips 28
phishing 75
physical breaches 75
physical privacy 57
Picasso, Pablo 112
pink slime 184
Pinterest 112, 152
PIPA. *See* Maryland Personal Information Protection Act
PIPL. *See* Personal Information Protection Law
Platform Accountability and Transparency Act (PATA) 35
Pom Wonderful LLC v. Coca-Cola Co. 151–2
potters marks, trademark and 133
PoW. *See* Proof of Work
Power and Progress: Our 1,000-Year Struggle over Technology and Prosperity (Acemoglu) 305
P2P. *See* peer-to-peer
PPC. *See* pay-per-click
Presley, Elvis 295
PRISM, program 223
privacy 3
　big data and AI 68–72
　big data and analytics 61–8
　categories 52–3
　concerns of 6
　cookies and 59–61
　and data breaches 74–7
　deepfakes and cyberscams 77–9
　defamation law and 173
　defining as right 51–3
　early constitutional history of 53–7
　metaverse and 72–4
　recognized forms of 57–59
　and right of publicity 79–81
　summary of 81–3
privacy rights, erosion of 66
profiling, potential for 67
Proof of Work (PoW) 243
propaganda 183
Prosser, William L. 52
public display, exclusive rights 99–100
publicity, right of 58, 79–81
Putin, Vladimir 192–3

Qiu Ziming 191
Qualcomm 267–8

ransomware attacks 75, 202–3
Raymond, Billy 29
reaction videos 114
real-time location data, sale of 65–6
Reddit 2, 31, 187
Reno v. American Civil Liberties Union 4, 26
reproduction, exclusive rights 99
reproduction rights 105–6
reputation, defamation law and 173
return on investment (ROI) 254
Revenue Share Agreements (RSAs) 268
right of publicity 79–81
"Right to be Forgotten" 70
"right to be let alone," concept 52
"Right to Privacy, The" 51
Ripps, Ryder 244
Roberson v. Rochester Folding Box Co. 54
Roe v. Wade 66
Rogan, Joe 180
Rogers v. Grimaldi 143
Rogue One: A Star Wars Story 295
ROI. *See* return on investment
Roommates.Com, LLC v. Fair Housing Council of San Fernando Valley 167

Roshan, Hrithik 298
Rothschild, Mason 142–3
Rowling, J. K. 156–7
Royal Society for Public Health 24
RSAs. *See* Revenue Share Agreements
Russia, defamation law in 193

SA. *See* Share Alike
SAG-AFTRA. *See* Screen Actors Guild–American Federation of Television and Radio Artists
Salesforce 64–5
Sandals Resorts International Ltd. v. Google, Inc. 175–6
Sandbox 72
Sandy Hook Elementary School 179–80
Saturday Evening Post 171
Savva Terentyev v. Russia 44
Scandalum Magnatum 168
Schenck, Charles 25–6
Schenck v. United States 25–6
SCMGA. *See* Stop Counterfeiting in Manufactured Goods Act
Scorsese, Martin 294–5
Screen Actors Guild–American Federation of Television and Radio Artists (SAG-AFTRA) 81, 297
SEC. *See* Securities and Exchange Commission
Second Circuit Court of Appeals 116
Section 230. *See various entries*
Section 106A, VARA 92–3
Securities and Exchange Commission (SEC) 154, 186–7, 196, 256
self-esteem 34
SESTA. *See* Stop Enabling Sex Traffickers Act
Share Alike (SA) 110
Shein 22
Sherman Antitrust Act of 1890 265–9
Shopify 141

SiriusXM 277
Slack 23
SLAPP. *See* Strategic Lawsuit Against Public Participation
smart contracts 236–9, 256–7
Smith, Lorie 28–9
Snapchat 2, 5, 9, 24, 33, 302, 304
Snowden, Edward 222–5, 230–1
Social Dilemma (film) 248
social media sphere
  balancing freedom and control in 15–16
  challenges to regulating content 34–7
  concept of appropriation in 113–14
  defining digital discourse 24–30
  EU voluntary code of conduct 41–6
  and false advertising 151–4
  and future of digital media law 302–5
  impact of digital media on freedom of expression 18–24
  importance of freedom of expression 16–18
  international perspectives on 37–41
  policies on regulating free speech 32–4
  state lawmakers and 30–2
  summary of 46–7
social privacy 58
societal impact. *See* deepfakes, deceptive realm of
software 101
Sony 17
Sony Corporation 115–16
Sony Music Entertainment 88
SoundCloud 114, 152
Southeast Asia, defamation law in 189–90
SpaceX 173, 289
speed over accuracy 182
Spotify 21–2
Stability AI 106
Stable Diffusion 106

Index

state-specific challenges, digital media and 311–12
Statute of Anne 90
Stop Counterfeiting in Manufactured Goods Act (SCMGA) 141–2
Stop Enabling Sex Traffickers Act (SESTA) 142
Strategic Lawsuit Against Public Participation (SLAPP) 176
Stratton Oakmont v. Prodigy 178
Sugar Trust Case. *See United States v. E. C. Knight Co.*
suggestive marks 144–5
Sullivan, L. B. 170
superhero, term 148–9
Supreme Court
    and antitrust laws 264–74
    and big data cases 66–8
    boundaries of fair trademark use 154–6
    and copyright laws 95–6
    and defamation law 169–72
    and early constitutional history of privacy 53–7
    fair use cases 114–21
    and history of trademark law 138–9
    landmark decisions in speech, online expression, and creativity 24–30
surveillance
    increase of 66–7
    privacy 58
    significant cases of 222–6
Swift, Taylor 78
synthetic media 293–4, 299–300
synthetic performers, focus on 297

Taft, William Howard 54–5
Taiwan Semiconductor Company (TSMC) 310
Tam 154
targeted advertising, potential for 67

TEAS. *See* Trademark Electronic Application System
tech giants, clash between state lawmakers and 30–2
technological protection measures (TPMs) 101
teenage girls, Facebook and 33–4
Telecommunications Act, Section 230 of 4
temporal autonomy 58
temporal privacy 58
Temu 22
Tencent 280
Tesla 173, 289
Tesla Motors 184
Texas, defamation law in 169–70
Thaler, Stephen 96
Thermos, term 146
Thermos LLC 146
Third Amendment, US Constitution 56
"This Is Your Digital Life" 63–4
Tiffany (NJ) Inc. v. eBay Inc. 147
TikTok 17, 23, 225–6, 282
    and fair use 112
TMA. *See* Trademark Modernization Act
Toeppen, Christopher 140
Tools and Weapons (Lilly) 24–5
TPMs. *See* technological protection measures
Trade Desk 255
trade libel 180–4
trademark
    boundaries of fair trademark use 154–6
    development of modern trademark law 134–6
    dilution 149–51
    and false advertising 151–4
    foundation of brand identity 144–6
    history of trademark law in United States 137–43

infringement 146–9
international trademark law 156–61
origins of trademark law 132–4
overview 131–2
summary of 162–3
TRIPS Agreement and well-known marks 161–2
Trademark Act of 1881 137
Trademark Act of 1905 135–6
Trademark Act of 1938 136
Trademark Clarification Act 140
Trademark Counterfeiting Act of 1984 139–40
Trademark Electronic Application System (TEAS) 142
Trademark Law Revision Act of 1988 140
Trademark Modernization Act (TMA) 140
Trade Mark Registration Act of 1875 135
Trademark Trial and Appeal Board (TTAB) 139
Trade-Related Aspects of Intellectual Property Rights (TRIPS) 160–2
traditional AI 293
Travis, Randy 295–6
TRIPS. *See* Agreement on Trade-Related Aspects of Intellectual Property Rights
TRIPS Agreement. *See* Trade-Related Aspects of Intellectual Property Rights
Triumph of the Nerds: The Rise of Accidental Empires (Jobs) 112–13
Trump, Donald 78, 181
TSMC. *See* Taiwan Semiconductor Company
TTAB. *See* Trademark Trial and Appeal Board
Tucker on X 181
Tumblr 112
Turkle, Sherry 1

2020 SolarWinds cyber espionage case 202
Twitter 9, 16, 24, 32, 147–8, 152, 173, 177, 187, 191, 272
Twitter v. Taamneh 29–30

UCLA. *See* University of California, Los Angeles
UCPA. *See* Utah Consumer Privacy Act
UDAAPs. *See* unfair, deceptive, or abusive acts or practices
UGC. *See* User Generated Content
UIDAI. *See* Unique Identification Authority of India
unfair, deceptive, or abusive acts or practices (UDAAPs) 186
Union Pacific Railway Co. v. Botsford 53
Unique Identification Authority of India (UIDAI) 77
United Kingdom 38, 40, 48, 96, 98, 125–6, 188, 225
United Nations Human Rights Committee 194
United States
　data protection laws in 212–13
　history of antitrust laws in 264–74
　history of trademark law in 137–43
　landscape of defamation law in 169–72
　national security concerns 220–2
　reach of GDPR to 209–10
　roots of defamation law in 168–9
　trademark laws in 157–9
United States Patent and Trademark Office (USPTO) 138, 149
United States v. Alcoa 266
United States v. American Tobacco Co. 266
United States v. AT&T 267
United States v. Auernheimer ("Weev") 228
United States v. E. C. Knight Co. 266

United States v. Keys 228
United States v. Microsoft Corp. 267
United States v. Nosal 228
United States v. Paramount Pictures, Inc. 266
United States v. Visa U.S.A., Inc., and MasterCard International Inc. 267
Universal City Studios v. Sony Corp. 115
Universal Music Group 17, 88
University of California, Los Angeles (UCLA) 118–19
Unsworth, Vernon 173–4
U.S. Copyright Act 92
USA PATRIOT Act 221
US Constitution. *See* First Amendment
US Copyright Office 96
user-generated content 4, 16, 20, 26, 30, 88, 102, 113, 122, 126, 153, 163, 178
User Generated Content (UGC) 2
USPTO. *See* United States Patent and Trademark Office
US Technology Licensing Agreement 161
Utah Consumer Privacy Act (UCPA) 218

Van Buren v. United States 227–8
Van Haren 159
VARA. *See* Visual Artists Rights Act
VCDPA. *See* Virginia Consumer Data Protection Act
VCRs. *See* video cassette recorders
Venezuela, AI-generated propaganda in 183–4
Verizon 76
video cassette recorders (VCRs) 115
videos 102
Vine 152
Virginia Consumer Data Protection Act (VCDPA) 217
virtual games 301–2

virtual reality (VR) 257, 293, 301
 concept 247–51
 Digital Millennium Copyright Act and 121–3
 key differences 251–4
virtual worlds 247–51
Visa. *See United States v. Visa U.S.A., Inc., and MasterCard International Inc.*
Visual Artists Rights Act (VARA) 92–3
visual privacy 58
Vizio 185
volume of information 182
Vossough, Angel 290
Voxels 72
VR. *See* virtual reality

WAF. *See* Women's Action Forum
Wall Street Journal, The 33–4, 68
Walt Disney Company 10
Walters, Mark 194–5
Walters v. OpenAI 195
WarGames (film) 226–8
Warhol, Andy 103, 119–21
Warner Bros. Entertainment 157
Warner Music Group 17, 88
Warren, Samuel 51
Washington Post 222
WCT. *See* WIPO Copyright Treaty
Web 1 247–8
Web 2 248
Web 3 248
Webster, Daniel 90
Webster, Noah 90
Whalen, Coles 29
Whistler House Museum of Art 91
White, Byron 266–7
WikiLeaks 224–5
Winkelmann, Mike 241–2
WIPO. *See* World Intellectual Property Organization
WIPO Copyright Treaty (WCT) 101, 160

wiretap privacy 58
Women's Action Forum (WAF) 189
workplace privacy 58
World Intellectual Property Organization (WIPO) 160–1
World Trade Organization (WTO) 93, 160
Wozniak, Steve 8
WTO. *See* World Trade Organization

XAI 173
X (Twitter) 2, 187, 196, 212, 244, 272
  and importance of freedom of expression 16
  as influential space 187
  interests protected by defamation law 173
  policies on regulating free speech 32–3
  state lawmakers and 30–2
  and trademark infringement 147–8

Yahoo! 75–6, 223
Yelp! 153
YouTube 5, 9, 16–17, 17, 103, 112, 114, 124–5, 152, 174, 209, 212, 273, 296, 311
  case against 29–30
  Digital Services Act 46
  and EU voluntary Code of Conduct 43
  and fair use 112
  major copyright infringement case involving 88
  policies on regulating free speech 33
Yo-Yo, term 146

Zalando 298
Zephyr Apparel 158
Zeran v. America Online, Inc. 26, 178
Zipper, term 146
zone of privacy, identifying 56
Zoom 23
Zuboff, Shoshana 263
Zuckerberg, Mark 5, 78, 251
  state lawmakers and 30–2

About the Author

Michael E. Jones, professor emeritus, taught law and directed the Legal Studies Program at the University of Massachusetts Lowell, for many years. A pioneer in many legal fields, including sports law, he created the first undergraduate course and wrote the first textbook for non-lawyers. As an analyst in sports, entertainment, art, media, and artificial intelligence law, he has contributed to the *Huffington Post* and numerous media broadcast and podcast outlets.

Academically, Jones holds a BA in Economics from Denison University, an MBA from the Wharton School at the University of Pennsylvania, a JD from the University of Miami, and an MLA from Harvard University.

A few years ago, he was named a Fulbright-Nehru Specialist by the US State Department, teaching intellectual property law at Jindal Global University Law School in India. He has also held roles as a visiting professor at the University of London and has spoken before Nobel laureates and leading technology pioneers at the Santa Fe Institute. Jones has extensively researched and written on copyright, trademark, publicity rights, artificial intelligence and media law globally.

An accomplished visual artist, he designed the official triathlon poster for the US Olympic Committee for five consecutive summer games. His paintings have also appeared on PBS cooking shows. As a former elite swimmer, runner, and triathlete, he medaled at the Penn Relays, qualified for the Olympic trials and won gold at the Pan American championships. He served as an appeals court judge at the Tokyo Summer Olympic Games and now helps to lead an international tribunal for multisport disputes.

Jones has been a board member and chairperson for *Provincetown Arts* magazine and has served on bank and nonprofit boards. He has written six books and over twenty-five peer-reviewed legal and business articles, including *Art Law* (2nd ed.), *Rules of the Game: Sports Law*, and *Intellectual Property Law Fundamentals* (2nd ed.). With his spouse, Christine M. Jones, he coedited the award-winning book *Timeless: The Photography of Rowland Scherman*.

About the Author

His diverse career includes four terms as a state legislator and over two decades as a trial court judge adjudicating civil and criminal disputes. He has received many awards, including the 2019 Fulbright-Nehru Specialist honor. He currently cohosts a salon where people from diverse backgrounds discuss contemporary societal issues. He continues to teach Digital Media Law and Ethics in the Arts and Design and Digital Media departments at the University of Massachusetts Lowell.